The Mbappé Project
Making a Superstar

ALSO BY PHILIPPE AUCLAIR
(in order of publication)

Cantona: The Rebel Who Would Be King

Thierry Henry – Lonely at the Top: A Biography

PHILIPPE AUCLAIR

The Mbappé Project
Making a Superstar

First published in Great Britain in 2026 by Quercus

Part of John Murray Group

1

Copyright © 2026 Philippe Auclair

The moral right of Philippe Auclair to be
identified as the author of this work has been
asserted in accordance with the Copyright,
Designs and Patents Act 1988.

PICTURE CREDITS (in order of appearance):
Introduction – ALEX DIBBON / Getty; 1, 5 – Magali Delporte;
2 – Trinity Mirror / Mirrorpix / Alamy; 3 – Pete Kiehart / Redux / eyevine;
4 – Offside / Presse Sports; 6 – XAVIER LAINE / Getty; 7 – Anthony Dibbon / Getty;
8 – Arturo Holmes / Getty; 9 – FEP / Getty; 10, 12 – JEAN CATUFFE / Getty;
11 – KIRLL KUDRYAVTSEV / Getty; 13 – Lars Höglund / TT News Agency via AFP;
14 – AFP, Franck Fife / Getty; 15 – Franck Fife / Getty; 16 – Frank Castel / ABACAPRESS.COM /
Alamy; 17 – AURELIEN MEUNIER / Getty

All rights reserved. No part of this publication
may be reproduced or transmitted in any form
or by any means, electronic or mechanical,
including photocopy, recording, or any
information storage and retrieval system,
without permission in writing from the publisher.

A CIP catalogue record for this book is available
from the British Library

HB ISBN 978-1-52944-677-7
TPB ISBN 978-1-52944-678-4
EBOOK ISBN 978-1-52944-680-7

Typeset in Minion by CC Book Production

Printed and bound in Great Britain by Clays Ltd, Elcograf S.p.A.

Papers used by Quercus are from well-managed forests and other responsible sources.

Quercus
Carmelite House
50 Victoria Embankment
London EC4Y 0DZ

John Murray Group
Part of Hodder & Stoughton Limited
An Hachette UK company

The authorised representative in the EEA is Hachette Ireland,
8 Castlecourt Centre, Dublin 15, D15 XTP3, Ireland (email: info@hbgi.ie)

To Richard and Jonathan

Contents

Foreword   ix

Introduction   1

1. Never in doubt   13
2. Jirès Kembo: the birth of the project   27
3. Bondy   39
4. Education, education, education   49
5. Clairefontaine   63
6. Monaco: the springboard   75
7. *Cherchez les femmes*   87
8. *Mbappé et compagnie*   101
9. *Je t'aime, moi non plus*: the PSG years – 1   121
10. *Je t'aime, moi non plus*: the PSG years – 2   137
11. The president's man   153

12. *Je t'aime, moi non plus*: the PSG years – 3	171
13. Stockholm	189
14. *La vie en bleu: Capitaine Kylian*	203
15. Mbappé power	223
16. *La débâcle*	239
17. The Ballon d'Or and beyond	253
Kylian Mbappé Milestones	269
Sources	277
Index	283

Foreword

You may notice that, unusually for a book of this kind, it is devoid of thanks or acknowledgements, aside from its dedication to the two people who made it happen, my literary agent Jonathan Harris and my editor Richard Milner of Quercus Publishing. It was originally my intention to seek the collaboration of Kylian Mbappé, his family and the very small group of friends, relatives and advisors who have accompanied him throughout his progress from boy wonder to global superstar – the initiators and executors of the 'Mbappé Project' which, rather than the footballer himself, was the subject of my work from the outset. A biography, authorised or not, was not what I had in mind. There was no point in chronicling the life of a young man who had just reached the halfway point of his footballing career and stood to achieve far more in the years to come; in any case, it was not *what* he had achieved which interested me, but *how* he had done it. The nature of my own project also demanded that I should remain independent from whichever narrative would be favoured by Mbappé himself, something I expected to be on the lines of 'whatever it is that you set yourself to do, dare to dream, and it will come true'; something I could just about accept if it came from his lips, but which I found hypocritical and repulsive in a wider context.

The idea, therefore, was to open a channel of communication with the player and his camp through which questions could be asked and answered. Kylian and his family, however, did not wish to cooperate. I should add here that, to their credit, they did not try to obstruct me in any way. None of the people I spoke to, some of whom had and still have direct dealings with the player in his football and business affairs, turned me down because they had been asked to; yet, with the exception of a handful of friends and colleagues who had been witnesses of rather than actors in the Mbappé story, none of them wished to be named either, a telling trait of the nature of a 'project' in which control is paramount and participants know how far they can go, and, more to the point, how far they can't. My thanks to them: they know who they are, no-one else will. I am also grateful for the work of fellow journalists that has provided me with a wealth of sources, in particular to the writers of *L'Equipe*, *L'Equipe TV*, *France Football*, *Envoyé Spécial* and *Le Parisien* who have chronicled Mbappé's career over the past decade.

This presented a challenge I had not encountered when writing two previous books about Eric Cantona and Thierry Henry. Eric's friends, former team-mates, managers and family had provided me with the material I needed to paint a nuanced, ambiguous – but ultimately loving, I hope – portrait of a man who, despite the regular yet unpredictable eruptions of the Cantona caldera, was far more nuanced and ambiguous himself than the headlines and the carefully wrought legend would suggest. As for Thierry, I had followed him week after week from the day he arrived at Arsenal and conversed with him regularly. I'd seen him exultant, I'd seen him despondent, I'd seen him disarmingly charming and candid, I'd seen him curt and angry, including with myself. Times had changed since Eric and Thierry had retired, not for the better for us journalists. Training grounds were turning into fortresses guarded by paranoid press officers who blanched when they heard you'd got hold of the mobile phone number of a club physio or of a second-team player. They had turned into the human equivalent of broken bottles, barbed wire and electric fencing. Their favourite word was 'no'. It's got worse since.

I knew Thierry well enough (and quite a few of his Monaco, France and Arsenal team-mates and coaches too) to work my way around those defences. Not so for Kylian Mbappé, but I soon realised that it was immaterial in the context of what I had set out to do. The world Mbappé has constructed for himself and inhabits as a person, a footballer, a businessman, a brand, has nothing to do with the worlds Cantona and Henry lived in. Nobody who is not already part of it will be let in, unless that nobody, who will remain a nobody, can bring something of value to the table. This is what fascinated me. I shouldn't fool myself. Whatever I tried, I would never, ever be part of that world, and neither would anyone else in my position. The few outsiders I met who had been shown the green light, always fleetingly, were the first to warn me that there was no genuine way in. That world's boundaries had been defined in such a way, and for so long, that you could not cross them unless you were waved in on someone else's terms – Mbappé's. You'd be shown a seat in the antechamber, then perhaps, if lucky, taken to one of the *salons* readied for special guests, then taken back to the door with the utmost courtesy. You'd be left with the illusion of proximity, but none the wiser for that.

The paradox is that Mbappé's communication skills are developed to a degree which is unprecedented among athletes of a comparable status, an admittedly narrow field. He comes across as polite, approachable, quick-witted, attentive and sharp, funny too, even mischievous in the best possible way. He is always impeccably dressed and groomed when he appears in public but makes no effort to present himself either as a demi-god like Cristiano Ronaldo or, on the opposite side of the spectrum, a scruffy couldn't-care-less like Lionel Messi. He is the ideal son-in-law: clean-cut, talented and rich, very rich. His rather large nose endears him to the nation of Cyrano de Bergerac, Serge Gainsbourg, Jean-Paul Belmondo, Valérie Lemercier and Astérix, in which it is a sign of intelligence, wisdom and courtesy; and quite sexy too. Yet, however remote we are from the stars we see flicker on the screen, I believe that we are closer to them than we are to Mbappé, who gets to act in the flesh in front of tens of thousands of fans but never sets foot in our shared reality, unless it is reality of a virtual kind, fragmented and conditioned to suit the purpose of others. I did not always feel that way. I was as thrilled as anyone when the teenage Kylian broke through at Monaco, cocking a snook at the continent's best defenders as if it all were just a wonderful joke. I marvelled at the improbable volley, a marvel of skill and balance, he scored in the 2022 World Cup final, when the ball fizzed on the grass as neatly as the blades of a master tailor cutting through obedient cloth. That much hasn't changed. As to the rest, let's find out.

Introduction

'Il n'y a de nouveau que ce qui est oublié.'

'There is nothing new except what has been forgotten.' What Marie Antoinette's dressmaker Madame Bertin had in mind when she made her *mot* was that the fashions she wanted to create for her mistress would not have existed had it not been for the fashions which came before her time; but she hit on a truth that was valid beyond the world of her craft. It certainly is in football, where 'new', supposedly revolutionary ideas more often than not resemble something which coaches, players and spectators would have been familiar with almost a century ago. The shape of Pep Guardiola's most successful Manchester City sides, for example, could be described as the famous 2–3–5 'pyramid' which was thought to have sunk into oblivion between the two World Wars. Similarly, sporting superstardom was not an invention of the twentieth and twenty-first centuries. Famous athletes of the past may have been forgotten, but the aura which surrounded them has barely changed in nature.

The exploits of Milo of Croton, a six-time Olympic champion so strong he is said to have carried a bull on his shoulders, Leonidas of

Rhodes, a sprinter and one-lap runner who collected twelve victor's laurels in four successive Olympiads, and Theagenes of Thasos, a boxer and wrestler who went through 1,406 bouts unbeaten, were known throughout the Greek-speaking world in Antiquity. Aristotle, Herodotus and Cicero celebrated Milo in their writings. Two thousand five hundred years before devotees of Diego Maradona founded his church in Rosario, the Iglesia Maradoniana, statues of Theagenes were to be found throughout the Mediterranean basin and even – according to historian Pausanias – in the 'Barbarian world', where they attracted pilgrims who believed they possessed healing qualities. Two millennia on, his profile still adorns the crest of his native island's football club, A.O. Theagenes Thasou.

The Romans too had their sporting stars, chariot racers and gladiators first among them. Syrian gladiator Flamma, who so loved fighting in the arena that he turned down the chance to be freed four times, became a favourite of the Roman populus. Charioteer Gaius Appuleius Diocles, who competed for three of Rome's four racing stables in the second century AD, is said to have won close to thirty-six million sesterces in prize money over the twenty-four years of his career, that is thirty-six times the value of the property a Roman citizen had to own to be allowed to sit in the Senate at the time of Augustus, and the equivalent of ten billion pounds sterling in today's money. Complaints about athletes being paid far too much for kicking a ball, driving a car, or indeed a chariot, are nothing new: the satirical poet Juvenal raged against those racers who made a hundred times more in the Colosseum than the best-paid lawyers in the capital of the Empire.

Closer to us, W.G. Grace, not the kind of man to miss an opportunity to add to the money he made from practising medicine in his spare time, was the first sports figure to endorse a non-sports product, long before Denis Compton advertised Brylcreem and Lionel Messi munched Lay's crisps in television commercials. Posters from the early 1900s show 'The Doctor' walking out of a cricket pavilion with the caption: 'Colman's Mustard – like Grace – Heads the Field'. He'd already lent his name to Lillywhite, Frowd & Co so they could launch a W.G. Grace line of bats, pads and gloves. His fame was such that a British garden furniture maker used his likeness to decorate the top of the legs of their metal chairs, as I found when visiting an Olde Worlde pub in Sussex, where those chairs were still in use a century later. Grace was, as C.L.R. James wrote in *Beyond a Boundary,* 'the best-known Englishman of his time', in an era where England's imperial dominance meant he was also the best-known well beyond Britannia's borders.

Fame of that kind spread in what was already a virtual world, the world of the imagination, a world in which sports lovers lived almost exclusively until the last three decades of the twentieth century. That world and those legends were born and travelled around the campfires of the Roman legions which conquered Europe, the Levant and north Africa. Later, they spread by hearsay, in gazettes and almanacs, then shaky Pathé newsreels in which crowd reaction shots outnumbered footage of goals being scored, radio broadcasts and finally, for the minority who could afford a TV set, the rare occasions on which a match was broadcast live. One thing remained the same: what we now call 'stardom' spread like a scent borne by the wind, very much real, but immaterial, fuelled by an age-old and quasi-mystical awe of sporting prowess.

The reputation of football greats such as Matthias Sindelar, Giuseppe Meazza, Duncan Edwards, Alfredo Di Stéfano and even Jimmy Greaves or George Best rests primarily on accounts of their heroic accomplishments, most of which are now lost to everything but memory. Taken together, they constitute football's Golden Legend, the chronicle of its Age of Miracles, in which faith counts for more than proof. There is no footage of the goal Pelé considered the best he had ever scored, at São Paulo's Rua Javari, in 1959; but all eyewitnesses told the same story, which we are happy to believe. The 18-year-old received a cross from the right on the volley just outside the box and, running towards goal, juggled the ball above the heads of three Clube Atlético Juventus defenders, in succession, before playing the same trick with their keeper and nodding it into an empty net. And he may well have done, just as Milo may well have lifted his bull. If foundation myths and folk songs can be passed unchanged through generations, why should it be so different for sporting tales?

Yet the virtuality in which we live now is a different beast altogether. Imagination no longer has a place or a role to play in that world: artifice has taken its place. In football, it comes in the guise of slow-motion replays, close-ups, multiple exotic camera angles and edgy editing which aims to accelerate the action, with a disregard for logic and bearing no resemblance to what spectators experience in the stadiums, giant screens or no giant screens. This is no longer the Age of Miracles, but the age of the spectacular, an age made for those footballers who trade in it, as Kylian Mbappé arguably does better – more spectacularly – than any of his contemporaries. Mystique and achievement used to be the pillars on which sporting stardom was born. This is no longer the case. There is no unseen left, no sacred place which can only be accessed by the mind's or the soul's eye. In this regard, whether we like it or not, there will never be another Milo, another Pelé or another Maradona. Deep down, we all know that Mbappé will not join them in that Pantheon. The veil has been lifted for good.

Consequently, if sporting superstardom and its exploitation for material gain are nothing new, the shape they have taken has shifted beyond recognition. Nothing escapes the scouts, the data analysts, the *Football Manager* gaming obsessives, or, in Mbappé's case, the cameras any longer. It is possible to watch every single minute of his appearances in official competitions since he made his first-team debut for Monaco on 2 December 2015, as a very late substitute in a 1–1 draw with Caen. It was one of the first records he broke. At 16 years and 347 days, he was just a month younger than Thierry Henry was at the time of his debut for ASM, back in 1994. We did not care a jot about such things back then. As a child prodigy who got his first sponsored kit before he was 10, Mbappé was already well used to having cameras trained on him anyway, starting with his father Wilfrid assiduously videoing his son's exploits in the Bondy youth teams, and didn't mind it one bit. Unlike the megastars his younger self hoped to emulate, his childhood idol Cristiano Ronaldo first among them, Mbappé is a late millennial who grew up in a digitally connected world he took to and learnt to use to his advantage as soon as his talent revealed itself.

It can feel like social networks have been a defining part of our reality for much longer than they actually have, when they only became a significant presence a little over a decade ago. Even YouTube, which seems so ubiquitous, only became accessible to the general public in 2005, when a Nike video featuring Ronaldinho facing a 'crossbar challenge' became the first to attract a million views. Cristiano Ronaldo had won an FA Cup and a League Cup with Manchester United and been capped thirty-nine times by Portugal at senior level before Twitter went live in July 2006, and four years would pass before he and his publicity team joined the platform. Ronaldo was 25 years old then. By the time the footballers' social network of preference Instagram was launched, in October 2010, the player who'd just left Manchester for Madrid had added a Ballon d'Or, three Premier League titles, a Champions League and a Club

World Cup to his honours. The same goes for Lionel Messi, Cristiano Ronaldo's cadet by two years and four months, who came to Twitter as a multiple La Liga, Champions League and Ballon d'Or winner in 2013; the year in which the @KMbappe handle appeared on the same platform for the first time. He'd just left Clairefontaine to join the academy of AS Monaco and would not play with the club's reserves for another couple of years. No-one knew what a meme was then. Barely anyone outside of the football world knew Kylian either.

In Messi's and Ronaldo's case, achievement had preceded the brand. They were, in many ways, the last of the traditional football stars as well as the first to cross into the viral-virtual world and make it theirs. They had more endorsements and earned far more money than their predecessors would have dreamt possible but had become headliners in the sports world before they had gained their first follower on social media. Even Neymar Jr, who is only six years older than Mbappé, already was a household name in his native Brazil (and a priority target for European clubs such as Chelsea – who made a £20 million offer for him when he'd just turned 18) when he caught up with the new trends. By the time Mbappé's future team-mate at Paris Saint-Germain launched his Instagram account, in 2012, he'd been capped by Brazil and won a Copa Libertadores, three Paulista championships and a Copa do Brazil. The huge following all three superstars built in record time on every platform followed on-field achievements which had made them superstars – or superstars-to-be in Neymar's case – the world over; Mbappé's own story is different. Ronaldo, Messi and Neymar rode a wave. Kylian was born in the ocean.

What sets him apart from previous footballing superstars is that his world is also the world which most of his fans inhabit, those fans who commune with other fans through video-sharing and rarely set foot in football arenas. The average age of stadium-goers and season-ticket holders has gone steadily up in Europe since the turn of the century, with several studies suggesting that the typical Real Madrid match-going supporter will be a 47-year-old male, and that only 8 per cent of La Liga spectators are aged between 18 and 24; part of the somewhat glibly-named 'TikTok generation', a generation which is also Mbappé's. It is not by chance that the French player is followed by almost 25 million people on TikTok, when Leo Messi's account is attracting less than 400,000, only twice as many as Kylian's younger brother Ethan. Cristiano Ronaldo's PR team hasn't even bothered creating one. It is a case of synchronicity, one which is central to our understanding of why and how Mbappé's career could be moulded into a unique sporting and commercial project by his family, a small entourage of carefully picked advisors and, above all, himself.

Everything about him, from his on-field acrobatics down to his casualness off it, chimes with the aspirations and desires of a generation for whom football is an individual game played in a collective context, in which a star player should be able to parade the skills of a freestyler, bicycle-kick for fun, crack a joke and goof for the camera. Watch him in the videos that those fans share by the millions, and compare them with Cristiano Ronaldo's, for example. Unlike his hero, Mbappé never tries to appear superhuman, even if some of the tricks he conjures would suggest he is. He is a comic book hero, a japer, a fun guy, not a video game Hercules who can behead five goblins in one arc of his sword. He acts and looks cool because that's what he is, *au naturel*. He loves being the centre of attention but is not narcissistic for that. There's never been a footballer like him. There have been a few who were just as good, or even better than he has shown himself to be until now. But Mbappé is a different animal, one which only his contemporaries truly understand. Older fans will be able to share their admiration, but as to what sets him apart – what are they even talking about?

This is one of the reasons why a book about Kylian Mbappé could not be a conventional biography. It's not just that at 27 years of age it is too early to tell a story that has a long time to run (his family and his advisors agree with this, as I found out). Should his body sustain the strain, he will add plenty of goals to the hundreds he's already scored and plenty of titles to those he's already won. The Champions League win he has chased from PSG to Real Madrid and the Ballon d'Or he covets more than any other distinction might not escape him much longer. He is only a couple of seasons into what are considered an elite footballer's best years. Such a biography would not even have an open-ended ending; it would have no ending whatsoever. What Mbappé's story is about we will only be able to tell once he enters the next chapter of his life, perhaps as a coach, as he told PSG's legendary striker Pauleta in a 2019 interview, perhaps as a football club owner, which he is since the investment fund he and his family set up bought French Ligue 2 club Stade Malherbe Caen in the summer of 2024.

The other reason is that the story which is worth telling is not the story of a uniquely gifted athlete who was earmarked for greatness almost as soon as his parents could find football boots small enough for him. It is how first Kylian's family, then himself, very much the master of his own destiny, devised a project around this unique gift, and bypassed all of the football business's usual conduits to make it a success. Potential pitfalls were identified from the outset and scrupulously avoided thereafter. Predatory agents were shown the door. Every aspect of the child's upbringing was tailored to ensure he could progress in a safe environment and acquire the skills he'd need to survive and prosper as a super elite player. Clubs were chosen not for monetary reasons – well, *not just* for monetary reasons – but for how well they fitted the project at a particular stage of Kylian's development. Clubs were left for the same reason. Financial and legal advisors had to submit to job interviews before being brought into the project; tellingly, none of those who were retained had had anything to do with football beforehand, and most were women.

Yet this is not the story of pushy parents smothering their precious child's spontaneity, of bullies screaming at coaches and referees on the touchline, of a wunderkind abused into abeyance. This is the story of how Kylian blossomed as a player and as a young man, the story of how he succeeded on the field, captained his country and became a regular guest at the Elysée presidential palace, never looking out of place or anything other than his relaxed, urbane, cheeky self whichever environment he was thrown into. He took part in two World Cup finals by the time he was 24, winning the first and scoring a hat-trick in the final of the second. He might yet become what the project has outlined for him: his sport's greatest star, the hero of a generation, then a great coach or, who knows, France's future Prime Minister.

Madame Bertin was only right to an extent. There is a 'new', which is just that, even if it is built on some of the foundations of the old.

1
Never in doubt

Kylian at Clairefontaine, 2011.

Journalists were no longer welcome at English training grounds in February 2017. And it was then that a friend who did PR for a small group of players and managers suggested I travelled to Middlesbrough to see for myself the training methods of her client Aitor Karanka, the former Real Madrid and Athletic Bilbao defender who was then in his third season at the Riverside Stadium. Middlesbrough were struggling. They hadn't registered a single win in the Premier League for two months and were about to be sucked into the relegation zone, from which Karanka was unable to extract them, leading to his departure at the end of the season. However, the opportunity to sneak into what had become a no-access area and witness the inner workings of a top-tier side was too rare to turn down. The only times media could access the inner sanctum by then were the open 'training sessions' held by the bigger clubs before European fixtures for the benefit of photographers and broadcasters. These exercises were by and large set up purely for show, with players jogging around the pitch and light-heartedly engaging in *rondos* which bore no relation to their actual preparations for a game. This promised to be different.

The abiding memory I have of that day spent at Rockliffe Park is not of the conversations I had with Karanka, pleasant and instructive as they were, nor of the various routines he and his assistants put the squad through. Middlesbrough's sports director at the time was a fresh-looking, bespectacled Spaniard named Victor Orta, who'd already built an impressive CV at the age of 39. He was only 27 when he'd been hired in a similar role by Real Valladolid, where he was spotted by Ramón Rodríguez Verdejo, better known as 'Monchi', the legendary sports director of Sevilla FC and the man who'd discovered the likes of Jesús Navas, José-Antonio Reyes and Sergio Ramos. Orta had been one of Monchi's closest collaborators for seven seasons in Andalucia before being poached by Russian club Zenit and, following a short stint back in Spain at Elche, joining Karanka's staff in 2015.

This is no insult to Karanka's coaching merit to say that having a close look at his training regimen took second place in my mind when I was told that Orta was willing to sit down and talk about his time with Monchi and shed light on the methods used by football's undisputed scouting guru of the time, methods which had acquired a quasi-mystical aura. These were still the days when sports directors did not rely primarily on reports drawn by data analysts, for a simple reason: the data which was available then was crude in comparison with what is on offer today. No-one had access to the number and breakdown of high-intensity sprints a player would commit himself to over ninety minutes. The notion of 'expected goals' remained a proposition discussed by academics and had yet to find a practical application within the sport. The data collection agencies which now routinely monitor and dissect low-level competitions – as low as the seventh or eighth tiers in some countries, including England – neither had the means nor the technology to be as detailed and exhaustive as they are now. As Orta explained, Monchi's astonishing ability to identify nascent talents in Spanish and European football was based on the work of some 700 independent scouts scattered throughout the Iberian Peninsula and beyond, who reported to him and his closest collaborators, the eyes of this modern sporting Argos.

There was an appealingly old-fashioned flavour to this work which, it should be remembered, was considered 'cutting edge' at the time. Almost every inch of Orta's desk was covered with piles of past editions of *France Football*, the weekly for which I'd travelled to Middlesbrough. This made sense, as *France Football* was the only magazine which published the full line-ups of all the teams that had taken part in official competitions during the previous week, down to the second and third divisions in the case of Europe's top leagues, and to the fourth and fifth for France. This information was not collated anywhere else. 'We have the full collection of your magazine in Sevilla,' he told me with a smile, adding that this was why he'd agreed to have a chat with its England correspondent.

I was particularly keen to put one specific question to him. How old – or how young – did a player have to be for you to track them?

More specifically, how long have you been aware of Kylian Mbappé?

Why Mbappé? Why would his name be the first that sprang to mind? Kylian, who was 18 at the time, had yet to make his debut for Les Bleus, despite being one of the stars of the show the French U19s had put on at their European Championships a year earlier, scoring five goals in a tournament which ended with France beating Italy 4-0 in the final. Monaco's manager Leonardo Jardim had used the teenager sparingly since giving him his debut as a late substitute in December 2015. As it happens, it was four days after I spoke to Orta, on 21 February 2017, that Mbappé started a Champions League game for the very first time, on the occasion of ASM's visit to Manchester City. Within a matter of weeks, following two exceptional displays against Pep Guardiola's team, he'd become Europe's most talked-about emerging talent; but he'd only been an episodic presence in Monaco's line-up until then, a passenger who'd spent most of his time in the waiting room while his team-mates battled through two tough qualifying rounds in Europe. Kylian's on-field contribution in that tournament so far had been a mere twenty-five minutes out of a possible 900, spread over three matches, and he'd remained on the bench for the 2–1 win over Spurs which guaranteed ASM would top their group.

Competition for places was fierce within the exceptional squad which Jardim had assembled and which could have gone on to far greater achievements if Monaco's billionaire Russian owner Dmitry Rybolovlev had been willing to keep it intact for another two or three seasons. Instead, its key elements – players of the calibre of Fabinho, João Moutinho, Benjamin Mendy, Thomas Lemar, Bernardo Silva and, of course, Mbappé himself – would all be gone within a calendar year of their winning the 2016–17 French title, eight points clear of Paris Saint-Germain and a prodigious 107 goals to the good, 12 of them scored by Kylian in the last four months of the season. But if the fuse had been lit, the explosion had yet to come.

So, why single Mbappé out? This was at least in part because of the media attention which had accompanied his decision to sign his first professional contract with Monaco in March 2016, when it was thought, with good reason, that he could have joined some of Europe's most successful clubs rather than ASM, who'd only rejoined Ligue 1 less than three years previously. Arsène Wenger, who was neither the first nor the last to compare Kylian to another teenage Monaco winger, Thierry Henry, had tried in vain to persuade him to join Arsenal before ASM got their man. Mbappé had already had a week-long trial at Chelsea in the spring of 2011 after being spotted playing for AS Bondy by Daniel Boga, the brother of Chelsea's *wunderkind* Jérémie Boga, who did scouting work in the Parisian *banlieue* for the London club. According to an interview he gave the *Athletic* shortly before the 2022 World Cup, Boga had been tipped off by a friend who worked for Kylian's sponsor Nike. Kylian had even played in a friendly against Charlton Athletic and kept a 'KYLIAN 10' shirt as a memento of his short stay in England. Kylian did not score in Chelsea's '6–0 or 7–0' (no one remembers exactly) win but made enough of an impression for the club to offer a second trial. According to Boga, Jim Fraser, Chelsea's long-standing youth development officer alongside Neil Bath, had made a comment which would be heard from others many times subsequently. 'Yeah, when he's got the ball he is amazing, etc,' he said. 'But we want to see this hunger.' Kylian would have to come back. According to what Boga told the *Athletic*, his mother Fayza, who'd been accompanied by his father Wilfrid and adopted brother Jirès on that trip, as per usual, retorted, 'No, we won't come again, if you want to sign him, you sign him now. In five years' time, you will come back for him for £50 million.' They did not do either.

Real Madrid too were interested in the youngster and invited him to spend a few days in Spain in December 2012. Kylian, who was about to turn 14, his parents and his uncle Pierre (Wilfrid's brother, a football coach himself and another influential member of the inner circle), were given tickets to a 2–2 home draw with Espanyol, in which the boy's hero Cristiano Ronaldo scored the Merengues' first goal. As Mbappé remembered it on his return, 'the morning after that, we went to the academy, which Monsieur Zidane made us visit for a bit'. (Monsieur Zidane, then Real's sporting director, would only start his ascension as a coach a year later, when he was put in charge of the club's reserves by Florentino Perez.) Kylian then took part in a training session and played an informal game with the club's youngsters, before being invited to a warming-down session with the A team a few days later. 'I took photographs with all of them,' he recalled. 'The Galácticos made me dream when I was 4 years old. I dream I can come back one day, through the main door.'

Real offered the prodigy a place at the club's academy, La Fábrica, 'the factory', which was declined. 'The euphoria died as soon as we received their positive response [sic],' Mbappé later told *France Football*. What he meant was that the joy of being judged good enough to be considered by Real was bound to be short-lived: the Mbappés had already decided to turn down whichever offer came from the Spanish club. 'I just wanted to prove [to] them I was a good player and feel they wanted me. There was also the fact [I'd have to] change countries, language and school. If there'd only been football, maybe I'd have gone there, but there was also the change of culture. If I have to go there, it'll be later.' Real Madrid was always part of the project, indeed its ultimate destination, but not just yet. There were further contacts with the club over the next couple of years. Kylian's father Wilfrid spoke with Zidane on a few more occasions, but these discussions stopped as soon as the sports director had been brought onto the technical staff of the first team, becoming Carlo Ancelotti's assistant in October 2013.

'I found it difficult to bother him [Zidane] for a 14-year-old kid,' Wilfrid said. 'Without him, we no longer had a point of reference. If he'd stayed with the young ones, we'd have gone for it. We spoke about everything, about the schools, not just about football. But what we were talking about was the arrival of a child, and that's why Caen were in the picture until the end. [Their] project, both in sporting and academic terms, was attractive to us; but Caen didn't get back to Ligue 1, and the project was fraying at the edges from then on.'

There was another reason why the Mbappés could do what very

few other parents of young footballers would have done and turn Europe's most successful club away. They could afford to, as Pierre Mbappé explained. 'He grew up in a very favourable environment,' he said. 'He was spoilt, but not spoilt rotten. My brother and my sister-in-law didn't want for money. That's why it makes me smile when I hear that the choice to join PSG [at a later stage] was motivated by money. Money never was the motivation. Priority was always given to the project built around the child.'

The same PSG had joined the beeline, but Kylian's parents were not convinced that the PSG of that era, which was entering its own gálactico stage and had just bought Zlatan Ibrahimović and Thiago Silva from Milan, plus Ezequiel Lavezzi from Napoli and Lucas Moura from São Paulo, was the right place for their son at that very early stage in his development. There was no guarantee that he would get the necessary playing time they believed his talent merited – or needed to grow into the star footballer they had the conviction he would become. But much of this – the approaches made by Arsenal, Chelsea, Real Madrid, PSG and others – only came to light later, once Mbappé had cemented his place at the top in the 2018 World Cup.

Orta confirmed that Sevilla too 'had been following him for a long time'. 'But it was already far too late for us to get involved by the time he was twelve,' he added. Not 'late', but 'far too late'. When Mbappé was twelve? 'Yes'. As Wenger had said, 'Unfortunately today, all these young players are in full view from very, very early on and all the big clubs want them.' Monchi and his team knew their place in football's food chain and looked elsewhere; not so paradoxically, fish smaller than Kylian would be a better catch for them.

Yet nothing was certain as we sat in Orta's office in February 2017. There was no guarantee that Mbappé would develop into a world-beater, even if it was obvious he had the talent for it. To start with, he was of slight build and his body was still growing. According to *Le Parisien*, PSG's unofficial newspaper, which chronicled the minutest details of his life and his career throughout the seven years he spent at the club, he would gain another 5 centimetres between 2018 and 2021. How would he respond to the greater demands put on his physique and the greater pressure put on his character? Tempting as it is to tell a story with a predictable ending, there were many ways in which things could have gone wrong for him and for the 'project'. You can't place bets by hindsight; yet the Mbappés never deviated from their methods or their objectives, certain as they were of Kylian's destiny.

Not every brilliant youth succeeds in football. The percentage who make it to a professional career is pitifully small, perhaps as low as 1 per cent in the top European leagues. It is estimated that half of those who sign professional forms at the age of 16 will leave football within two years of their first contract. This proportion grows to 75 per cent by the time they reach 21. Moreover, a 'professional career' means just that: it doesn't mean holding a place in a top team, it can mean being a squad member in a fourth-tier club. Talent is a prerequisite, not a guarantee. Almost every successful player can name academy team-mates who were more athletic, quicker and more skilful than themselves, could dribble the length of a field and slot it in the top corner, yet hit an invisible wall when it seemed nothing could stop them. Others make progress yet take an unexpected step back as they approach maturity.

Take Jean-Kévin Augustin. A year-and-a-half older than Kylian, he joined PSG's academy at the age of 12 and progressed smoothly through the ranks, winning caps for France in every age group, including the U19s who won their Euros in 2016. Mbappé scored five goals in that tournament. That was one fewer than Augustin, who was also voted the tournament's best player. One year later, he'd been signed by one of Europe's highest-rated finishing schools, RB Leipzig, for whom he performed adequately for one season before his form tailed-off and Ralf Rangnick got tired of his recruit's indiscipline. Augustin was sent on loan, first to AS Monaco, where he remained on the fringe of the first team, then to Leeds United, where he played a grand total of forty-eight minutes in the Championship for Marcelo Bielsa's side. A legal tussle which went all the way up the Court of Arbitration for Sport ensued, which ended up costing Leeds a fortune and wrecked what was left of the reputation of the player, who'd already damaged it by turning down a call to Les Espoirs, the French U21s, on the pretext he was injured – and then turning up in a friendly for his club. Augustin, now a free agent, moved to FC Nantes, for whom he failed to score a single goal in two years, after which it was Nantes's turn to let the former sensation go to FC Basel, where he failed again, finding himself unemployed at the age of 26. Augustin, now weakened by long COVID, last played – not very much – for Metro Lublin in the Polish Ekstraklasa and, at the time of writing, is clubless again. This was a footballer whom Lionel Messi had once chosen as one of 'five to follow' in world football.

Orta was as aware as anyone of the dangers all exceptional prospects must face in the crucial years of their development, yet told me that Mbappé was 'different' and that his future success was 'never in doubt'. The qualities which made him stand out from a very early age were also the qualities which would make him a contender for the Ballon d'Or. His first coach at AS Bondy, Antonio Riccardi, said he had 'two rockets for legs' and that he was 'able to combine this phenomenal speed with a technique which is out of the ordinary'. Training and match footage shot by Kylian's father Wilfrid when his son played for Riccardi, highlights of which were later used for an advertisement for EA Sports, supports the coach's words. The 8-year-old Mbappé displayed the same astonishing acceleration over short distances – and the ability to sustain his effort over the length of the pitch – which would later give nightmares to the likes of Gerard Piqué. His close ball control was as refined then as it is now. His bag of tricks was already packed to the full, in which he instinctively picked the one best-suited to the situation, as the boy was not just burning the grass like a lightning bolt but could think as fast as it fell as well. He could fizz the ball at pace into the net from tight angles from his favoured position on the wing, *à la* Thierry Henry, with this difference: the teenage Thierry had spent countless hours with his coach Claude Puel in Monaco to perfect what would become his signature move, whereas the boy Kylian could do it off the cuff as if to the manner born. His balance was exceptional. Everything he did was done at pace, with alertness of mind as well as swiftness and agility of body; and he carried those exceptional attributes through the age groups seamlessly, without being held back by his being usually a year (sometimes two) younger than his team-mates, without complaining, without getting hurt either. They couldn't catch up with him.

Ludovic Batelli, who coached France's youth teams from the U16s to the U20s between 2013 and 2017, hadn't seen Mbappé at first hand until 2014, when a friend insisted he should have a much closer look at the 15-year-old graduate from Clairefontaine who was on the verge of breaking into the first team at AS Monaco. Batelli did, and what struck him as much as anything was 'his *culot* ["cheek" as well as "nerve"], the way he didn't let pressure have an impact on him'. 'He loves football, he loves the game. He breathes it,' Batelli said. Then as later, and as will probably be the case until he retires, Mbappé was not one to track back or press his defender like other, less gifted and more malleable forwards will and most coaches insist they do. He knew – he'd always known – it was with the ball at his feet that he could have an impact, and this impact was so devastating that his managers, some more reluctant than others, accepted that the boy with the rocket legs should only ignite them when he felt it was the right thing to do. He wasn't found wanting in that respect. This was not laziness. Mbappé didn't shun or dislike training – he always turned up in good time and often was one of the last to leave the field, rehearsing his shooting technique on his own if he had to – but he trained to his strengths rather than to the demands of his coaches.

Batelli called the teenager to the French U19 squad as soon as he could, naming him in the starting line-up of France's first qualifier for the 2016 Euros, a 1–0 win over Montenegro on 3 March 2016. Mbappé would not miss a single U19 competitive game thereafter, until the time came for him to join the senior side. The trust Batelli put in the youngest of his players* was rewarded in spectacular fashion. It was Mbappé who got the goal against Serbia which sealed France's place in the final phase of the 2016 U19 Euros – a typical finish across the keeper, from the right flank on this occasion. It was Mbappé who scored an astonishing second goal in France's 2–0 crucial win over Croatia in the tournament itself. Twenty-four hours earlier, eighty-one people had died in Nice, when a lorry driven by an Islamic terrorist had rammed into the crowd. As Batelli reminded his players in his last team talk before kick-off, they would not just play for themselves or their families that day but also for a country in mourning. In a single blur, Mbappé ghosted past the Croatian

---

* Only one other player of the squad selected by Batelli for the 2016 U19 Euros was born in 1998, defender Faitout Maouassa, Kylian's elder by almost six months.

right-back at full speed, cushioned Issa Diop's long pass with the outside of his right boot, then controlled it with his left, dribbled past the keeper and guided the ball into the net, all in one fluid movement. Kylian did not celebrate that goal.

More were to come, starting with a brace against the Netherlands in the last group game. In the semi-final against Portugal – a revenge of the Euro 2016 final which the French A team had lost a few days previously – it was 'Kyky', as Batelli called him, who set up Jean-Kévin Augustin for France's equaliser after a breathtaking raid on the left wing and a mazy run in which he waltzed alongside the goal line like a highwire acrobat to cut through the Portuguese defence; after which he scored twice again, the second of his goals an unlikely, brave glancing header, perhaps the least Mbappé-esque goal he ever put his name to.

Every scout and recruiter in Europe, including Orta, had now seen the prodigy on what was the greatest stage that football could set up for a boy of his age. To most of them, it was not a revelation but confirmation of what they already knew. Mbappé was a generational talent whose future might eclipse that of all his contemporaries. No matter how early they'd noticed him, they were already too late. The Mbappés had been right. That future had never been in doubt.

2
Jirès Kembo: the birth of the project

The Zaïre 1974 WC team. Jean Uba Kembo is front row, second from right.

Unless you happen to be German or Polish, or have a particular fetish for the Adidas Durlast matchball, it is unlikely you will feel nostalgic about the 1974 World Cup. In my own, vague memories, it was played through a veil of fine drizzle, in stadiums surrounded by factories belching steam and smoke into a leaden sky, a return to black and white after the explosion of colour of Mexico 1970. Reigning champions Brazil played some of their games in an ugly shade of blue, which I suppose suited their new, brutal brand of football. The artists had gone: there was no Pelé, Tostão or Gérson; there was no Peru and no Teófilo Cubillas, who had failed to qualify. There was Johann Cruyff, but the Dutch failed at the last, against a West German team which, though superb in many respects, was the purest expression of everything the rest of the world loved to detest about them. Poland, with their attacking trio of Gadocha, Szarmach and the balding Lato (the competition's top goalscorer) provided some excitement, but as much because of the unexpected nature of their success as of the way in which they achieved it. They, too, fell to the Germans, by a single goal, in the one game they didn't win at the tournament, the one which mattered most. This wasn't a tournament for romantics.

One of the few enduring images of 1974 is of Zaïre defender Mwepu Ilunga haring out of his team's defensive wall after Brazil had been awarded a free-kick some 25 yards away from goal and smashing the ball upfield before the referee had blown his whistle. This gave TV summarisers of the time the perfect excuse to engage in comments which ranged from the condescending to the downright racist. Those Africans, eh. We knew they couldn't defend (Yugoslavia had put nine goals past Zaïre without reply in their previous group game). Now we also knew that they were ignorant of the most basic laws of the game as well. What those commentators didn't know was that Mwepu Ilunga's apparent moment of folly was in fact a protest against the appalling way he and his team-mates had been treated by their federation and by the regime of Zaïre's president Mobutu Sese Seko. Together, they had broken every promise made before the competition while basking in the reflected glory of their country's first-ever qualification for the final phase of a World Cup.

Their capitulation against Yugoslavia had been a direct consequence of this. The players had learnt prior to the game that the money which was supposed to reward their efforts had been embezzled by the officials and hangers-on who outnumbered them at their World Cup base. The team which had caused Scotland so many problems in its opening game, losing 0–2 yet forcing the respect of neutrals, was an empty shell, a phantom. The players had initially decided to go on strike and were only persuaded to turn up on the field hours before the start. Mobutu stepped in, in the manner befitting one of the most brutal dictators of his time. He issued threats to players who needn't be told twice they should take them seriously. Some of them reportedly were the target of assassination attempts when they returned home.

Mwepu Ilunga had had enough. No more of this. When Romanian

referee Nicolae Rainea awarded Brazil a free-kick 25 yards away from the Zaïre goal, he saw a chance to be sent off by surging from the box and kicking the ball away as hard as he could; all he got was a yellow card and a place of choice in YouTube compilations of 'mad' moments in football. 'We got back home without a penny in our pockets,' Mwepu Ilunga told the BBC in 2002. 'Look at me now, I'm living like a tramp.' He died in 2015, aged 65.

It didn't matter that this Zaïre team was at the time one of Africa's very best, a double winner of their continent's championship, in 1968 and 1974. It didn't matter that, to get to Germany, they had beaten powerhouses such as Cameroon, Ghana and Morocco – twice – on their way. It didn't matter that Fifa had allocated just the one World Cup berth to the African confederation and that, defying the odds, Zaïre had claimed it. They were the first sub-Saharan team to do this in the history of the World Cup. This exploit would not be repeated. Despite the enlargement of the tournament from sixteen teams in 1974 to the thirty-two who took part in the 2022 Qatar edition, Zaïre, now the Democratic Republic of Congo, has not qualified for the World Cup proper since.

The hero of their qualification was a diminutive, aggressive striker called Jean 'Pépé' Kembo Uba Kembo, nicknamed *Monsieur But* not just for his ability to score plenty of goals, but also for scoring them at the most crucial of times. Jean's 'take no prisoners' approach to the game was exemplified in a club match against CARA Brazzaville, in which he'd barged the opposing keeper with such force that both post and bar of the goal were shattered and local carpenters had to be summoned to fix them mid-game. Kembo finished the qualification phase for the 1974 World Cup as joint top goalscorer in the competition, with doubles against Ghana in the third round and in what amounted to a final against the Moroccans, in front of more than 70,000 home supporters. European football hadn't embarked on its wholesale pillage of African talent yet. Jean spent all of his career in Kinshasa's then pre-eminent club AS Vita Club, a key component of the team's famous so-called 'machine-gun attack', winning seven Zaïre league titles and an African Champions Cup in the thirteen years he spent there, a hero at home, an unknown elsewhere. His popularity was such that his federation had to backtrack after it suspended him for three years in 1971 for daring to complain about unpaid wages.

Jean Kembo Uba Kembo was part of that 1974 squad and played in all three of Zaïre's games in Germany: a starter in the catastrophic loss to Yugoslavia, a second-half substitute in the other two. He was on the pitch in Gelsenkirchen to witness at first hand Mwepu Ilunga kicking the ball downfield with everything he'd got against the Brazilians. Jean was also the biological father of Kylian Mbappé's 'adopted' brother, Jirès Kembo Ekoko. Bizarre as it may seem, the French 2018 World Cup winner had a direct family link to one of the most famous episodes of the 1974 tournament. That's not all. Without Jirès, there may well never have been an 'Mbappé project'. What is certain is that it wouldn't have taken the shape it did.

Jirès, who was born in 1988, eight years after his father retired from professional football in 1980, had been named after Alain Giresse, the footballing geometer with the sweetest of touches who, alongside Michel Platini and Jean Tigana, breathed magic into France's midfield in its European and World Cup campaigns from 1978 to 1986. Jean, all of 5 ft 5 tall, may have seen something of himself in the goalscoring midfielder who was even shorter than he was – by 2 inches.

In 1994, Zaïre was about to descend into civil war, with Mobutu hanging on to power by the most fragile of threads as head of state in a government cobbled together from two rival, briefly reconciled warring factions which soon started to fight each other again. Kinshasa was one of the most dangerous places on Earth at the time. Looting was commonplace, violence ever-present. Some 20,000 foreign nationals, most of them French and Belgian, had been evacuated from the capital city three years previously.

In neighbouring Rwanda, following the assassination of President Juvénal Habyarimana on 6 April 1994, militias from the Hutu tribal group had embarked on a genocidal campaign which would cost the lives of over half a million people in a single year, the vast majority of them ethnic Tutsis. The Hutus were ultimately defeated, and many of the perpetrators of the Tutsi genocide fled to Zaïre, which was renamed the Democratic Republic of Congo in 1997. The conflict is still raging nearly thirty years later and has led to the death of an estimated five million Congolese civilians.

Any parent would have wanted their children to escape this nightmare. In 1994, when he was just 6, Jirès was sent to live with an uncle who had settled in France. 'My parents wanted to give me a chance to have a better life,' he told French magazine *So Foot* in 2016. 'With hindsight, I can only salute what they did. It is not everyone who has the strength to do this.'

Things didn't work quite as hoped, not the way Jean and his wife intended in any case. 'I moved around quite a bit,' Jirès recalled, 'until I finally ended up in Paris with my new family, the people who now are my parents.' Wilfrid and Fayza, still childless, had been made aware of the youngster's precarious situation and offered him a place in their Bondy home, a modest – 59 square metres – but comfortable second floor flat in a small house a stroll away from AS Bondy's Léo Lagrange stadium. Later, Kylian and his younger brother Ethan would also grow up there. Jirès was never formally adopted but later became Wilfrid's legal ward and was treated as a son – a son who soon displayed exceptional qualities as a footballer. 'It was in my blood ever since I was born,' he said. 'It started in the schoolyard. I often was the first one to be picked in the teams. That was a good sign.'

In 1997, Jirès joined AS Bondy, where Wilfrid was already working as a coach and a mentor to the club's youth teams. 'It's hard to explain,' Jirès said. 'It is as if this person was destined for me. He was the father figure I hadn't had.' His progress was smooth and, in 2001, ten years before Kylian did the same, he joined Clairefontaine as a boarder, where he initially trained as a midfielder before his coaches saw he could flourish as a striker. Several French and foreign professional clubs, including PSG, had shown interest in him early on, but, in 2004, the teenager chose to go with Rennes, then a solid middle-of-the-table Ligue 1 club where he thought he would stand a better chance of breaking into the first team. That choice, which he insists he made himself, met with the approval of his new family. The Mbappés, though not quite as involved as they would later be with Kylian and, later, Ethan, had been careful to ward off the agents who'd circled around their charge at the Institut National du Football, 'people who do not necessarily work for your own good', as Jirès put it. 'The most important element in a player's success, or lack of it, is his entourage,' he said. 'I had the luck of being surrounded by good people, who gave me a lot of love and were first and foremost preoccupied with my well-being and not with what I could bring in for them.' Two years later, 'Kembinho', as he was nicknamed, a nod to 2005 Ballon d'Or winner and then Barcelona superstar Ronaldinho, signed his first professional form with the Breton club. Call-ups to the U20 and U23 France teams followed soon afterwards. The Congolese federation approached him, but Jirès, who had acquired French citizenship in 2008, turned down the chance to represent the country of his birth. He had his sights set on Les Bleus. His father Jean had died a year beforehand, at the age of 59.

This constituted remarkable progress for a teenager who, twelve years previously, had still been playing in the streets of Kinshasa. But Jirès was impatient by nature. He believed he already deserved a place in the starting line-up of Stade Rennais. He believed he should play and asked his club to loan him out to lower-division clubs on several occasions in order to test himself in competitions. Each time, Rennes turned down his request. To them, at least for the time being, he remained what the French call *le joker*, the kind of player who has the capacity to turn things round by himself but is only called upon as a last resort in the dying stages of a game. 'Be patient, your chance will come, you will play,' his management kept telling him. 'I had fire in my legs,' he said. 'I was killing it in training, and it wasn't an easy situation to live with.' When Rennes' main striker Jimmy Briand was injured just before the final of the 2009 French Cup, Jirès thought his time had come. His club's opponents were a local rival, Guingamp, then in Ligue 2, but it was from the bench that he saw US left-back Carlos Bocanegra give his side a 1–0 lead in the second half. It was only one minute before the final whistle that *le joker* was at last brought on, after Guingamp had scored twice in the space of ten minutes, far too late to have an impact on a match Rennes had been expected to win at a canter. He still extended his contract the season after that. 'To leave then would have been [an admission of] failure,' he explained. 'I didn't want to go without having really played for them.'

Yet it was not until 2011, by which time the Corsican Frédéric Antonetti had replaced Guy Lacombe as head coach, that Jirès was given an opportunity to show on a regular basis what he could bring to the club he'd joined seven years previously. Over two years had passed since he'd scored his first Ligue 1 goal, a powerful long-distance strike against Le Mans. The 2011–12 season brought him 13 goals, the most significant of them another long-range shot in a 1–0 victory in Marseille's Stade Vélodrome which finally cemented his place in the starting line-up. Jirès was only 24. This is when he took a decision no-one but him could quite comprehend. He was expected to sign a new, much-improved contract with Rennes, and, indeed, after months of negotiation, was days away from putting pen to paper. He accepted an offer from Emirati club Al Ain instead.

There could be no motivation other than money for such a move. Four years later, he maintained that it was a decision he'd mulled over for a long time and that he 'regretted nothing'. 'It was a life choice,' he said. 'There are still people who do not understand [why I did it]. It was an opportunity that might never present itself again, and as you never know what tomorrow will be made of in football . . .' He didn't finish the sentence. But yes, it was the money, and he admitted as much. 'When I talk about life choices, I also include the financial side. It clearly played its part.'

His career would not recover. Les Bleus never called. He won a couple of league titles in the United Arab Emirates with Al Ain and a Qatar Cup while on loan with El Jaish; but who cared about that? He'd thought of his move to the Gulf as a lucrative parenthesis in his career. Clubs which had coveted him interpreted it as a lack of ambition, and the parenthesis turned into a five-year hiatus, at the exact moment when he should have hit his peak as a player. While in the UAE, he talked about his desire to come back to Europe 'one day'. That day finally came in 2017, when he joined Turkish Süper Lig club Bursaspor. It proved a disaster. A first so-so season in Burse (four goals in twenty-four league appearances, five of them as a substitute) was followed by a nightmarish second, in which he was also injured and played a grand total of fourteen minutes in all competitions. Jirès Kembo officially retired on 1 July 2019, at the age of 31, a mere footballing footnote; a player who will be remembered as a wasted talent who took the wrong turn and could not trace his way back to where he really belonged.

Little brother Kylian idolised Jirès. He showed that you could come from Bondy and make it as a professional. 'Kyks' treasured the French jersey that Jirès had given him after playing for Les Espoirs. In the dreamland he inhabited, where he lined up footballs instead of fluffy toys in front of the TV to 'watch' a game and, aged 5 or 6, sang 'La Marseillaise', hand on heart, when Les Bleus were playing, Jirès was proof that if you believed enough, nothing was impossible. 'My parents said I was a bit crazy,' Kylian recalled. 'But the more it went on, the less they were saying it.' Jirès's departure to the UAE hit Kylian hard. 'It was his choice,' he remembered. 'But I didn't accept it. It was really tough for me. [Jirès] had just come out of a great season for Rennes and wasn't that far from the French national team. I thought he could do something. I cried. It was the love of a brother [which was expressing itself].' Kylian was only 13 at the time; but he knew, better than his elder, and he wouldn't make the same mistake himself.

Jirès was not a 'project' as Kylian would become. The family had supported and tried to protect him the best they could; but their approach had been primarily reactive, and when the time came for the biggest decision of his life so far – to leave Rennes and prioritise money over career prospects – they'd been unable to bend his will, if indeed they even tried to. Maybe they didn't fully realise then what the implications of that choice would be. Maybe they felt that at 24, Jirès had every right to do what he felt was correct. Maybe they weren't quite sure anyway. Unlike Kylian, neither Wilfrid nor Fayza ever publicly commented on the subject; but they did not forget what had happened. Jirès was not just an example of what could be achieved, but also of what should not be done: football must always be the priority. Money mattered, but no choice should be made on the basis of financial interest alone. That lesson would not be forgotten when Kylian himself faced similar career choices.

Jirès never left the inner circle, the 'clan', as the media called them. He accompanied his 'little brother' wherever he went in his early years, be it Chelsea or Madrid, together with uncle Pierre and family friend Alain Mboma. He had 'no fingernails left' when Kylian started with the pros at AS Monaco. He was in the room when Kylian signed his first professional contract with the Monégasques in 2016. On his side, Kylian made sure to maintain close contact with Jirès and his children after his brother's career came to an end at the age of 31. For the Mbappés, this did not constitute a rehearsal or a field experiment of what was to come; but they could also see how and why the career of Kylian's childhood hero had been ruined by a single decision borne out of impatience. Once was enough.

3

Bondy

A giant mural of Kylian celebrating 'Bondy, ville des possibles'.

As France prepared to face England in the quarter-finals of the 2022 World Cup, British newspapers turned their attention to the striker who'd already scored five times in the competition so far. Ordinary accounts of Mbappé's career were no longer enough; there'd been plenty of those published since he'd been voted 'best young player' at the Russian World Cup four years previously. New angles had to be found. So – who is he *really*? Where does he come from? The *Daily Mail* showed particular appetite for such questions. It told its readers that the 'free-scoring winger' who earned '£1.2 million a WEEK' and was 'linked to various high-profile women' had grown up 'in poverty'. His home town, Bondy, was 'part of the infamous Seine-Saint-Denis 93rd arrondissement – one of the [*sic*] France's poorest neighbourhoods which over the years has earned a reputation for sky-high crime rates and violence'; in other words, the kind of place where Mathieu Kassovitz could have shot *La Haine*, the 1990s film through which international audiences discovered the brutal reality of life in the Parisian *banlieue*. Three days later, the *Mail* completed its Mbappé one-two. The paper despatched a reporter to Bondy, who, by the sound of it, was looking forward to his Eurostar trip back to London as soon as he set foot in that urban hell-hole.

The piece mentioned the gigantic Mbappé mural which, since December 2019, has covered the side elevation of a high-rise apartment building at 21, rue Jules Guesde. A very young Kylian is shown asleep, cradling a football, dressed in the green of AS Bondy, dreaming about his older self wearing the number 10 for Les Bleus. This colossal piece of 'street art' was nothing of the kind: it had been commissioned and paid for by Kylian's principal sponsor Nike. The *Mail* journalist noticed that an unknown hand had written a threatening message directed at the player over the fresco, 'symbolic (. . .) of how Mbappe's image has been tarnished in recent years', he ventured. He also remarked that the crowds he had expected to congregate around the mural had 'gathered on a nearby bridge as emergency services tended to a body. Fished out of the river, apparently.'

The story wrote itself. Mbappé was another one of those young men from the immigrant community (Wilfrid was born in Cameroon, tick, Fayza's parents were from Algeria, tick again) for whom football represented more than a pastime or even a passion. It was a means to escape the nightmarish environment of *cités* rife with vandalism, drug dealing and violence, breeding grounds for feral children, criminals and terrorists. Ignored by the establishment and demonised by French right-wing parties (not just Marine Le Pen's Rassemblement National) these young men, *la racaille*, as president Nicolas Sarkozy had called them (a derogatory term of which 'riff-raff' is far too soft a translation), were staring at futures blighted by social rejection and unemployment, destined for the refuse heap of society – and, probably, jail. Football offered a way out, as did rap music. Nothing else. The one upside was that, as with the *villas miserias* of Argentina and the *cantegrils* of Uruguay, the footballers who grew up in the blighted *cités*, those who made it at least, had fire raging in their bellies, a hunger which set them apart from players who came from more comfortable environments. Think Diego Maradona and Luis Suárez – think Zinedine Zidane, the child of Marseille's notorious *cité* of La Castellane.

There is some truth in those common assumptions. Bondy is a world away from the sleepy quietude of bourgeois Versailles or gentrified Issy-les-Moulineaux and Vincennes. Bondy was not spared when violent riots shook the suburbs of Paris and other French cities in late October and November 2005. Over 10,000 cars – 1,400 on a single night, on 7 November – and 300 buildings were set ablaze by angry youths, embracing Paris in a ring of fire for a whole three weeks. The trigger of the violent unrest was the death, on Thursday 27 October 2005, of two teenagers from Clichy-sous-Bois, less than 6 kilometres away from Bondy, named Zyed Benna and Bouna Traoré, who had been electrocuted in an EDF substation. They'd been playing football all afternoon and wanted to be home in time for *Iftar*, the breaking of the Ramadan fast. A local man saw some youths enter a construction site and, thinking they were up to no good, alerted the police. The boys – Zyed was 17, Bouna only 15 – accompanied by a friend who survived the tragedy, panicked when they were approached by officers who misidentified them as the suspected intruders. They sought refuge and found death.

They'd done nothing wrong. They died not because of what they did or didn't do; they died because of a complete lack of trust: the man who spotted young men entering the construction site didn't trust them; Zyed, Bouna and their friend didn't trust the police. They literally 'died for nothing', as was written on a banner displayed at the front of one of the many demonstrations which followed the tragedy. A state of emergency was imposed in Bondy, as it was almost everywhere else in the suburbs of the capital and of most of France's main cities. Brest, Nantes, Strasbourg, St Etienne and Toulouse in particular witnessed appalling violence. That, what happened in 2005, was the reality of the *banlieue* in the eyes of those who did not live there and never set foot in it.

Yet, Bondy is not a lawless space where young men who can't get a job have no choice but to turn to crime to survive, even if the unemployment rate there is twice the French national average. It is by no means the most unsafe town in the *banlieue*; Sarcelles, Argenteuil and Saint-Denis have worse records in this respect. It may be the kind of place where outsiders should be careful to avoid certain areas, even in daylight, yet, over the last five years, there have been more murders in Torquay, Folkestone or Clacton-on-Sea, all of them towns with a similar population (just over 50,000 residents), than in Bondy.

The *Bondynois* themselves are not an homogeneous group, be it socially or ethnically. Paris is close-by, a sixteen-minute commute to Gare du Nord on Line E of the RER suburban network, about the same time it would have taken to walk from the Mbappé home to Bondy station. The most recent census shows that a notable proportion of *Bondynois*, over 7 per cent of them, are 'professionals', 'senior executives' or 'business people'. The Mbappé family didn't quite fit into that category but could be considered to be part of Bondy's lower middle- to middle-class, in a position to offer their children a safe, comfortable lifestyle far removed from the 'poverty' Kylian was supposed to have been born into. Wilfrid came from what could be considered a privileged, even aristocratic background in Cameroon. Djébalé, where he was born on 11 October 1970, is an island in the estuary of the Wouri river, part of the country's most populated city Douala. It is home to the Sawa people, a Bantu ethnic group of which Wilfrid's father Philippe Mbappé-Bessemé, who also settled in Bondy and was a constant presence in his grandson's upbringing, is a tribal chief. Kylian himself was ennobled by the 'Association of Sawa Monarchs of the Littoral' in November 2023, four months after he'd visited his father's village, dressed in full Sawa garb, to see for himself how money provided by his foundation had enabled the local community to rebuild their dilapidated 1930s school.

For most of Kylian's childhood, the family home was a second-floor flat in a four-storey house at 4, Allée des Lilas. Wilfrid and Fayza, who never married but entered into a civil partnership – *pacte civil de solidarité* – in December 2016, and separated amicably less than five years later, had moved there when Fayza was pregnant with their first son. The apartment, located in one of Bondy's more salubrious neighbourhoods, was large enough to accommodate a family of four – Ethan was born in 2006, the year Jirès joined Rennes – and enabled the brothers to organise impromptu one v one football games in their bedroom. 'I've only kept good memories of [Bondy],' Kylian remembered later, 'as when I was coming back from school, right in front of the stadium, with the ball in my satchel. I went straight to play, without even coming home first.' That school was the Groupe Scolaire Assomption, a private catholic school just round the corner from Allée des Lilas.

'People outside of France always speak of the *banlieues* in a negative way, but when you're not from there, you cannot understand what it's like,' he told the *Players' Tribune* in February 2020, in a 'Letter to the young Kylians' which is strikingly different in style and tone from similar pieces 'written' by other sports stars for that platform. The voice that can be heard in those lines sounds very much like his, not the embellished whispers of a ghost. 'There, we live in an incredible mix of different cultures – French, African, Asian, Arabic, from every corner of the world,' he explained. 'People talk about delinquents as if they'd been invented [in the *banlieue*]. But there are delinquents everywhere in the world. The reality is that when I was a little boy, I used to see some of the toughest guys in my *quartier* carry my grandmother's shopping. You never see that side of our culture on the news. You always hear about the bad stuff, never the good stuff.'

Kylian himself was not of those 'tough guys', and if he'd ever been tempted to become one or, given his slight physique, to join their hangers-on, his parents would have seen to it immediately. In any case, whilst he was a true *Bondynois*, the relative affluence of his family set him apart from most of the children he went to nursery school with. It's not every little *banlieusard* who gets given a miniature electric 4x4 car for his third birthday. 'There were pedals, everything,' he recalled. 'My parents let me drive it from our home to the football pitch on the other side of the street, as if I were a real footballer who drove to training. I was taking my routine very seriously. All I missed was my toiletries bag.' Kylian didn't want for anything, including replica shirts of his favourite players: *genuine* shirts, that is, something which made a strong impression on the friends he kicked a football with in the streets.

Growing up in Bondy was also a blessing for children who loved sport. Few towns of 50,000 inhabitants provide their residents with two football stadiums, both natural grass and synthetic pitches, an athletics track, a futsal indoor facility, a dedicated five-a-side space, two fully-equipped gymnasiums, a 'sports palace' complete with two boxing rings, a fencing school, indoor and outdoor tennis and badminton courts (five of them), as well as a dojo for judo, taiso and ju jitsu practitioners. All of these facilities are owned and run by the local authority and are made available to the population for little or no money since a visionary mayor, Claude Fuzier, decided in the late

1970s that everyone in his community should have full access to its remarkable sports infrastructure, regardless of whether they were officially registered with a federation or not. The local authority's significant investment in sport has paid rich dividends in terms of both social cohesion and civic pride, as a quite extraordinary number of young men and women from Bondy have gone on to represent their country in the world's greatest competitions. Sprinters Muriel Hurtis and Jimmy Vicaut both won bronze with Olympic French 4x100 relay teams; tennis player Quentin Halys entered the ATP's top 50 in May 2025; basketballer Thierry Zig played in the top divisions of France, Spain and Italy; judoka Audrey Tcheuméo won silver and bronze at the London and Rio Olympics on top of eight individual European titles. Then there are the footballers: Kolo Muani of Eintracht Frankfurt, PSG and Juventus and Jonathan Ikoné of Lille, Fiorentina and Como were both born in the annus mirabilis of 1998, just a few days before their future France team-mate Kylian in Muani's case. William Saliba of Arsenal, three years their junior, is the latest name to have been added to that prodigious list.

Then there are Wilfrid and Fayza themselves. Wilfrid, who never made the step up from amateur regional football as a player, found his true calling in coaching, first as a volunteer, then as a club employee, taking care of Bondy's seniors as well as every youth category from the U11s to the U17s. Fayza, who'd grown up next to one of the city's gymnasiums, took to handball in her teenage years, as several of her brothers had done before her, and progressed through the age categories to become one of the key players in the AS Bondy side which won the second division French title in 1998 and went on to play in a European competition, the Coupe Challenge, three years later. Jean-Louis Kimmoun, one of the club's senior officials at the time, recalled 'a fighter on the court, [someone who] should not be teased, not always the friendly type with her opponents. When you came across Fayza, you didn't forget it.' It should be remembered that handball is not a minority pursuit in France, but one of the most popular team sports, played in every college and high school, and which has earned the country four gold medals for its men's and women's teams at the Olympics. Fayza's team-mates included two genuine legends of the game, Svetlana Mugoša-Antić, a world and Olympic champion with former Yugoslavia, and Hungary's then most-capped player Éva Erdős, who scored over 700 goals in 277 games for her country. Fayza was a top athlete, a professional until 2001, when, aged just 27, she became a facilitator in a leisure centre, a logical choice for a young woman who'd graduated in educational studies, and which she only left to become a full-time advisor to Kylian. Add the Mbappés' ward Jirès Kembo to the mix, as well as a network of family members and close friends which included Wilfrid's younger brother Pierre, also a coach, and Patrick Mboma, another Bondy resident and one of Cameroon's greatest-ever footballers, and you have what looks like an almost ideal environment for a gifted child to flourish in. All that was required was to provide him with the right kind of education.

As it happens, Bondy could do that too.

4

Education, education, education

Kylian in his bedroom in Bondy.

Not all professional footballers love the game. Some will admit to it in public, like Marc-André ter Stegen of Barcelona, Ben White of Arsenal or Cameroon international Benoît Assou-Ekotto, formerly of Tottenham Hotspur, who never hid the fact that he was primarily motivated by money and did not fancy working 'all his life in an office for €1,500 a month' in order 'to buy a little suburban apartment or something' at the end of his career. Then there are those footballers who detest their profession and have good reason for this.

'S.' was one of these. He was an enigma to his team-mates, a loner who did not join in the dressing-room banter; but he could make the ball sing so well it is a mystery why he never received a call-up to his country's national team. His career spanned almost twenty years, which he spent in top-tier European clubs; he played well over fifty games in UEFA competitions, some of them in the Champions League; songs were sung in his honour. Yet he hated football.

Another footballer who'd trained at the same academy told me why: 'S.' had been abused by his own father for years. The pattern is well-known. Parents waking their child up at dawn for their morning run. Clips round the ear or worse after a bad game. Constant reminders that the family has invested so much time and money into the kid's future that every indifferent performance is a betrayal. 'S.' had gone through all of this; but he'd also gone through far worse. His father, a former amateur footballer himself, was a sadist. The family lived in the countryside, 9 or 10 kilometres from the academy. If he thought his son had failed to give his best in a training session, he'd stop the car as soon as they were out of sight. 'S.' would have to step out and run back home, his father driving behind him in first gear, with headlights on, left arm resting on the open window, shouting abuse and honking the horn if the child was slacking. It didn't matter how cold it was, it didn't matter if it rained or snowed, which it often did in that part of Northern Europe. It didn't matter if 'S.' cried or pleaded to be spared just this once. My informer knew this because he'd been in that car a few times himself and watched his friend, still in his training kit, pound the surface of the road in the dark. The father didn't give a damn if another child saw what he was doing to his son. The club must have known as well but did nothing.

But why did 'S.' stay in football, then, and for so long, long after he had earned enough to ensure he would never have to work again? He knew about nothing else, his friend said. He felt lost outside of the only world he knew. He'd finished school without any qualifications, so what could he do? More than anything, he was still under the influence of the man who'd tortured him throughout his childhood and his teenage years.

What 'S.' went through, countless children are also going through today, in France as much as anywhere else; France where this kind of parental obsession is now referred to in the media as – yes – *un projet Mbappé*. The bitter irony is that the actual *projet Mbappé* has nothing to do with this cruel simulacrum of care, in which ambition cannot be distinguished from coercion. It is so widespread now that it has become a branch of the football industry, as professional clubs realised how offering training camps to children as young as three was a lucrative business. PSG was charging €1,190 per child for its Easter six-day course in 2024, sweetening its offer with a 'free' tour of the Parc des Princes, a complete training Nike kit and 'awards for all participants' at the 'ending ceremony'. FC Barcelona now runs more than thirty of these academies spread over 180 campuses throughout the world. A ten-day course in Barcelona itself costs just under $3,200. Everyone is welcome, regardless of talent, as it is not about talent-spotting anymore. It is about making money by playing on the unrealistic aspirations of parents as much as on the passion of their children. Imagine going back to school and telling your friends what you did during the holidays just by pointing at the badge on your T-shirt.

Private football training schools and coaches are also doing well out of it, especially in France, to the extent that the *projet Mbappé* phenomenon made the national news in the autumn of 2024. Public broadcaster France Bleu had no problem finding a pushy father who not only paid a (non-qualified) trainer to put his 7- and 9-year-old sons through extra sessions every Sunday but had also bought all of the training kit needed for their exercises. One child the reporters spoke to had individual football tuition of this kind six evenings a week on top of his club's training programme. None of these youngsters had shown particular promise or been scouted by professional clubs. These are not isolated examples. More and more families are spending large amounts of money on individual tuition in the misguided belief that this is what Kylian's parents did themselves. They did not. What they did was to provide the education best-tailored to Kylian's own needs, which were many, and talent, which was exceptional.

When French TV network Canal+ questioned him in December

2024 about the *projet* which now bore his name, Mbappé exploded. 'Stop it, cut it out, cut it all,' he said. 'My parents never put any pressure on me. My dad never made me run round the pitch at six in the morning with a stopwatch in his hand. They let me have fun.' Kylian went on, talking about himself in the third person, something he's not known to do usually; but the moment was well-chosen. The 'icon' was talking, a then 25-year-old man who knew how the story of his own progress to the top had become a fanciful roadmap for the 'next Kylians', as he called them in his *Players' Tribune* column. In November 2021, together with *L'Équipe*'s resident cartoonist Faro, Mbappé published an autobiographical comic book, *Je m'appelle Kylian*, which sold a quarter of a million copies in France alone. The book's message was clear: 'If you believe in your dream, you'll make it come true', a child-friendly version of his sponsor Nike's advertising mantra *JUST DO IT*. One of the three Mbappé murals in his hometown shows Kylian in his PSG kit with this slogan: *Bondy, ville des possibles* ('Bondy, city of possibilities'). *Yes, you can. Why? Because I did it.* Should he be so surprised that those who admired him the most would take him at his word?

'When it started to become serious,' he explained, 'it's true that, very early on, I had a discussion with my parents. "What do you want to do? Do you want to be a footballer? What kind of footballer do you want to be?" I told them: "I want to be a great one. I want to be one of the best in the world. I don't want anyone in front of me." But *I* made the choice. It's not my father who imposed it on me, even though he's mad about football. He was very happy I'd taken this decision but [choosing] football, it must come from [the children]. Let them have fun. Don't worry, there'll be a time when it'll become serious. If it has to become serious, it'll become serious.'

*

When this discussion took place is not known. The Mbappé family folklore is full of stories about Kylian the baby, who was given a football when his mother was still in the maternity ward, the toddler who didn't go anywhere without it, and the little boy, who was so obsessed with the game that he told everyone – aged 4, or 5, depending on the storyteller – that he'd go to Clairefontaine to start with, then to Rennes, like big brother Jirès, then to Real Madrid, like his idol Cristiano Ronaldo and Zidane. He'd watch every game that was broadcast on television, stand to attention when 'La Marseillaise' was played, eyes closed, hand on heart. He'd sneak into the team talks that his father Wilfrid gave AS Bondy's senior team on matchdays. He played a version of 'Let's Pretend' in which he took the role of a star footballer answering questions from journalists at a press conference; but all of this came from him, and him alone. There are no tales of Wilfrid holding his newborn son aloft and proclaiming 'one day, you will play for France!', as Thierry Henry's father Antoine is said to have done.

Wilfrid later told *L'Équipe* that 'before Kylian even started to play with AS Bondy [when he was 6 years old], he went downstairs to play in the street, and that was good. I wanted it to come from him. I didn't want it to be: "hey, I'm off to work [as a coach], come along and play some football". I waited until I was sure it was his wish. He insisted I should be his coach, and I wanted to be as well, so it was perfect – even if I wasn't too keen on it at the beginning. I wondered if I could step back enough to make the distinction between the dad and the coach.' He could, though not always. Once, when AS Bondy were playing against neighbouring Bobigny and losing 0–1 at half-time, Wilfrid spent almost all of his team talk tearing into his son for his poor performance, not just out of frustration, but also from a desire to show Kylian's team-mates that he was not giving preferential treatment to his own flesh and blood. Only much later did he come to realise that he'd gone too far, even if a second-half double from Kylian overturned Bondy's one-goal deficit.

It was only from the age of 8 that Kylian's dream of becoming a professional footballer, and a 'great one' at that, was taken seriously by his family, when Kylian took part in a tournament in Burgundy at which rival teams asked to see the boy's licence in order to check he really was that young. 'When you see what he does, it's impossible he could be a débutant,' they said. 'He's far too far ahead of the others.' Yet Kylian was the smallest player in his team, so slight that one of his nicknames was *la crevette* ('the shrimp'). 'This is when you tell yourself there's talent there,' Wilfrid commented. This is also when things 'became serious', as his son would put it, and the real *projet Mbappé* was set in motion. Football coaching was at the heart of it, but so was education. Kylian never had to run home in front of Wilfrid's car as if caught in the criss-crossing searchlights of a prison camp.

All his former teachers agree: Kylian Mbappé was no ordinary pupil. He was charming yet unruly, disruptive and close to unmanageable on occasions. He was smart and clearly well above average in terms of academic potential, yet, more often than not, unable or unwilling to concentrate and make the most of his aptitude. As is the case with many gifted children, he was easily bored and hated school. All he could think about was the next break, the next impromptu game in the schoolyard. He once undertook an IQ test while in the equivalent of Year 6, doing brilliantly until the school bell rang for a pause, which he was not allowed to join in. He then sulked his way through the second half of the test and registered a sub-par score as a result. He received regular warnings as to his 'dissipated' conduct in class and came close to being expelled on a couple of occasions, as when one of his teachers grabbed him by the hand at a break and Kylian responded by scratching him with his fingernails. It was obvious that the boy was not just gifted with quicksilver feet but a quicksilver mind as well, which only increased the frustration of those who were given the task of looking after him at school. Yannick Saint-Aubert, his headmaster at Bondy's newly opened Olympe de Gouges primary school, half an hour's walk from the Mbappé home, remembers a child who could and would just 'drift away, because of nonchalance or because [he was lost in] a daydream' and who was 'lucky to have teachers who were willing to take him as he was'. 'They had to accept to do things differently [with him],' he said. 'His parents and us were into "co-education"; as to me, I represented the rules, the law.'

Things became so 'complicated' – Saint-Aubert's word – that Fayza took to coming to school every afternoon to find out what mischief her son had been up to that day. Yet Kylian never repeated a year throughout his schooling. He could always cram in extra studying when push came to shove. As his uncle Pierre said, 'as soon as he wanted to, he could do it. When he had to be shaken up, we'd do it, and he responded'. One subject in which he showed exceptional aptitude was French. 'He mastered all the orthographic, syntagmatic and lexical rules,' Saint-Aubert said. 'It was a tool for him, another way to make the stars he had in his head shine even more brightly.' As Saint-Aubert put it, '[Kylian] knew when the cannonball was about to whistle past his ear' and would do just enough to make sure it wasn't fired by his parents. 'He was a child who could blow a fuse if he didn't get what he wanted,' according to family friend Alain Mboma. 'His schooling was always a concern. Succeeding in football was the only thing for which he had space in his head. There is no doubt he was exactly the kind of kid who could have exploded in a *cite*.'

But Kylian did not grow up in a *cité*. His parents were aware of how challenging their son could be, his mother Fayza in particular, who went to inordinate lengths to make sure Kylian kept to the straight and narrow. It was decided that to avoid mixing with children who might have had a negative influence on him, Kylian would be sent to a private school. After five turbulent years spent at Olympe de Gouges, the ten-year-old boy was enrolled at L'Assomption de Bondy, a private ecumenical Roman Catholic institution catering to boys and girls of all faiths or none, which was also much closer to the family home, just a ten-minute stroll away past the Stade Léo-Lagrange. Money was not an issue: the Mbappés were comfortable enough to afford the fees as, like most other French private schools, L'Assomption was affiliated to the state education system and received public funding. A year's tuition – lunch included – would have cost less than €2,000 per child, at the time.

Save for a couple of hours a week devoted to religious education, the school's curriculum was identical to what was taught in every other *collège* in the country. The intake was different, though, with a larger proportion of the pupils coming from white, more affluent backgrounds, mostly from the southern *quartiers* of Bondy. Discipline was stricter too, not that Kylian was any easier to deal with than at Olympe de Gouges: the opposite, in fact, as it was now obvious that becoming a professional footballer was no longer a child's dream, but a genuine prospect for him. Much bigger clubs than AS Bondy knew of his potential. Agents had started to circle around the young player who was scoring bagfulls of goals against teams of boys much older than himself. Kylian himself could see it, which only increased his frustration at being forced to sit still in a classroom when he could be having fun with a football instead. Wasn't he meant to become a pro anyway?

Wilfrid and Fayza did everything in their power to keep their son in check and broaden his horizons beyond the game which was obsessing him. Kylian was given swimming and tennis lessons, joined a children's theatre troupe and somehow managed to attend music lessons for a full six years at Bondy's Conservatoire de Musique, another ten-minute walk from Allée des Lilas. His chosen instrument was the classical flute, which he only stopped studying when he went to Clairefontaine. He was also singing in the conservatoire's choir, which would often be called upon to perform in the small park which surrounds Bondy's town hall. His singing teacher Céline Bognini remembered a boy 'full of life, a real ray of sunshine, always hyperactive, whom you needed to feed in every sense, with culture, with sport, with the arts' – and who could apparently sing a very presentable version of Serge Gainsbourg's politically incorrect 'Couleur Café'. His flute teacher Françoise Ducos was more struck by Kylian's unusual willingness to play in public than by his ability ('ordinary, normal, neither hyper-gifted nor bad'). 'He always wanted to be the first,' she remembered. 'Often, when you ask children, "who'd like to play first?", there's nobody. But he always wanted to do something.'

Things came to a head in Kylian's last year at L'Assomption, which was also his last year in the standard French education system. Clairefontaine would follow, where the football scholars benefited from a curriculum tailored for the needs of elite athletes, then the Lycée Jean-Jaurès of Rueil-Malmaison, which offered its pupils a similarly structured curriculum. He was in *cinquième* at L'Assomption then, the equivalent of Year 8 in England, and was now deemed 'uncontrollable' by some of his teachers. As is commonplace in France, a psychologist was assigned to follow him throughout the year. Fayza, who'd always kept a very close watch on her son, now insisted that his teachers filled in a form which had to be ticked every single hour, to indicate how he had behaved in class. Kylian's luck was that he still bonded with some of his educators, none more so than Nicole Lefebvre, who taught him French for the two years he spent in the Catholic institution. She remembers a 'puny child' and a 'joker', but also 'a very good pupil, who had an extraordinary mental agility', 'a leader in the classroom, who drew others to a higher level and hated injustice'. He could not always express his feelings as well as he wished, but 'had determination'. 'What he wants to do, he will do,' she said. 'His tenacity astonished me.' He could also be very funny, knew it, and knew how to use it to his advantage.

Nicole Lefebvre has told how 'one day, one of his schoolmates teased him a bit, and Kylian made a mocking comment about his jacket. So [Fayza] dressed him in flares, which had been out of fashion for twenty years, and worn-out sneakers for a week. And he looked at me, saying, "*Je suis beau, madame, hein*?" I told him, "Yes, it's ok." He said, "It's thanks to you, madame." But as he knew I liked him, and I believe he liked me back, it was a kind of amused complicity. Even when he was punished, he could accept punishment without taking it badly.'

It was not just his talent for football which set Kylian apart, nor his intelligence, his command of the French language and his speed of thought, which everyone had remarked upon from a very early age. The rebellious boy who seemingly couldn't and definitely wouldn't pay attention in class, or disrupted his lessons by constantly chatting with whoever was sitting next to him, knew 'how much he could go too far', as Jean Cocteau put in. There always came the moment when he checked himself and did just enough to get back in line. 'Taylor', one of his neighbours at the time, spoke of 'a child who wasn't like us'. 'He was a phenomenon on the football pitch,' he said, 'and a discreet kid outside of it. He didn't hang out. He didn't do anything silly. He visited his friends from time to time, that's all. His life was school, football and so to bed', a child's equivalent of the Parisian commuters' *métro, boulot, dodo*. A rebel? Only up to a point, and one who didn't lose sight of the lines others drew in the sand for him. There lies the foundation of the real *projet Mbappé*: the almost perfect alignment of a child's dreams and ambition with his parents' own, the very opposite of the suffocating pressure other, less gifted but also less well-protected, and perhaps less loved children are put under by families desperate to see their sons become rich and famous thanks to football – *comme Kylian*. There was no need to 'push' Kylian, to make him run back home in the rain if he'd misbehaved. There was no need for harsh punishment; the occasional telling off was balanced with constant attention, care and affection. He could push himself well enough. The school clown knew that the education that was forced on him would serve him well in the future: indeed, that he wouldn't succeed if he did not do what was asked of him, much as he'd prefer to kick a ball or daydream in a bedroom plastered with photographs of Cristiano Ronaldo. This may sound trite but is no less true for that.

In October 2018, Kylian went back to Bondy to address a 4,000-strong crowd which had gathered at the Stade Léo-Lagrange to salute the city's first world champion. Then-mayor Sylvine Thomassin had an unusual present for him: a classical flute. Visibly moved by the occasion, he accepted it with a large smile, but stopped short of playing a tune. Thomassin knew the Mbappés well – her husband was none other than Kylian's former headmaster Yannick Saint-Aubert. 'His parents didn't want him to have nothing but football in his life,' she later recounted. 'They were taking him to museums.

They made him study music at the Conservatoire. They wanted to broaden his horizons and I believe that's what made him the man he is now: accomplished, collected and self-confident.' It is the simplest of secrets. Mbappé never was a footballer *malgré lui*.

5
Clairefontaine

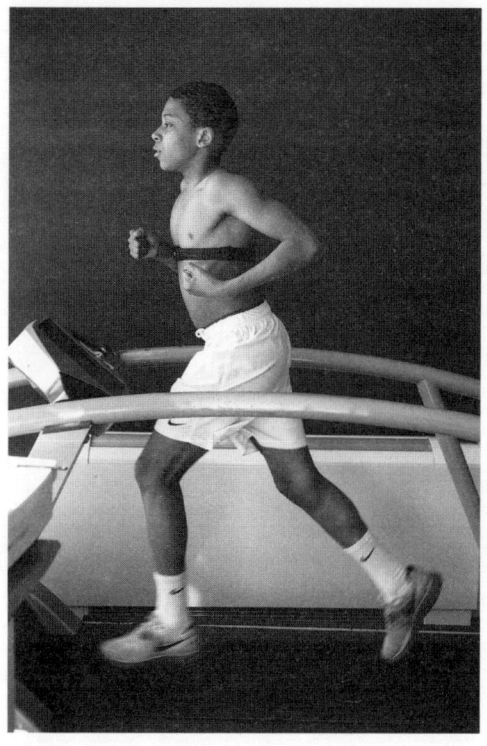

Kylian undergoing fitness testing at Clairefontaine, 2011.

It was 4 May 2011. An unusually large cortège of cars was queuing at the entrance of the Domaine de Montjoye, the 56-acre estate where the Clairefontaine academy has been welcoming the crème de la crème of young footballers from the Parisian region since 1988. The French FA had invited the media to attend the last of its 'detection tests', when forty boys aged 12 and 13 – girls would only be admitted from 2022 onwards – would be competing for one of the twenty-three places on offer at the elite boarding school. Kylian Mbappé was one of them. Those final tests, which included psychological evaluations, physical and technical tests and seven- or nine-a-side games, had never been held in public before. It's not that the federation had called in the press to mark a special occasion, an anniversary or the visit of a very special guest; it was an exercise in damage limitation, after investigative website Mediapart had published a week earlier a leaked conversation which had taken place at the Direction Technique Nationale, the top echelon of the French FA, in the presence of then-manager of France's senior men's team Laurent Blanc.

The topic of conversation was a delicate one. More and more young players who went through the coaching programmes of the

French FA were of foreign, mostly, though not exclusively, African heritage, and were eligible to represent a country other than France at international level. Of the youngsters who attended Clairefontaine at the time the discussion took place – in November 2010, five months before a recording was passed on to Mediapart – two would go on to play for France U19s, while three were capped at senior level by Senegal, Congo and the Democratic Republic of Congo. Erick Mombaerts, the coach in charge of the U23s, Les Bleuets, went straight to the point: 'Do we set a limit to the number of kids who can change nationality?'

It was a legitimate – if loaded – question. A fair, logical answer would have been another question: 'Does it really matter?' France, now established as one of world football's most powerful nations, was in no danger of seeing a crack player opt for another country, unlike, say, Ireland, who saw Declan Rice opt for England after having played three games for the Republic, or Argentina, who lost two-time Ballon d'Or winner Alfredo Di Stéfano to Spain. Those youngsters who switched allegiances usually did so when they realised that their chance of representing France had passed them by. But this is not how Blanc replied to Mombaerts.

'As to me, I am fully in favour [of setting limits],' he said. 'Sincerely, what is happening in football at the moment bothers me a lot.' It is at that stage that the conversation took a rather different, and highly problematic turn. 'It feels like we're training the same prototype of players: tall, strong, powerful,' Blanc said. 'Today, who is tall, strong, powerful? *Les Blacks*. That's the way it is. That's a fact. The Spaniards told me, "we don't have a problem. We don't have *Blacks*."' Mombaerts suggested that club academies were not taking care of 'small-sized white players'. U20 manager Francis Smerecki was the only person present at the meeting to say that setting limits on the number of 'bi-nationals' in academies was 'discriminatory'. It is then that National Technical Director François Blaquart dropped the bomb. 'We can organise ourselves around a certain type of unspoken quota,' he suggested. 'But it shouldn't be made public.'

The French FA, finding itself under attack from anti-racist organisations, had to do something: Blaquart was suspended (but resumed his position a few months later); Blanc made a public apology (and carried on); and the gates of Clairefontaine were opened to the media, so they could see for themselves and tell the country that there were no quotas in place and that the selection process was non-discriminatory; which was true. Clairefontaine, in fact, was proof that the French system was meritocratic. It so happened that Kylian was one of the exhibits put forward by the FFF to proclaim its innocence in what would be remembered as *l'affaire des quotas*. Kylian could have chosen to play for Cameroon, his father's country of birth, or Algeria, where his mother Fayza's parents came from – but the *projet* had always been about France.

Being accepted by the Institut National du Football, be it at Clairefontaine or at one of the French FA's seventeen other regional *centres de pré-formation*, is not an obligation for young French footballers who aspire to become professionals, nor is it a guarantee that they will. While Nicolas Anelka and Thierry Henry are alumni of France's elite football school, Zinédine Zidane and Antoine Griezmann aren't. On average, out of the twenty-three scholars who are admitted every year at Clairefontaine, over half will have left football behind them by the time they are 21. It still is a dropout rate which compares favourably with what is seen in most club academies, where failures outnumber successes by a factor of ten to one or more; and there are exceptional vintages, in which most of the graduates – who are 14 or 15 by the time they leave the Institut – will be offered a professional contract by a professional club. Kylian's group was one of those exceptional crops. Lilian Thuram, one of France's revered 1998 World Cup winners and the most outspoken critic of Laurent Blanc during *l'affaire des quotas*, had made the trip to the academy on the opening day of Kylian's first term. He intended to watch his son Marcus, who was about to start his second year there – and would later set up Mbappé's equalising goal in the 2022 World Cup final against Argentina. 'It looks like a very good group of players, technically speaking,' he said; but his eye had been caught by the newcomers, who 'looked more promising'. He was right. Ten years on, seven of Kylian's fellow boarders are playing in the first tier of European leagues, from the Italian Serie A to the German Bundesliga, from the Swiss Super League to Spain's La Liga, where Mbappé came across his old Clairefontaine schoolmate Yvan Neyou, now a fixture in Getafe's midfield, twice in the 2024–25 season, as well as a Cameroon international – another of those 'bi-nationals' which so exercised Blaquart's Direction Technique Nationale.

Mbappé did not stand out just because of his outrageous talent, but also because of his atypical background. His extrovert personality and his sense of humour enabled him to fit in, but only to an extent. He was not 'one of the boys' – not really. To start with, he was just too good for that. Everyone was aware of it, Kylian included. He'd been invited by Zinédine Zidane to visit Real Madrid, for goodness' sake. Then-director of Clairefontaine Gérard Prêcheur later said that 'what [he] immediately liked about him was the "natural" side of his character'. But not everyone shared that view, as Prêcheur conceded. 'He wasn't always well perceived by his coach and his team-mates. It could be mistaken as arrogance. But it wasn't how I perceived him.'

Then there was the way he spoke, his accent as well as his choice of words. Two reporters from *Le Monde*, Rémi Dupré and Henri Seckel, who had also been there when the FFF had invited the media back in May 2011, followed Kylian's group day-to-day for two whole years and wrote a fascinating chronicle of life at Clairefontaine, in which Mbappé appears as one of the main characters, by chance more than by design. The story Rémi tells differs from the 'everything was wonderful' narrative which is commonplace when Kylian's schoolmates and coaches are asked to reminisce about the time they spent with the prodigy. On one hand there was the 12-year-old Mbappé who told him with a straight face: 'I know that work and attention to what is said bring their reward. I just do not want to have any regret if I happen to fail.' On the other, there was the prankster 'who couldn't be arsed and would infuriate his coaches', as Dupré remembers him. 'Jean-Claude Lafargue was one of those who criticised him the most.'

Lafargue's view of his most famous charge had mellowed by the time *L'Equipe* interviewed him for an in-depth portrait of the superstar shortly before the 2018 World Cup. 'Plenty of players run a lot, but, in the end, there's a lot of waste,' he said. 'That wasn't the case with him. You'd have thought he was sparing himself, but that wasn't the case: every time he tried something, there was an end product.' More importantly, when there was a problem with Kylian, as Lafargue agreed happened on quite a few occasions ('no player is a saint'), he had 'no worries'. 'I knew they put him back on the right path,' he said, they being Wilfrid and Fayza, who were just as attentive to their son's progress at Clairefontaine as they had been in Bondy when he was driving his teachers to distraction at L'Assomption.

The influence of Kylian's parents also struck some of his fellow boarders. Guillaume Péria, now an assistant project manager in a successful Parisian architecture practice, has kept fond memories of the boy who was nicknamed *Mbébé* (for his tendency to sulk like a baby when something displeased him), *Chicots d'or* ('Golden gnashers', because of the yellowish colour of his teeth) and *Cacahuète* ('Peanut', as he was the smallest of his class). 'Donatello', in reference to the Teenage Mutant Ninja Turtle of the same name, would come later, in his first season as a PSG player. 'He was always laughing, always involved in silly chat,' Péria remembered. 'He was well-managed. If I compare him to myself, for example, maybe the choices I made were not the right ones, and maybe if I had taken more time to choose another club [Péria joined AJ Auxerre's academy in 2013 and quit competitive football two years later], my life would look completely different today.' But Kylian's life was already completely different by then. Nike had been supplying him with free equipment since 2006, when he was still yet to celebrate his eighth birthday. For Péria, what singled him out, apart from the care and attention he received from his parents, was that he turned up at the Clairefontaine trials with a brand new pair of trainers. Kylian also ingratiated himself with his fellow scholars when he gave away the spare boots he had no use for.

Most of Clairefontaine's boarders had had a modest upbringing. The vast majority of them came from the *banlieue* and were the children of first- or second-generation immigrants who could not dream of taking their families to Dubai for their summer holidays, as the Mbappés did at the end of their son's first year at the academy. Bondy was only just over an hour's drive away; the home he came back to every weekend was spacious and comfortable; and he had a big brother to look up to. Jirès too had spent two years at the Institut National du Football a decade previously and was about to have his most prolific season with Rennes; he'd already had a trial at Chelsea in the spring; and of the twenty-three boys admitted to Clairefontaine in 2011, he was the only one who was offered professional forms with a major club while at the Institut, in his case AS Monaco (though the documents were only signed after Kylian left Clairefontaine, in July 2013).

If Clairefontaine represented a once-in-a-lifetime opportunity for many of the boys Kylian boarded with, it was not the case for him, who had every reason to believe – who already knew – that his footballing future was assured. Clubs had already lined up for him and, to start with, according to Wilfrid, his son was reticent to join the Institut National du Football. Kylian knew a few other footballers of his age who had joined the youth teams of Ligue 1 clubs and wished to follow their example. His father disagreed: Kylian was still too young. Clairefontaine fitted in with the project not because it was an indispensable step in his progress but because it provided him with a safe space in which he could benefit from high-quality coaching outside of the far harsher environment offered by club academies. Kylian would be protected at a particularly delicate moment of his young life, as he was about to hit puberty. As then-director Gérard Prêcheur, later to be called on by the Mbappé family to work at their club Stade Malherbe Caen, explained, 'here, they are not in competition with each other'. 'The change is going to be abrupt when they join a professional club's academy, where adaptation is difficult,' he warned. 'They won't be asked the same things there.' The young Mbappé agreed. 'Rivalry was more pronounced at the beginning of the season,' he told Dupré and Seckel. 'We've learnt to live together since then. We are cut off from the outside world, so we are united.' It was to be different in Monaco.

What was asked of Clairefontaine boarders was to show their willingness to improve, to be the best they could be, which is not the same thing as to be better than the others. They were expected to abide by the rules and not neglect their academic studies. As the selection process had already taken place, no child lived in fear of being told to go home or to be dropped for the next game. The Institut's first- and second-year teams had taken part in national U16 and U17 competitions until 2010 and had even won the Coupe Gambardella – the French equivalent of the FA Youth Cup – back in 1988; but no longer. Clairefontaine was about personal development, not competition. There were games, of course, hundreds of them, which Wilfrid often followed from the touchline, whereas Fayza involved herself with the coaching staff as she had with her son's teachers in the past.

The time spent at the Institut could have felt like a blissful two-year holiday. Kylian's schoolmate Allan Momège could not believe that he'd seen does wander out of the Rambouillet forest to graze on the lawn of the château. The food was prepared by the same chefs who cooked the meals of France's national team. The training pitches were in better condition than what could be found at most Ligue 1 clubs. The Collège Catherine de Vivonne in Rambouillet, where they studied for the *brevet* – the French equivalent of GCSEs – gave the scholars preferential treatment, with reduced class sizes and a timetable tailored to their training schedule. 'We're better here than at Barça!', another of Kylian's fellow boarders joked.

Yet so much was at stake for most of the scholars, dependent on whether they could attract the attention of a club while at the academy or not. Those who did – about half of Kylian's group signed forms in their second year at the academy – at least stood a chance of proving themselves in a professional environment. The rest would go back to their small clubs and, barring a miracle, drift into obscurity. There was no formal selection process within the academy: it was all about the judgement of the scouts and recruiters who watched the training sessions and the games from the sidelines. Some of them came every day of the week. Some were despatched by a club.

Others were freelance agents who sometimes pretended to be family members in order to gain access to the grounds. All were tolerated by the academy officials as long as they did not cause any trouble or disturb the players and coaches at work. Come half-time, they went up to the parents who were watching from the stands to discuss their child's future. Some, nicknamed the 'vultures', would offer money to be mandated as representatives. 'It can feel like a cattle fair,' one bona fide recruiter told the reporters of *Le Monde*. 'The kids already are in the professional circuit,' Laurent Blanc deplored. 'They're caught in a mad race.'

It was a race in which Kylian Mbappé had long since been ahead.

6

Monaco: the springboard

Kylian celebrates in trademark fashion one of his two goals in the first leg of ASM's Champions League quarter-final against Borussia Dortmund, 12 April 2017.

It could have been Caen, and it very nearly was. The first contact between the Normandy club and the Mbappé family had taken place in September 2009, three months before Kylian's eleventh birthday. Caen's recruitment team had been so struck by the child's qualities that its head Laurent Glaize wondered if 'he wasn't too big for us'. They still made a proposal which they knew to be on the – very – low side. Wilfrid's reaction was to ask whether there was a page missing in the documents. 'You want to catch a shark with an angling rod?' he asked Glaize. Other, more established and wealthier French clubs were trying to attract the prodigy: Bordeaux, who were one of the last to give up on his signature, PSG, Rennes, Sochaux and RC Lens, where Kylian went for a trial which might have led to something more if the club hadn't dropped to the second division at the close of the 2010–11 season. 'He showed a rare potential,' then head of the Lens academy Marc Vesterloppe said. 'He didn't just seek to "provoke" players, he also looked up to ask himself, "Should I dribble? Should I pass the ball?" He was able to play with the others, which showed a great intelligence.' And for a while, Lens were first in the queue.

Unlike Lens, Caen had survived, just, and had a trump card to play in the race to secure Kylian: their manager Franck Dumas, a Normand himself, the former Newcastle United player with whom Caen had climbed to fifth place in Ligue 1, and who'd been in charge of the first team as a head coach since May 2005. His profile and personality fitted what Wilfrid and Fayza had in mind for their son. Dumas was an extrovert, a man who 'worked on instinct' and found it hard to hide (and sometimes control) his emotions, who fell foul of football's authorities on several occasions but also inspired fierce loyalty within his staff: his heart was as big as his mouth. The Mbappés visited him on the eve of a game which would decide whether Caen would be demoted to Ligue 2 or not. The last training session to take place before the match was to start shortly after 2 pm, the time at which the family arrived at the training ground. Dumas had never seen Kylian play himself but trusted the judgement of Glaize and of his chief scout for the Paris region David Lasry. He instructed his assistant Patrice Garande to take over the pros for the afternoon, opened the windows of the meeting room, lit up a cigarette and sat down with Wilfrid and Fayza.

This was the kind of commitment the Mbappés were looking for. Twenty-four hours before one of the most important games of the season, Dumas had chosen to leave his team aside to discuss the future of a child he only knew about from hearsay. The discussions went on for several months after that, and another season had started before Wilfrid gave his verbal assent to the move: deal done, Kylian would join Stade Malherbe Caen at the conclusion of the 2011–12 campaign. A letter was drafted by the club to inform the Institut National du Football of Clairefontaine that their pupil was about to sign his first form with a professional club. Others may have proposed more money than Caen; but they didn't have a Dumas.

Yet the move collapsed at the eleventh hour. Wilfrid would later suggest that Caen's failure to stay in Ligue 1 was the determining factor in their decision to walk away from their informal agreement; the story Glaize tells is different. Caen were to pay the Mbappés a signing-on fee of €120,000 or €180,000 depending on which division they'd play in 2012–13 and, at the last minute, the club's executives decided this was too big a sum to disburse for a child when they'd just been relegated and were struggling to balance Caen's accounts. It fell to a heartbroken Glaize to phone Fayza and break the news to her. This was the first and last time Kylian Mbappé would be turned down by anyone; and it worked out to his advantage in the longer term.

With Caen out of the picture, the problem for the Mbappés was not to wait for another club to declare an interest in Kylian, but to choose the right one. Despite Real Madrid entering the fray, welcoming his family and offering him a place at their academy just before Christmas 2012, it would be AS Monaco who played their cards perfectly, and had the right man to do it. Their head of recruitment Souleymane Camara already knew the Mbappés from following Kylian's adopted brother Jirès in the past. Camara saw the young Kylian play an 'exceptional' game in his second year at Clairefontaine, in which he assisted a goal and scored another one. That was the clincher.

This was late in the spring of 2013, in his last term at Clairefontaine. Monaco had been bought by Russian billionaire Dmitry Rybolovlev eighteen months previously and were about to embark on an unprecedented €170 million spending spree which would transform the club's fortunes over the following five years and turn it into a French champion and a semi-finalist in the Champions League. As Camara recalled it, 'We knew the stars were on their way [to Monaco], and we had to position ourselves [for Kylian]. He was a little shrimp. But we had the arguments to convince them – and the big one was that he would play, with the U17s and the U19s.' It also helped that the three-year contract Monaco offered to the 13-year-old Mbappé came with a signing-on fee of €400,000, over twice as much as Caen had been proposing before throwing in the towel. Wilfrid, who did not want his son's head to be turned by Monaco's money, told him that they paid a mere €15,000 for his signature and did not divulge the real figure until Kylian turned fully professional.

The time had come for the prodigy to find out how he could cope outside of the protective cocoon woven by his family until that point. It was to be a brutal awakening.

Monaco was a risky choice, as Kylian's uncle Pierre told Wilfrid. It made perfect sense in purely footballing terms, as ASM were renowned for the excellence of their academy, where players such as Manuel Amoros, David Trézéguet and Thierry Henry had made the transition from hopeful talents to full internationals. The financial terms were excellent too, especially when taking into account the privileged tax status of footballers domiciled in the principality. The problem was the break-up of the family nucleus which had supported the teenager until then. Wilfrid took a year-long sabbatical and rented an apartment in Monaco which he shared with his son, but Fayza stayed behind in order to look after Kylian's younger brother Ethan, who was still only 6 years old at the time. Big brother Jirès was now playing for El-Jaish in Qatar. The rest of the extended clan which had functioned as a support group for the prodigy – the Mbomas, uncle Pierre Mbappé and Wilfrid's parents, who had so often looked after the child when Wilfrid and Fayza were at work – turned up for occasional visits, Pierre in particular, but the structure was broken at the exact moment it was needed the most.

Monaco integrated the 14-year-old into their U17s, as Souleymane Camara had promised his parents, but not in the first team of that age group. Its manager Bruno Irlès was frustrated by what he saw as deficiencies in the youngster's approach to football – above all the way he neglected his defensive duties – and decided he deserved to be taught a lesson. 'The aim was to show him what was missing from his game and what was required for high-level football,' Irlès explained a few years later. 'I didn't find him very receptive to these remarks which would have been constructive for him.' Kylian was frozen out and found himself playing for the reserves of the U17s when he was playing at all. He was also stung by the comments Irlès made during training sessions, overheard by his team-mates and ever-present father, such as 'here, you're not at Real Madrid'. The relationship between player and coach deteriorated to such an extent that Irlès was confronted by Pierre Mbappé on several occasions. 'He [Irlès] considered that Kylian had to play with the amateurs,' Kylian's uncle recalled. 'That's his problem, and I have no comments to make on that. This said, what I can comment on is the way the club and Mr Irlès managed the situation.' For Patrick Mboma, 'When you have a big machine like Kylian, you don't manage it like the others. When you have a jewel, you have to try and polish it to make it make quick progress, and it's not by putting him on the bench that it will work.' Mboma and the Mbappés shared the conviction that Monaco ought to bring Kylian to the top level 'as fast as possible'. This was the first time in Kylian's progress so far that the individual project had clashed with a collective interest – or at least what a coach believed to be his club's collective interest.

Things came to a head when Irlès and Kylian's parents were called in for a meeting by the club's management. It was decided that he would no longer be demoted to the reserves of the U17s and be forced to play in the lowly Division d'Honneur; but neither would Irlès be forced to field him in the first team. Kylian finished that miserable first season at Monaco training on his own with his coach's consent. The Mbappés must have thought that things would take a turn for the better when Irlès was despatched on a mission to Monaco's partner club Arles Avignon and left ASM's youth set-up a few months later. Moreover, Kylian, still only 15, was also called up for the first time to the French U17s in September 2014. Things were improving, albeit perhaps not as quickly as he and his parents had wished. Kylian now featured regularly in the U19 first team and sometimes took part in the amateur CFA championship with the reserves but barely figured in the Monaco side which played in the UEFA Youth League, with half-an-hour of game time, as a substitute, in the six matches the Monégasques played in Europe in that 2014–15 season.

The French U17 manager Jean-Claude Giuntini, taking a leaf from the Irlès coaching manual, judged that the winger he'd given two caps to a year previously had an attitude problem and did not contribute enough defensively; and so Kylian was left out of the group Giuntini took to the European title in 2015, with Odsonne Edouard, later of Crystal Palace, having a superb tournament as his replacement. In November 2015, when many of his first-team players were away on international duty, Monaco's manager Leonardo Jardim finally invited the teenager to train with the professionals who had stayed behind, and was so taken by what the youngster showed in his first training session that he told ASM's sporting director Luís Campos that 'that kid would never go back down to CFA, would work with us and get his chance'. That chance would eventually be offered to the teenager, but only after Monaco came close to losing their best prospect. Kylian had only eight months left on his contract and was growing impatient. He was not included in Monaco's Ligue 1 matchday squad until 2 December 2015, coming off the bench for a two-minute cameo at the end of a 1–1 home tie against SM Caen; he was an unused substitute in the following fixture in Bastia; he spent twenty minutes on the pitch when Saint-Etienne visited the Louis II stadium; then disappeared again for three matches before coming on when ASM were leading 3–0 against Toulouse on 24 January 2016, with five minutes to go until the whistle.

Come June 2016, ASM could have been left with nothing but regrets for their investment. Aware of the uncertainty surrounding Mbappé's future, the Arsenal manager Arsène Wenger travelled to Monaco, where he had won his first major title, a French championship, back in 1988, to try and convince the Mbappés that London was the one place where their son could flourish. Liverpool made enquiries as well. Paris Saint-Germain's sporting director Olivier Létang set up several meetings with Kylian and his family, which kept the door open with the Parisian club almost until the last minute – until a chance meeting between Fayza and Luís Campos tipped the scales in Monaco's favour.

Both have told the same story. Campos had been mandated by the club to resolve the situation and turned up at a training game which Fayza also happened to attend, something she did only on rare occasions. ASM's sporting director walked up to Kylian's mother and sat next to her in the stands. The conversation lasted for forty minutes, with Campos doing most of the talking. It was too early for Kylian to leave, he said. That time would come, but only later, when Kylian would be able to walk into the dressing-room of a club like Arsenal or PSG and be greeted by team-mates with big egos who would say, 'welcome Kylian, thank you for helping us'. 'It was an act of God,' Campos said later. 'This is something they understood very well; and it was the correct decision.' In truth, the Mbappés needed to be reassured rather than convinced: Wilfrid, in particular, felt that Kylian's opportunities would be even more limited at PSG, as their manager Laurent Blanc could count on Javier Pastore and Lucas Moura to complement a formidable attacking trio composed of Ángel Di María, Edinson Cavani and Zlatan Ibrahimović.

Kylian signed his first full professional contract on 6 March 2016, which would take effect on 30 June. He received a signing-on fee of €3 million and was guaranteed a monthly salary of €85,000 in the first year of his three-season deal, which would be raised to €100,000 in the second and €120,000 in the third. These were unusually generous terms for a 17-year-old who'd only played the equivalent of two matches when committing himself to the club; but he'd scored his first senior goal for ASM a few days before, wearing number 33, in the dying seconds of a 3–1 win over Troyes. It was a decent finish, nothing to make the sparse crowd jump out of their seats, but a clean enough strike from just beyond the penalty spot which wrongfooted an over-committed keeper. Kylian had not perfected his trademark cross-armed celebration yet. He just ran away, arms aloft, a huge smile across his face, before attempting an elaborate, awkward-looking dance move cut short by the congratulations of his team-mates.

Yet this goal did not kick-start his Monaco career. He shone for their youth team, scoring twice in the final of France's most prestigious U23 competition, the Coupe Gambardella, and was Les Bleuets' most influential player in their victorious run in the European U19 championships; but Leonardo Jardim kept ignoring him. Come April, following a run of eight games with the seniors, most of them as a substitute, Kylian was back playing with the reserves in the fourth tier, starting four matches on the trot and scoring a couple of goals which did nothing to alleviate his frustration. The 2016–17 season didn't start better than 2015–16 had ended. Selected in the starting line-up for the first Ligue 1 game of the new season, he suffered concussion and had to be replaced just before half-time. More bit-part appearances followed, in the Champions League as in Ligue 1. His disappointment at being left out for a crucial 2–1 win over Tottenham in the latter competition was such that he broke down in tears and disappeared for three hours. Despite being fit again, he played just eight minutes of Monaco's five Ligue 1 games which followed. Once again, the Mbappés felt that Monaco had not been true to their word. The clan decided to counter-attack. As the club was deaf to their private entreaties, perhaps they'd listen if the player's grievances were made public.

There was only one place to do this: in France's sports daily *L'Équipe*, which had been following Kylian's progress with club and country very closely since he'd left Clairefontaine for the principality. Contact was established with journalist Vincent Villa, who interviewed Wilfrid and was convinced that the family was acting in accordance with a plan devised with Kylian's assent. One sentence stood out. 'We'll have to think about the *mercato* [winter transfer window] in January,' Wilfrid said. It was not a veiled threat. The message was not aimed at *L'Équipe* readers, but at the AS Monaco hierarchy: things had to change, and fast; and they did. Whether it was because of the pressure exerted by the family, of a quiet word in Jardim's ear, or of Jardim deciding the time had come to see what Kylian could offer, eight days after the publication of Villa's piece, Kylian was in the starting line-up of the first team for a spectacular 6–2 win over Montpellier, scoring one goal (with a header, a rarity in Kylian's catalogue of finishes), assisting another and gaining a penalty. This was the start of a quite extraordinary second half of the season, in which Mbappé, now an automatic starter, scored a further 14 goals – from only 28 shots – in Ligue 1 (including his first-ever hat-trick at senior level, against Metz), most of them as a second striker alongside the marvellous Colombian centre-forward Radamel Falcao. All of Europe knew his name now, as he was even more effective in the Champions League, scoring six in six in Monaco's progress to the semi-finals of the tournament, including two in two against favourites Manchester City in the round of 16.

A call-up to France's A-team followed, as everyone knew it would. Didier Deschamps gave him his debut in a routine 3–1 away victory in Luxembourg on 25 March 2017. He wouldn't miss a game for Les Bleus until a hamstring injury kept him out of a Euro qualifier against Albania in September 2019. By then, the 20-year-old already had 13 international goals and 34 caps to his name.

His elevation from almost-outcast to superstar-in-the-making had been both long-drawn-out – as he and his family, for whom nothing could come fast enough, saw it – and sudden; according to his former headmaster Yannick Saint-Aubert, his head was turned for a while, but Fayza was there, as ever, to correct him. Not long after he'd turned 18, Kylian's mother had noticed how her son had left his dirty boots behind in the dressing-room, trusting unseen, unknown hands to take care of them. She exploded. 'Do you realise what it means, socially, to have someone else clean your shoes?' she asked Kylian. 'You come from the *quartier nord* of Bondy, which is a rich place – in human terms – but you cannot enter this kind of cycle. I forbid you to have someone else clean your shoes from now on.'

Kylian had arrived, as he believed he would. It had been a long, frustrating run-up, but he'd hit the springboard full on the sweetest spot; and as soon as he did, it was clear he would fly. The project had always been to move; and, from that moment on, to build up the Kylian brand, like no other teenage footballer's brand had ever been built, not even Ronaldo's, Messi's nor Neymar's. And it was Neymar, the world's most expensive player, for whom PSG had paid €222 million, alongside whom Kylian was to play at Paris Saint-Germain in the new season.

7
Cherchez les femmes

Kylian Mbappé's lawyer Delphine Verheyden sitting next to Fayza Lamari, at the France–Denmark game, 2022 World Cup.

The Mbappés did their utmost to keep outsiders at arm's length from the outset. The agents – dozens of them – who approached them to become Kylian's representatives ever since the 8-year-old was making fun of defenders twice his size with AS Bondy were all rebuffed. The financial advisors who offered their services to broker sponsorship deals met with the same response: father Wilfrid would take care of his son's sporting career, mother Fayza of all the rest, with Kylian having the final word in any decision involving his future, be it on or off the field; and so it has remained to this day. Kylian does not have a Fifa-registered agent. Nobody but the closest members of his family gets a cut from the deals he signs with clubs or commercial partners. This is not to say that nobody else is involved in the *projet*. Luís Campos, now sporting advisor for all of the clubs owned by Qatar Sports Investments after fulfilling a similar role for Lille and AS Monaco, remains a trusted confidant, as he's been since playing a central role in smoothing out the difficulties the young Kylian had encountered at AS Monaco. Former *L'Équipe* journalist Bilel Ghazi, who, though unlicensed by Fifa, has been working with players like Rayan Cherki (whom Kylian's mother Fayza also represented for a short while), has provided media guidance to the Mbappés. Neither Campos nor Ghazi are part of the inner circle, however.

Yet the time came when the Mbappés could no longer rely solely on themselves and family friends like the Mbomas to take care of the player's interests, as Kylian would soon sign his first professional contract with Monaco. As they wouldn't entrust his affairs to a traditional agent, they set their sights on recruiting a lawyer – the best they could find; and they did. It has been written that Fayza held auditions to pick the right candidate, but this is not quite correct. It was Fayza who approached the 44-year-old Assas University graduate Delphine Verheyden in 2015, not the opposite.

'I didn't know Kylian, I don't know anything about football, I accept that,' Verheyden told *Ouest France* in 2022, in one of the handful of interviews she has granted to a French newspaper. 'And that's exactly what [Fayza] was looking for. This extraordinary woman touched me, I wanted to help her.' Regardless of what she claimed about her knowledge of football, sport was far from a terra incognita for her. In the mid-90s, when still studying for the bar, she'd done an internship with a Boston legal firm which specialised in looking after athletes and had not forgotten how one of her mentors had told her that, soon enough, lawyers would take over a lot of the business of traditional agents. It was already happening in the USA; it would happen in France as well, as 'France tends to lag twenty years behind the States'.

Back at home, Verheyden came across another lawyer, Jean-Jacques Bertrand, whose name was better than well-known in sporting circles. It was Bertrand, another Assas graduate, who had taken care of Jacques Anquetil after the quintuple Tour de France winner retired at the very end of 1969. It was Bertrand who sat by Eric Cantona's side when he delivered his famous 'seagulls' speech before his appearance at Croydon Crown Court in 1995. It was Bertrand whom Cantona also made a director of his short-lived 'Cantona French Wines Ltd' and 'Cantona French Brandy Ltd' companies, later sat on the Court of Arbitration for Sport and co-founded the International Association of Football Lawyers. It would have been difficult for Verheyden to find a better-connected and more experienced mentor to guide her in her chosen field. The two published *Le Sportif et son Agent* in 1999, the very first book in the French language to look at the relationship between elite athletes and their representatives, which she followed up with her own *Agent de Sportifs: Pleins feux sur une profession en développement* ('Sports Agents: Spotlight On A Developing Profession') six years later. The foreword was provided by Frédéric Dobrage, a former professional keeper and the agent of 1998 world champions Robert Pirès and Bixente Lizarazu among others; so maybe Verheyden knew rather more about the football world than she liked others to believe.

What is true is that 16-year-old Kylian was her first football client. She had done some work for the French Rugby Union Federation when an employee of the August Debouzy law firm, at the very beginning of her career. Moving to another practice, Vivien & Associés, of which she was made a partner, she landed her first big – very big – name, the multiple world and Olympic judo champion Teddy Riner, in 2007. Other great Olympians followed suit: biathlete Martin Fourcade, canoeist Tony Estanguet, pole vaulter Renaud Lavillenie and skier Perrine Laffont, all of them household names in France. Verheyden, who has run her boutique practice since 2014, first with collaborator Jean-Rémi Cognard, then on her own, insists that she has never approached anyone herself. Word of mouth was enough. Those who knocked at her door came of their own accord. 'Would you trust a doctor who recruits his own patients?' is how she put it to *Le Parisien*. She had, and has, other, more powerful arguments.

She deals with superstars but does not seek attention for herself. Despite the company she keeps, photographs of her never appear in the gossip media. She owns a holiday home in the Vendée region but insisted its location should be kept a secret on the one occasion when she met journalists there. Her motto could be the concluding line of Florian's fable *Le Grillon*: 'To live happily, let us live in hiding.' She is a tough negotiator, who will fight tooth and nail for a few thousand euros more if she believes this is what her client is entitled to. She understood how an elite athlete is not just a performer, but also a brand, an image, long before anyone else did in the agenting world – at least in France. Her profession has made her wealthy, but she has never taken a penny in commissions, as she charges the same hourly rate to everyone, regardless of their fame or the value of the contracts she is negotiating: what she fears is that, should she take a cut, self-interest would impair her judgement; that she'd be tempted to favour choices which would prove detrimental to her charges and, in the longer term, to herself as well. Whoever asks her for advice does so knowing that the amount of money she is in line to earn will have no bearing on the opinion she formulates; and if that were not enough, the finicky lawyer who will dispute the placing of a comma in a contract is also a master strategist who is able to see the 'big picture', and will know, for example, which sponsors fit best with the image her client wishes to project and protect (the fewer the better) and which offers to turn down (most of them). 'It's not just about saying yes or no to a brand. It's about building a strategy over time, while remaining at a distance from the choices,' she said.

Delphine est parfaite. Everyone I have spoken to when writing this book expressed respect, even admiration for Verheyden – how she is not just a 'brilliant legal mind' but 'brilliant', full stop ('brilliant', here, only conveys part of what is meant by the French *brilliante*, as the French do not share the English ambivalence about people who might just be, you know, too 'clever'). Her clients love her. 'She gives me serenity,' Martin Fourcade has said. 'Many offers are made to you when you reach a high level in your sport, and you can quickly find yourself surrounded by the wrong kind of people. Delphine knows how to keep her distance, she brings a lot of balance to all of this.' Colleagues praise her attention to detail and her ability to mix silk and steel in negotiations, a combination which was also in evidence during the only opportunity I was given to talk to her.

Verheyden was the first name on my 'to contact' list. I'd been told by journalist friends that she was to Mbappé what Argus Panoptes was to the mythical Io, the perpetually vigilant eye whom nothing and no-one can escape. I could try my luck and approach Kylian's parents – but given the nature of my own project, it was unlikely they'd agree to speak to me without seeking Verheyden's advice first. Wilfrid had a reputation for being easy-going, and a friend of mine who had done some business with him offered to make an introduction, which was turned down. Wilfrid had receded into the background of Kylian's career a while ago already. He clearly enjoyed being his son's father; this was his VIP pass to the parties, functions and sporting events he so enjoyed attending, especially now that Kylian had outgrown the need for the kind of professional advice he, a player and coach of modest achievement, could provide. Wilfrid does not play any official role in the multiple companies Kylian and Fayza have set up to monetise the player's image and look after his interests in France and abroad. The son still leans on the father for support, of course, but the nest the child flew years ago cannot be rebuilt.

Fayza, whose own influence had grown as Wilfrid's had waned, was a trickier proposition. She was known to invite journalists to impromptu chats near the flat she'd moved into after splitting up with Wilfrid in the spring of 2020 (the two had signed a 'civil solidarity pact', but never married, and separated on amicable terms). Fayza now resides close to the *Église de la Madeleine*, where the great and good of Paris must have their nuptials just as they have to be buried in the Père Lachaise. Some who'd met her there or outside the media suites which she often frequents when Kylian is playing, painted her to me as approachable, down-to-earth and great fun to be with. Others contented themselves with a 'Fayza, oh la la . . .'

I sent Verheyden an email in which I outlined the work I was planning to do as clearly and honestly as I could, insisting that I had no intention of writing the biography, authorised or not, of a football player who had just turned 26. Verheyden agreed this would be nonsensical. It was the 'project' which was of interest to me, the 'project' she was a key part of, which I believed to be unlike any other in the world of football, especially when it came to the degree of control exercised by the star of the show. There too, she agreed, and said she would ask Kylian himself whether he'd be ready to hear from me directly or not.

Perhaps surprisingly for a biographer and investigative journalist, I have never managed to get rid of a natural unease when addressing strangers in the course of my work. I always feel like an intruder in such circumstances, and have only succeeded in learning how to hide it a bit better; but not this time. Verheyden was a delight to talk to when we discussed my proposal on the telephone. She 'got' everything I told her instantly. She was straight to the point, but unhurried; she didn't give anything away but was happy to tell me I was on the right track when I mentioned a couple of my angles of attack to her; she set clear boundaries from the outset but did so with the utmost courtesy. A mere twenty minutes of conversation were enough for me to understand why everyone found her *brillante*. Verheyden was true to her word and approached her client on my behalf, but came back with a polite 'no', adding a personal 'good luck' message which I admit touched me rather more than I would have expected. I regretted, of course, not to have a chance to put questions to the Mbappés themselves; but I regretted even more not to be able to do the same with their lawyer, whose role had only increased in scope as years went by. For if Kylian, Fayza and Wilfrid refused to cooperate, so would Delphine, whose whole professional life now revolves around the Mbappé project: she coordinates, together with her small legal team, the work of the thirty or so full-time employees who look after her number one client's image and investments. No wonder she has only taken on a handful of new clients since 2018, the year Kylian joined Paris Saint-Germain.

There is one question I would have loved her to answer more than any other. In a football world which is almost exclusively dominated by men, how can it be that Kylian Mbappé's career is primarily managed by women, what's more, women who have very little experience of men's football and barely any contacts within? There is Delphine, the guide, the enabler, the rock. But there is also Patricia Goldman, one of the biggest names in the public relations business, who helps define Kylian's communication strategy, a job she does for no other sports personality: her clients are superstar chefs like Alain Ducasse, business figures such as Alain Afflelou and global companies, Air France and Renault among others. There is Marie-Alix Canu-Bernard, a criminal lawyer who came to prominence when Mbappé had to fight and was cleared of allegations of rape in the autumn of 2024. There is Barbara Uzzan, a Parisian accountant who moved to Los Angeles in 2007 and specialises in providing tax advice to French citizens and companies which seek to establish a presence in the USA; it is Uzzan who is the agent for Zebra Valley LLC, the company which Kylian and Fayza incorporated in California in April 2022, just before signing a representation deal with US agency WME Sports and announcing a multi-year 'content creation' partnership with the NBA.

And more important than anyone or anything else, there is Fayza.

It took Fayza Lamari a long time to accept that she too was a public figure. It was only in October 2021, following constant encouragement – needling, in truth – from her son and Delphine Verheyden, that she agreed to speak at length to *Le Parisien*, the daily in which she used to look for the weekend's results when she was a professional handball player. She set the rules of engagement: the questions, which were not vetted by the Mbappé team prior to the interview, would not be asked by journalists but by readers of the newspaper. There was nothing random about the timing of the exercise. In her own words, Kylian, 'the ideal son-in-law', had become 'a little devil' in public opinion, and she wanted to set the record straight. She had had enough. First, in late June, Kylian had missed his penalty kick in the shootout which saw Switzerland eliminate France in the round of sixteen of the European Championships. The Swiss, who had last beaten Les Bleus in 1992, came back to win from 1–3 down with nine minutes to go. Mbappé, who had played every single minute of that Euros without scoring, was crucified on social networks. He no longer was the impish winger of Monaco's glorious Champions League campaign nor the golden boy of Russia 2018; he was an established superstar and, therefore, a target, not that all of the criticism he received was undeserved.

Two weeks before Fayza sat down in the office of *Le Parisien* with Delphine Verheyden at her side, PSG had beaten Metz 2–1 in Metz thanks to a goal scored by their right-back Achraf Hakimi in the dying seconds of added time. Instead of celebrating with his team-mate, Kylian ran towards Metz keeper Alexandre Oukidja and goaded him in full view of the crowd and of the cameras, then ran away as an incensed Oukidja chased him. Mbappé hid behind Neymar in the group of PSG players who'd congregated by the corner flag, not looking too proud or too reassured it must be said. His rampart Neymar pushed the keeper to the ground and was booked, while Mbappé got away with his taunting. The Metz manager Frédéric Antonetti was not impressed. '[Mbappé] had better behave differently if he wants people to love him,' he said. 'I adore this player. He is very, very strong, but he would benefit from behaving differently. He would benefit from being a bit humbler.' Others put the same sentiment in more forceful terms. This was the reason why Fayza, with her son and his lawyer's consent, had chosen to speak out. It made for a fascinating read; fascinating, but also frustrating, which was perhaps unavoidable. She turned on the charm and the humour, shared a few family anecdotes and painted a portrait of her relationship with her son which contained enough rough edges to pass as the whole truth. She too disapproved of Kylian's behaviour towards Oukidja. She agreed: Kylian was a *sale gosse* ('naughty kid'); but he didn't mean harm.

She revealed enough of 'human interest' value to keep more delicate matters at bay. For example, Kylian never carried cash nor credit cards on his person, she said; but she didn't add that this was a characteristic he shared with many other multi-millionaires who, like him, are constantly accompanied by assistants who do the paying for their employer. Yet it enabled her to add that he 'wasn't a big spender', when the penthouse he was renting in the 16th arrondissement at the time cost him €35,000 a month. She explained how they 'didn't touch the money for three years' after Kylian signed for PSG, without mentioning that his previous contract with Monaco was already worth over €1 million a year. She said that they suffered from 'poor people's syndrome'; but neither Wilfrid nor her were 'poor'. Their parents may have been (though Wilfrid's father was a tribal chief and a landowner in his native Cameroon), but they were well-off enough to take the family on holiday to Dubai when Kylian was at Clairefontaine and to offer him an electric toy car he could drive to the local stadium in Bondy before he was 10. This was not dissembling. This was a sincere attempt at humanising a young man whose talent and achievements had turned into a subject of contempt, even hate, for some.

That sincerity shone through when she spoke to *Le Parisien*, in a lengthy interview published in October 2021, of how she, the mother, had struggled to cope with the quick-as-a-flash rise to stardom of her son. 'I wondered what was going on,' she said, speaking of the reaction to Kylian scoring his first Champions League goal, on 21 February 2017 against Manchester City, when he outpaced his marker to send a rising shot into the roof of Willy Caballero's goal. 'He'd become Justin Bieber, and it scared me.' She put on 24 kilos in the space of six months between that game and Kylian signing for Paris Saint-Germain. 'It [was] so difficult in the beginning,' she said. 'I was not prepared for that.' With time, she learnt how to deal with the constant attention – and criticism – Kylian was receiving, primarily by 'switching everything off'; but it was impossible to 'switch off' completely. 'This summer, Kylian became the one who had to be shot in the public square. The mother intervened. He [was] young, he was always going to make mistakes, he didn't deserve what came to him. I came out like a she-wolf.'

She also felt that Kylian himself was partly responsible for the negativity which surrounded him since his failure at the European championships. 'He has to learn how to open himself to others a bit more,' she said, adding that she had tried to convince him to be the subject of an autobiographical documentary for two years, in vain. 'People already know everything about my life,' her 22-year-old son had retorted.

What Fayza had not spoken about – just mentioned *en passant* – was that she had also become a businesswoman whose business was her own son, the unofficial chair of what could be called Mbappé Inc, and that she hadn't waited for Kylian to go to PSG and succeed there to start building the enterprise. Delphine Verheyden had been recruited in 2015, when Kylian was struggling to get a game in the Monaco reserves. The first two companies dealing with her son's image rights, Assini and Saziley Communications, were registered in Paris on 25 August 2017, a week before Mbappé officially became a PSG player. The project had been underway for a while.

Other football superstars had followed a similar route, but none of them so early. Cristiano Ronaldo was already 24 years old, with three Premier League titles, the UEFA Champions League and the FIFA Club World Cup on his honours list, when the CR7 trademark was registered in June 2009, just under a year after it had been used for the first time to promote a line of underwear. The Manchester United player had also scored 22 goals in 66 games for the Portuguese national team. He'd taken part in three major international tournaments and reached the final of the 2004 European championships. Everything – including a dreamt-of move to Real Madrid – was in place to monetise his personal on-field achievements as no other footballer had ever done before him. Cristiano was different. He had the talent, the looks, and, more importantly, a near-exhibitionistic keenness to be filmed, photographed and admired.

Kylian Mbappé was different too, but in another way. The image he projected as a very young man exploding onto the French football scene was that of a happy-go-lucky, slightly mischievous, even cartoonish character who was out to have fun – and make fun of others, too. You could imagine him looking back and thumbing his nose at the defenders he regularly left in his trail, his heels kicking sparks and clouds of dust off the pitch. He giggled when he saw his face projected on the giant screens of the Stade de France. He had the charm of a Parisian *poulbot*. He was the imp with a winning smile, not a frowning footballing superman gifted with the physique of a kouros.

Yet Kylian didn't wait as long as Cristiano and his protector Jorge Mendes did to make sure that the commercial rights associated with his name were protected. In August 2017, when, still 18, he had played a grand total of 40 games in Ligue 1 with Monaco, the French law practice Cabinet Flechner filed the 'Kylian Mbappé' trademark with the British registration body UKIPO. The project had entered a new phase. Control must be asserted over every dimension of Kylian's commercial potential. The time had come to make some serious money.

8
Mbappé et compagnie

Kylian with NBA commissioner Adam Silver, 2022.

I have used the adjective 'unique' in conjunction with the 'Mbappé project' on a number of occasions in this book; but I did not infer by that that it was conceived *ex nihilo*. There have been precursors to the model which Kylian, his family and his advisors have built over the past decade and more, and the one which bears the closest resemblance to it is the strategy followed to build the brand of one of Kylian's team-mates at PSG, Neymar Jr.

Like Kylian, Neymar was a natural-born footballer whose gift had been obvious from a very young age, a gift so outrageous that his father, Neymar Sr, a former lower league player like Wilfrid Mbappé, chose to devote his life to honing it. The father had been forced to retire after a car accident in which his baby son, then only a few months old, miraculously escaped unharmed. Mogi das Cruzes, the satellite town of the São Paulo conurbation where Neymar Jr was born, did not have a club worthy of his talent, even though it was the one in which his father had eked out a living as a footballer; so the family relocated, first to São Vicente, then to Vila Belmiro, the *paulista* neighbourhood of Santos FC, where the prodigy signed forms in 2003, at the age of 11. Just like they would later try to entice Kylian in

2012, Real Madrid invited Neymar Jr and his family to Spain in 2005, where the teenager trialled for ten days with the Merengue youth team; and in the same way that Wilfrid and Fayza would turn down the offer of the multiple European champions, Neymar Sr decided that it was far too much to deal with, and far too soon to leave home; and just like Wilfrid and Fayza, he made sure the agents who were swarming around the Santos sensation got nowhere near his son. It was not an agent that the Neymars needed: it was a lawyer, the best there was. Marcos Motta, Neymar's Delphine Verheyden, stepped in.

Motta, an alumnus of the University of Warwick and of Harvard Law School, served as a director of *carioca* club C.R. Flamengo from 1997 onwards, when he was only 26, and advised the Brazilian government on the so-called 'Pelé law' a decade later, before starting his own practice. His claim to have been Brazil's first-ever dedicated sports lawyer is not misplaced: Neymar Sr could not have found another better-connected and better-informed lawyer to guide him and his son. Better-dressed, too: I remember Motta telling me how proud he was to have been voted his country's third most elegant gentleman by *GQ* magazine. He had a smile on his face when he said that, the smile of a man who was making fun of his own vanity. Charm too is a weapon.

Together, Neymar and Motta devised a plan for the rising star of Santos who, within a year of making his debut for the Peixe, aged 17, rose to become the key player of their triumph in the 2010 Campeonato Paulista and Copa do Brasil. Fourteen thousand people signed a petition to implore then-national team manager Dunga to take the teenager to the South African World Cup – in vain. Neymar Jr had become the latest (and most convincing) prodigy to be hailed as the next Pelé. It would have been easy to seek an immediate way out of Brazil and join a top European club. FC Barcelona had already declared a firm interest, but Motta and Neymar Sr rejected the move. To everyone's surprise, they even sold 40 per cent of the player's sporting rights to a strategic partner of Santos FC, the DIS Esporte Club. This fitted in with the three-stage strategy they'd devised: first, develop the Neymar brand regionally, in the state of São Paulo; second, move up to the national level; third and last, go global.

In sporting terms, this meant staying at least one extra season with Santos, which was to be the club's most successful since the Pelé era. They retained their state title in 2011 and won South America's number one club trophy, the Copa Libertadores, for the first time since 1963. Neymar Jr was voted 'Man of the Match' in the return leg of the final against Uruguay's champions Peñarol. An astonishing solo goal against Flamengo in the Brazilian league earned him Fifa's Puskás Award. The *seleçao* was now built around him. Surely he must leave now? But he did not. He signed a contract extension with Santos until 2014, despite being voted South American Player of the Year and finishing in the top ten of the Ballon d'Or that year. More titles followed: the Recopa Sudamericana in 2012, another *paulista* crown the same year. It was only in May 2013 that it was announced that Brazil's great hope would join Lionel Messi at Barça, with €40 million of the €86.2 million transfer fee going to his family.

In parallel, Motta and Neymar Sr built a large portfolio of commercial partnerships, first restricting themselves to deals with local companies which only spent the equivalent of a few tens of thousands of dollars to associate their brand with the footballer. *Chi va piano va sano,* slow and steady. This was the mantra. Stick to the three steps: regional, national, global. Build the brand, establish Neymar Jr as *the* player who embodied the *jogo bonito*. As the goals and the titles added up, those sponsors gradually made way for bigger names, now including international brands. Nike had been first to make their move, signing him up when he was still a child, as they did with Mbappé, and making the Brazilian their 'ambassador for South America' in 2011 for a reported $10 million. It was only after Neymar was presented to over 53,000 fans at Barcelona's Camp Nou in June 2013 that the big contracts rolled in for good.

The parallels with Mbappé's own project are striking in terms of both methodology and longer-term strategy; yet the similarities are less revealing than the differences. In commercial terms, the 'three-step' Neymar plan aimed to maximise revenue by multiplying partnership deals. The brands he lent his name to reflected his on-field progress from regional to national to global football star, not his inclinations or personality. At least thirty-five brands have been associated with the Brazilian over the past fifteen years, and this is probably an underestimate, as more names keep being added to the list, even now that the perennially injured Neymar has gone back to Santos to play out the final years of his career. What mattered, what still matters for him and his advisers, is numbers. The website set up by his image rights company Neymar Sport e Marketing S/S Limitada, which is run by his father and his mother, Nadine Gonçalves Santos, focuses solely on the reach its number one product can offer advertisers. Neymar expects money from his 'clients', as they are described on that website, and nothing else; Mbappé is looking for much more, and picks commercial partners whose own image reflects favourably on his own or, at the very least, does not taint it in the eyes of the general public; the brands he promotes also promote *his* brand. It works, and very well, as a two-way image-building system.

Kylian will never become a 'global ambassador' for PokerStars, for example, as Neymar did in 2015. Neither will he accept an offer to be the public face of a brewer, as the Brazilian did when he promoted a full-strength Brazilian beer called Cerveja Proibida back in 2017. Mbappé favours brands evocative of 'class', hipness and luxury. Aside from his longstanding kit partner Nike (his ten-year contract is said to be worth $15 million per year until 2029), gaming giant EA Sports and Panini, through whom he sells autographed memorabilia, the handful of brands he's endorsed include Swiss watchmaker Hublot, where he succeeded Usain Bolt as 'global ambassador'; Oakley glasses (he recently fronted an international advertising campaign for Oakley's 'smart' glasses, developed with Meta); fashion house Dior; high-end 'home entertainment systems' Loewe, in which he took a 10 per cent stake in 2024; crypto card-trading platform Sorare; exclusive German luggage manufacturer Rimowa; and Accor hotels. Less than ten partners in total, a far cry from the dozens collected by other superstar footballers like Cristiano Ronaldo and Lionel Messi, a man who will literally advertise anything, including the Saudi Arabia tourist board.

The task of managing Kylian's image rights, selecting and dealing with the right partners, is primarily entrusted to the indispensable Delphine Verheyden and to his mother, Fayza. As Mbappé's lawyer explained in the French *Pause* podcast in 2019, the emphasis is put on control. 'My work consists of ensuring that athletes are not dispossessed of their image,' Verheyden said. 'We are moving into Web 3.0, and I believe that the individual image and its ownership will be cardinal virtues. We must not give up anything in our age, otherwise it will be a catastrophe for the people who have a [public] image.'

Where Neymar Jr was happy to let his father and their lawyer conduct all commercial and business affairs on his behalf ('My father takes care of things, my finances and my family,' he told CNN in 2012. 'He is the one who is in charge. He's the boss'), Kylian will, almost always, have the last word in this regard. 'Almost always', but not 'always'. Fayza has told how her son buckled when she turned down a particularly lucrative advertising campaign. 'You made me lose €6 million!' he said, half-jokingly. 'I'm still your boss, no? Can you explain it to me?' She did. 'The values [of the campaign] did not correspond to what he is. The benefit, when you have money, is that you don't have to sell your soul to the Devil.' You can still sell your image, however, and must do it properly, which is what the Mbappés did from the beginning, with Verheyden's help, setting up their own business structure, on their own patch, on their own terms.

There is nothing remarkable about rue Henry Monnier, a Parisian street which looks like dozens of others in the Saint-Georges quarter, south of the Pigalle district, a straight line bordered by five-storey houses built in the late nineteenth century. The brothel which Emile Zola visited there, at number 6 – for research purposes, this being said without irony – has long since been divided into flats located above a minuscule grocery store. The house next door, at number 4, in which poet Louise Colet, Gustave Flaubert's great love, welcomed Dumas, Hugo and Baudelaire to her *salon* in the 1840s and 1850s, has been turned into a Japanese restaurant. It is true that Zola's and Colet's Paris died a long time ago. The *bobos* who can't quite afford to rent a flat in a more affluent arrondissement but earn enough to escape the *banlieue* have replaced the true bohemians.

There is nothing remarkable about number 17 either. It used to be flanked by a charming neighbourhood restaurant, Le Petit Canard, which lowered its shutters for the last time a year ago. To the right is a hairdresser's which specialises in anti-lice treatments; and sandwiched between the two is Sofradom, a company which offers *domiciliation d'entreprises*, meaning that its own address can be used to register businesses which have no physical presence on the site. Close to a thousand companies have chosen to do so, from film producers and electricians to convenience shops and tech advisors, who pay as little as €22 plus taxes per month for the service, with €9 on top if they wish to re-direct their business correspondence to another place. This is where the Mbappés have located the vast majority of their companies since July 2017, not long before Kylian signed his first contract with PSG, on 31 August of that year.

It is a long list and, I fear, not the most riveting of reads; but such is the nature of that particular beast, which has the merit, at least, of illustrating how Kylian's business affairs are intimately linked with his parents' interests, and with Fayza's in particular, as Wilfrid's role has ebbed over the years.

The first Mbappé company to appear at 17, rue Henry Monnier, on 17 July 2017, remains the most important of them all: Interconnected Ventures, the mothership, far more than the 'PR and communications consultancy' it started as. Previously known as KEWJF (the initials of Kylian, Ethan, Wilfrid, Jirès and Fayza), Interconnected Ventures borrowed its name from another company which had been registered in Bondy but doesn't seem to have been linked to the family. It is now 100 per cent owned by Kylian himself, with Fayza registered as the company's president. Assini, which appears to deal with property management, and whose president and sole shareholder is Kylian's father Wilfrid (using his actual first name Elie), was added to the registry a few days later, on the same date as management company Saziley (president and sole shareholder: Fayza; turnover: close to €6 million in 2024), which later expanded into two other entities, Saziley Prod, a film production company which was set up in 2020 and ceased activities in 2024, and Saziley Communications, which was dissolved in 2024 as well and does not seem to have generated any significant revenue. There is also Newpie, managed by Wilfrid until Fayza took over in 2025, which deals in real estate (founded 2019), and associates Kylian and both his parents, who hold half of its shares; Ohzora (real estate management, 2020), originally owned by Wilfrid and Fayza, of which Kylian now controls 499 of the 500 shares, with his mother keeping just the one; SCI Falam (2022, used by Fayza and Kylian to manage properties they rent); FLA (which remained dormant and was dissolved in 2024); and Fayza's PR company Tathou, a more recent addition (2024). Only one of Kylian's French companies is registered elsewhere, the one which bears his name and which he fully controls, 'Kylian Mbappé Lottin', at 57bis avenue de Rochechouart, a non-descript building which has seen better days and which serves as a post box rather than as an actual office. It is that company which trademarked Kylian's goal celebration in February 2018 as well as two of his most famous quotes, first *'Moi, tu m'parles pas d'*âge' ('don't talk to me about age', trademarked in March 2021) then *'le football il a changé'* (trademarked in June 2023, one year after he employed the expression twice in a press conference; yes, football has certainly changed).

Interconnected Ventures, whose turnover rose from €12 million to €32 million between 2021 and 2024, when a new French law made such financial information confidential, has four subsidiaries: Cultural Factory, whose accounts are not publicly available; Collective Motion, which generated €7.3 million in 2023; Zebra Valley Holding; and Zebra Valley France. The last two were created in 2023 as the French pendants of Zebra Valley LLC, the entertainment and sports content production company Kylian and Fayza had set up in California a year previously.

It was the first time the Mbappés had domiciled one of their companies outside of France. Having a visible presence on the US market was the first step towards making the Mbappé brand truly global, but it didn't quite work out as hoped or planned – the 2026 World Cup may change that – despite some high-profile deals, none more so than the 'multi-year partnership' signed with the NBA in June 2022 'to foster dialogue between global communities and make cultural conversation more relevant', according to a statement attributed to Kylian himself. In practical terms, Zebra Valley had a broad remit. It was intended to produce film and television projects, including animated movies, on sport, music, art and gaming.

To bolster this new venture, Kylian and Zebra Valley also signed a representation deal with the sports division of William Morris Entertainment, part of the colossal Endeavor entertainment group, a global agency which calls itself 'the original advocate for the world's most extraordinary artists, content creators, and talent', with offices in London and Sydney as well as in Beverly Hills, Nashville and New York City. Kylian was the first and, to date, the last soccer player to sign with the representatives of, among others, Charlize Theron, Denzel Washington, Matt Damon and Michelle Obama. Yet, more than three years later, there is nothing to show for this ambitious move. The only sports stars featured on the WME website are three tennis players: Iga Świątek, Carlos Alcaraz and Frances Tiafoe. No project has been announced. The only sign of activity on the Mbappé side has been a capital injection of €2.5 million in Zebra Valley Holding in 2024, which suggested some imminent action; but that company's last available filings show a negligible turnover and a loss of €78,000 which had been carried over from the previous set of accounts. It is of course too early to talk of a stillborn project: things can take a long time in Hollywood. Just ask Francis Ford Coppola.

I hope this avalanche of names, dates and figures is forgiven. I could have added a few more, but none of them would have been of particular significance. The point I wanted to make is of a different nature: what is remarkable about the business affairs of Kylian Mbappé and his family is not their relative complexity. It is that it should be possible to provide so much detail about them. All of the directorships, statutes and share structures of their companies are publicly available, a number of financial statements too. All that is required to access these is a computer, the URLs of a handful of registries and some tenacity. Type 'Fayza Lamari' in the main resource for this type of research, the OpenCorporates database, and all of her company appointments will be listed, like the names of Kylian and Wilfrid (or Elie) Mbappé will appear when searched on the multitude of sites which store French company details.

This transparency is unusual in the sports world, where the majority of elite athletes tend to channel their earnings and store their assets through opaque holding companies, especially when this money derives from the exploitation of their image rights. I'd have been unable to provide anything like this wealth of detail if my subject had been Cristiano Ronaldo or Lionel Messi, and that's before mentioning Neymar Jr, whose use of offshore structures was at the heart of the problems he encountered with the Spanish and Brazilian tax authorities after he signed for Barcelona. It is a well-trodden path. Gibraltar, with its zero per cent corporate tax rate for non-residents, has been especially popular with footballers in the past, like the US state of Delaware, which also charges no tax and where financial data is kept confidential, and has long been a favourite with NBA and NFL multi-millionaires.

The Mbappés chose to steer away from such arrangements and deserve credit for it, all the more so since the French corporate tax rate was still a comparatively high 33 per cent when Interconnected Ventures was set up in 2017. Kylian himself has always paid his taxes and social security contributions in France, bringing an estimated €261 million to the French Treasury in the seven years he spent at Paris Saint-Germain. Whether he remained a 'tax patriot' after his move to Real Madrid or not, as Karim Benzema was throughout his fourteen-year stay in Spain, is another matter; but he and his family have played by the rules all along. Not everyone else has.

Judging by the suggestions which pop up without prompting when a footballer's name is keyed into a search engine, guessing their wealth is a popular game. In Kylian's case, according to Google, Bing and Duck Duck Go, estimates of his worth vary between €250 million and half a billion. The only thing that can be held for certain is that all of those numbers, every single one of them, are wrong, even the ones which might bear some relation to reality, should we ever know what reality is in this case, which we won't. They are educated guesses at best. We have a fair idea of what Mbappé's gross salaries have added up to since he signed his first professional contract with AS Monaco in 2015 – €310 million gross, including what he was to receive in his first two seasons at Real Madrid – but usually forget to factor in what he paid in income tax and social contributions, what he claimed in tax relief, and how much of that income went into financing his various businesses and paying the family members, assistants and advisors on the Mbappé payroll.

As to the rest, we do not know. Sponsors do not release information of that kind. All we can say is that the 27-year-old captain of the France football team has enough money in the bank to do pretty much as he pleases. He has built up a collection of so-called supercars which he cannot drive, as he doesn't hold a licence: three Volkswagens – a Tiguan, a Tuareg and a Caravelle; at least one Ferrari, either a 488 Pista or an SF90 (some say both); a V-class

Mercedes van; a Cadillac Escalade and a BMW i7 which he was given as part of the German manufacturer's deal with Real Madrid. All we can say is that the car collector is wealthy enough to be a serious investor and that, to do this properly, he set up a specific structure in December 2023, Coalition Capital, whose registered office is located on rue Henry Monnier as well. Before that, the player had made his business investments as an individual 'angel', aside from the real estate deals which were channelled through companies created for that specific purpose.

The 'angel' has fallen to earth on at least one occasion. The fantasy sport cryptocurrency game Sorare was valued at $4.3 billion when Kylian, whom the French 'unicorn' had signed as its global ambassador, decided to put some of his own money into the venture in June 2022. Other sports stars like tennis player Serena Williams and footballers Gerard Piqué and Antoine Griezmann had already done so. Sorare did better than most NFT ventures, inasmuch as it is still operational, whereas the monkeys of the Bored Ape Yacht Club have seen such a depreciation in value that they are now a species on the verge of extinction; but the heady days are gone. Only a fraction of the two million users who traded digital player cards at the height of the game's popularity remain active on the platform. The alpha investors such as SoftBank and Atomico, who had flocked to Sorare and raised a record $680 million to finance its development in 2021, are now resigned to writing off most of their investment.

Like all first- and second-generation 'Web 3' products, once the initial frenzy had fizzled out, Sorare experienced a severe downturn in customer uptake, which was compounded by repeated warnings from regulators in France and Britain about its modus operandi, which they suspected to be a form of sports betting, an activity which the company was not licensed for. Sorare denied any wrongdoing and pleaded not guilty when appearing in a Birmingham court in October 2024. Collectors could trade their player cards using cryptocurrency, the Ethereum blockchain in Sorare's case. The value of those cards fluctuated according to their scarcity, but also to their desirability, which is not the same thing. I remember being intrigued by the sudden, spectacular rise in value of a certain Belgian player who had just been singled out as 'one to follow' by a journalist who had a sizeable number of followers on social media at the time and whom I knew to be a Sorare card collector. There may have been nothing to it; but it illustrated how, if one put their heart into it, the market could be manipulated in order to make a profit.

According to French investigative website *L'Informé*, the company's turnover shrank by 53 per cent in 2023 and by a further 27 per cent in 2024, to €43 million, when its losses totalled over €300 million for the same period. It is to be hoped for Kylian that his stake in Sorare was a modest one, and that what he earned in cash or kind as its ambassador softened the financial blow he must have suffered. This was the last significant deal of this kind that he did on his own before Coalition Capital was set up.

Coalition Capital, which is ultimately controlled by Interconnected Ventures and therefore by Kylian himself, serves as a holding company for the management of his wealth, image rights excepted, and has been very busy in the first two years of its existence, generating a revenue of nearly €4 million and a pre-tax profit of €2.76 million in the 2024 calendar year, quite a decent return for a balance sheet of €18.7 million during that period. The investments that were made are in line with the brands the footballer has endorsed, projecting the image of a young man who is effortlessly chic, embraces luxury but not bling, and is always on the lookout for new trends in culture or technology. Thus, in January 2025, through Coalition Capital, the global ambassador for Hublot and classic watches aficionado became a shareholder of Wristcheck, a secondary market platform operating from Hong Kong, Macau and New York, through which collectors buy and sell high-end timepieces without fear of burning their fingers. Two months later, Kylian himself announced that, in tandem with another of his sponsors, the Accor hotel chain, Coalition Capital had invested in France's SailGP team. For the uninitiated, SailGP (main sponsor: Rolex) is to catamaran close-to-shore racing what Formula 1 is to motor cars, quite a posh and expensive affair, conducted in twelve 'iconic' destinations, most of which are playgrounds for the rich and famous of our age, Dubai and Saint-Tropez among them. France, skippered by yachting Olympian and America's Cup helmsman Quentin Delapierre, finished a respectable fifth in the 2025 championship season.

Then there is Coalition Capital's biggest and riskiest investment to date, its purchase of Stade Malherbe Caen in July 2024. Who, these days, apart from nation states and private equity funds, would dare to buy a football club? Mbappé did, and it proved as fraught a venture as could be feared; but that is a story which deserves to be told on its own.

Before I get there, let me add a postscript. What struck me when I was looking at Mbappé's investments was more than their 'exclusive' nature. They fitted in within the project and complemented it. They reflected the tastes of a young man who was rich enough to indulge them, and why shouldn't he? One thing puzzled me, however. Mbappé's business affairs did not just involve himself and his companies, but his foundation Inspired by KM (or IBKM) registered at 17, rue Henry Monnier, as well. The SailGP deal was conditional on the yacht-racing tour naming IBKM as the 'official charity partner' of the France team. Seven of the 98 young boys and girls IBKM has taken under its wing (Kylian was born in 1998, hence this number) since the foundation was set up in 2020 flew to New York to 'immerse' themselves in SailGP in October 2025. Kylian's sponsor Accor footed the bill.

Similarly, when Kylian's Zebra Valley signed its cooperation deal with the NBA in 2022, thirteen children accompanied Mbappé on his visit to the USA at the expense of the foundation and of its partners. One year later, it was Oakley's turn to host an event at which the footballer mingled with the foundation's *étoiles*, the children and teenagers which IBKM has been associated with since its beginnings. In April 2024, a tour of the Dior Gallery was organised for them. A month later, it was Nike's turn to help IBKM stage a sporting and cultural extravaganza ('Victory Mode') on the Champs Élysées for 300 youths; Kylian and his brother Ethan dropped by towards the end of the day's festivities. Accor, again, intervened to pay for nineteen teenagers to visit Madrid, take in the views and talk to their hero after he'd joined Real in February 2025.

To me, this feels like instrumentalisation; to most others, it won't. It has always worked that way. Even before the not-for-profit association was launched in January 2020 in Bagnolet, not far from Bondy, another of Kylian's commercial partners, the French subscription baby food service Good Goût had been brought in to finance a cooking class for children attended by their ambassador. There is nothing reprehensible about this *per se*. Kylian makes it a condition for his sponsors to support his charitable work, which is not restricted to what IBKM is offering its 98 beneficiaries, 49 boys and 49 girls from the Parisian region who were all aged between 9 and 16 when the foundation was created. The appearance bonuses he receives when he plays for the France national team go to charities like Premier de Cordée, which promotes the use of sport as therapy, especially with sick children. IBKM has spent millions financing the building of schools and football fields in Cameroon, Algeria, and, more surprisingly, Ancón, Peru, which may not be unrelated to the fact that the full-time 'strategic digital manager' of Interconnected Ventures is a Peruvian national based in Paris, Maria Fe Giha Brigneti.

To be clear, I do not doubt that Mbappé's generosity is genuine, as genuine as his rapport with the children he gets in contact with. They worship him. My friend Vincent Duluc of *L'Équipe* told me how he once nearly started a riot in a provincial school after taking the shirt Kylian had worn in his last game with Les Bleus out of his bag. Vincent found himself surrounded by dozens of screaming boys and girls who all wanted to touch the hallowed jersey. It is no surprise that the one book that was commissioned and published by the Mbappés, *Je m'appelle Kylian*, should have been a comic strip aimed at under-15s which sold over a quarter of a million copies, to the astonishment of the French publishing industry. Children see themselves in him, and vice-versa. He values them and interacts with obvious pleasure, without condescension and affectation; and there mustn't be many sports superstars who pass on 30 per cent of the profits generated by their companies to their foundation as he does – at his mother Fayza's insistence, who initially wanted him to devote *half* of that income to IBKM. When Kylian says, 'I have a desire to help, to make [children] benefit from what I earn and from my fame' or 'I am happy to make [sick] children smile; they're far more courageous than we are. It doesn't take any courage to play for France or PSG, anyone could do it' or, speaking about IBKM, 'this is what I derive the most pride from', these aren't empty words.

The caveats? Some of the foundation's initiatives – the NBA trip to

New York, for example – feel like brand-building exercises designed with PR messaging and photo opportunities in mind; and IBKM is also a conduit through which members of Kylian's family and entourage can be remunerated in a tax-efficient way, starting with Fayza, very much the driving force of the association, whose salary is not made public. IBKM's last available accounts were filed in 2021 and showed an income of €692,256, a more than respectable figure keeping in mind that the accounting period coincided with the worst phase of the COVID pandemic; but since then, nothing. This is unexpected, as French law demands that not-for-profit associations with a significant turnover publish their accounts in the *Journal Officiel*, which IBKM hasn't done for four years. The blurring of boundaries between charity and self-interest may be unavoidable; it doesn't make it less challenging or questionable for all that.

9
Je t'aime, moi non plus: the PSG years – 1

French president Emmanuel Macron, Kylian,
FFF president Philippe Diallo and PSG chairman Nasser Al-Khelaifi.

Mbappé's transfer to PSG was finalised on 31 August 2017, the very last day of that summer's window, in the form of a one-year loan with a mandatory purchase option which valued the player at €180 million. The lateness of the move should not suggest that it had been in serious danger of not happening; at least not once Mbappé had made it clear that if he really had to leave Monaco, it would be to join PSG, not Real Madrid – as Monaco would have preferred, using the interest of the Spanish club to drive the hardest possible bargain from the Qataris. 'Nothing is ever certain,' he said, 'as you can never be certain of anything. That's bullshit. Nobody will write that you're certain to play in your contract; but I felt I would have more chances to play in Paris than in Madrid.' His father Wilfrid shared that feeling.

Talks between the player, his family and PSG had entered their final phase in June 2017, but proved trickier than expected, even if the issue remained beyond doubt. Mbappé played ASM's opening game of the Ligue 1 season, then watched the three matches which followed from the bench, as any injury could have scuppered the transfer at the eleventh hour. Those two weeks of inactivity felt like an eternity to him. 'I could not understand [why I didn't play for Monaco],' he said, adding, 'I was still an important player.' His inactivity, short as it was, opened his eyes to another facet of his profession, as he watched the clubs haggle and various intermediaries trying to get their pound of flesh from the most expensive transfer of a French player in history. 'I didn't know that world,' he told *L'Équipe*. 'It's a world I discovered and, seriously, I do not wish on others to discover it. This is not the true face of football. I had ideas [about the football business] in my head – but when it is other people who talk about it, it goes in one ear and goes out of the other. It's not the same thing when it happens to you. It really is a world to avoid.'

Eight days after signing his contract, Mbappé was in the starting line-up of the Parisian team which won 5–1 in Metz, the newcomer scoring one goal and assisting another, setting the tone for what was to follow. 'I join Paris Saint-Germain with a lot of joy and pride,' he gushed. 'For any young man who comes from the Parisian region, it often is a dream to wear the red and blue jersey and to sample the unique atmosphere of the Parc des Princes. I was attracted by the club's project, it is one of the most ambitious in Europe.' PSG's chairman Nasser Al-Khelaifi predicted that with Mbappé's arrival, 'more than ever, our team will make the hearts of the supporters beat faster'.

It was not all about the sport, though, as the PSG 'project' had always been about more than the sport. The Qatar-engineered transformation of the occasionally brilliant and perennially troubled club into a merciless winning machine had inspired hostility rather than envy in the rest of French football. Since 2012–13, the first full season to follow the completion of Qatar Sports Investment's acquisition of the club, PSG had only left four of the fifteen major titles on offer (Ligue 1, Coupe de France, Coupe de la Ligue) to what could no longer be described as 'the competition'. Marseille still saw themselves as *the* rival and had the fan base to back that claim but lacked the financial clout to be considered more than an irritant. Rybolovlev's wealth had enabled Monaco to assemble a formidable squad, especially in attack – they'd scored 107 goals on their way to winning the league in 2017 – but that investment was a one-off: by 2018-19, every single one of the players who'd been instrumental in the conquest of that title had gone, bar Radamel Falcao. Bernardo Silva and Benjamin Mendy were the first to leave, both of them for Manchester City; Mbappé was the third. Fabinho, João Moutinho and Thomas Lemar followed suit a year later.

What escaped no-one, the Qataris included, was that PSG's dominance had been built on recruiting established foreign stars rather than by making the most of the club's privileged access to the greatest reservoir of talent France – and perhaps Europe – had to offer: the Île-de-France, where Kylian was born. As Mbappé had said, 'for any young man who comes from the Parisian region, it often is a dream to wear the red and blue jersey'; but a dream it remained for almost all of them. Many of these young men had joined the club's academy since the Qatari takeover, but hardly any had managed to get a taste of the first team, let alone become one of its regulars. The eight recruits who joined the club in the summer of 2012, the first time QSI used their financial muscle to bully their way to the top of Ligue 1, were all foreigners: Thiago Motta, Thiago Silva, Ezequiel Lavezzi, Marco Verratti, Zlatan Ibrahimović, Lucas Moura, Gregory van der Wiel and David Beckham. The first five would constitute the nucleus of Carlo Ancelotti's and Laurent Blanc's teams over the five years to come, with the addition of Edinson Cavani and Marquinhos a year later. Of the thirteen players who left the Parisian club in 2015-16, eleven were French, including current or future internationals like Lucas Digne, Yohann Cabaye and Alphonse Areola. The likes of Kingsley Coman, Mike Maignan, Xavi Simons, Moussa Dembélé and Jonathan Ikoné all trained at the club since before the age of 10 but made a combined total of fourteen league appearances for PSG, most of them as late substitutes, before flourishing at other clubs. A direct consequence of the Qatari modus operandi was that there was only one PSG player in the starting line-up of the French team which lost 1–2 to Sweden in a World Cup qualifier two months before Mbappé's signing: midfielder Blaise Matuidi, who was then sold to Juventus. Mbappé had been capped for the fourth time by Didier Deschamps on that occasion.

This explains why Nasser Al-Khelaifi chose to frame his welcoming address to Kylian as he did. 'It was crucial (*"primordial"*) for French football to keep such a talent and help him progress in our league,' he said. 'In our colours, among great players, Kylian will keep progressing in a way which will also benefit the French national team over the months and the years to come.' Mbappé's signing was one of those 'statements' which Al-Khelaifi and his paymasters were fond of and which, at the time, constituted their approximation of a strategy, as Zlatan Ibrahimović's, Neymar's and even David Beckham's signings had been. The club of the City of Light had to attract the most rutilant of butterflies to live up to its name.

Mbappé's capture differed in one respect; it was not just another deafening cymbal crash announcing that the orchestra was in town. The message was that PSG *cared* and was aware of the responsibilities that came with the quasi-absolute power it now exerted over French football, off the field as well as on it. Ligue 1's dependency on Qatari money had kept on growing since Al Jazeera Sport, soon to be incorporated in the beIN media group – with its chairman Nasser Al-Khelaifi – had acquired its international broadcasting rights for the 2012–18 period in June 2011, not so coincidentally at the time when QSI was acquiring a majority stake in PSG from US investment fund Colony Capital. Year after year since then, the Qatari network had increased its share of Ligue 1's TV market to the detriment of its 'historical' broadcaster Canal+, who'd owned the club from 1991 to 2006, and found itself in a position where it could dictate its will to the league without fear of meaningful opposition. That hand was to be kissed, not bitten.

Al-Khelaifi was a former tennis professional of modest achievement who had worked himself into the favour of Crown Prince and future emir of Qatar Sheikh Tamim bin Hamad al Thani, who made him a minister without portfolio in 2013. He had added to his portfolio of official positions accordingly. 'NAK' was first elected to the board of the Ligue de Football Professionnel (LFP) in September 2014, then, in October 2016, replaced former Milan executive Umberto Gandini on the board of the UEFA Professional Football Strategy Council as a representative of the European Club Association (ECA), an appointment which automatically gave him a seat on ECA's executive board. The clubs that PSG were simultaneously keeping alive through the largesse of beiN and swatting away in their stadiums week after week gave their blessing to NAK's spectacular rise, at least in public. Their fans thought and said otherwise. Some, like the Bastia ultras, deployed banners which accused Qatar of financing Islamist terrorism. Others, like the Marseille *fadas* ('nutcases') satisfied themselves with the customary insults and obscene chants. Away from the stadiums, French media were at last discussing how the acquisition of PSG by the Qataris may have played its part in securing the support of French president Nicolas Sarkozy for Qatar's ultimately successful bid for the 2022 World Cup.

It is a story I know well, as I wrote a significant part of it myself, together with my *France Football* colleague Eric Champel. UEFA president and Fifa vice-president Michel Platini had been invited shortly before the 2 December 2010 Fifa vote to the Elysée, only to discover that Crown Prince Tamim and Qatari Foreign Minister Hamad bin Jassim Al Thani were also in attendance. The informal, non-minuted gathering was discussed at a French Cabinet meeting in January 2013, and made headlines in most places where newspaper editors think their readers care about football. Unbeknown to us, a cascade of legal letters rained on our editor Gérard Ejnès's desk after we made that revelation. He ignored them and did not tell us he'd received them until much later. As Eric and I saw it, the timing of PSG's acquisition by Qatar was – at the very least – troubling. It could be seen as a reward for France's decisive role in securing the backing of UEFA members of Fifa's Executive Committee at the crucial vote. Platini later admitted that he'd switched his support from the US bid to Qatar at the last minute, with other European ExCo members imitating their president, adding that he had only been subjected to 'subliminal' pressure and that he'd come to believe that Qatar genuinely was the best destination for the 2022 Fifa tournament. So many articles and books have been written on the subject, and so many documentaries of varying merit been made in the wake of the 2015 FBI raid on the Fifa grandees' favourite Zurich hotel, the Baur au Lac, that I don't think it is necessary to go into further detail here. What matters is that Nasser Al-Khelaifi and Qatar had their work cut out to placate French football fans who not only despised the new Molochs of Ligue 1 but were also convinced that they had not just bought but corrupted their ascent to the top of the game. Just like beIN had 'saved' French football by paying over the odds for its TV rights, PSG had 'saved' Kylian Mbappé for the country. For once, unlike what had happened with Zinédine Zidane, Thierry Henry and Paul Pogba, our finest prospect would stay at home and make 'the hearts of the fans beat faster'.

The €180 million PSG would have to put on the table in 2018 had not just bought a superb player. It had also bought the goodwill of rival clubs who knew that their stadiums would be packed when Mbappé and Neymar visited them, and that the value of the TV rights on which they depended for their survival would be enhanced by having such stars on show every weekend. The media might now think twice about printing more horrors about the bad Qataris if they knew that this would limit or even end their access to the PSG stars, as had happened to us after our 'Qatargate' dossier was published. Things would change with time, when Gérard Ejnès retired and another editor spent a couple of days in the Qatari desert to write an 'intimate portrait' of Al-Khelaifi. That editor later became PSG's director of communications. Ah well.

If PSG was part of the Mbappé project, the opposite was just as true.

For Kylian, leaving Monaco, a club which had just been crowned champion and had dazzled Europe in a run to the Champions League semi-final, for another which had just lost its title and found a way to surrender a four-goal advantage to Barcelona in that tournament, made perfect sense in the skewed landscape of Ligue 1. It could happen that another club took advantage of PSG's inability to think beyond the next big signing and pounced to poach the title. It had happened before; but when it happened, it could not be repeated. Montpellier did it in 2011–12 (when the Qatari flag had only just been raised at the Parc des Princes), and so did Monaco with Mbappé in 2016–17. Lille would make a splendid champion in 2020–21, only to lose all of their best players afterwards. Every time, PSG bounced back and reclaimed their due.

Monaco's affront was dealt with in spectacular fashion. That summer, one of the main architects of Barça's *remontada*, Neymar Jr, scorer of two goals in that 6–1 epic, joined the club he'd put to the sword for a world record – which still holds – of €222 million.

Uruguayan striker Edinson Cavani, the scorer of an astonishing 49 goals in 50 games for PSG in 2016–17, remained untouchable; the irreproachable Ángel Di María warranted a place in Unai Emery's starting line-up alongside him and the undroppable Neymar; but Mbappé's path was not blocked for all that. Emery would play all four attackers. Given the colossal amount of money PSG had parted with to have all four forwards in their squad, plus crowd favourite Javier Pastore and perennial hope Julian Draxler to make up the numbers from then on, he might not have much of a choice, or perhaps even a say, in the matter. At least Kylian would play. It would have been much more complicated in Madrid.

Mbappé father and son knew that there was no way that Zinédine Zidane – on his way to a third Champions League title in a row as a Merengue manager – could accommodate Kylian in his starting XI on a regular basis. Real's rather narrow 4–3–3, which sometimes took the shape of a 4–4–2 diamond, was built around the exceptional understanding and devastating partnership that Cristiano Ronaldo and Karim Benzema had developed over eight seasons spent together at the Bernabeu. Gareth Bale, when fit, slotted in as an inverted winger on the right flank; and when Bale was unavailable, the versatile Isco, who'd just had his most prolific season with Real (with 10 goals in 30 games, when he sometimes played in midfield), had proved that he could be depended on. Game time, Kylian had said over and over again, was what mattered most to him. 'The Galácticos made me dream when I was 4 years old,' he'd said after being invited to visit the club when he was 12 years old. 'I dream of coming back there one day, through the main door.' Had he gone then, in 2017, he'd have had to knock on that door for a while to be let in. So there would be no uprooting, not yet.

The family moved from Bondy to Paris, where Kylian's starting salary of €18 million gross – eighteen times what he earned at Monaco – soon enabled him to rent a sumptuous 600 square metre penthouse in the 16th arrondissement, the chicest of the *quartiers chics*, conveniently located a short drive away from the Parc des Princes, with a rental bill of €35,000 per month. PSG footed most of the bill and also paid for a private chauffeur, while the family would be entitled to five VIP passes for every home game. 'We did not "negotiate" the finances with PSG,' Fayza told French TV programme *Envoyé Spécial* in 2024. 'We worked by deduction. I remember I told him, "well, you're 18, we'll make it your salary, in millions". It went completely over the head of his father and over mine. It's like we were hallucinating.' Fayza might have overplayed her naivety in this case, as she had been laying the foundations of the next stage in her son's career since 2016 and had already built up the spine of the corporate structure which still looks after her son's assets and interests, as well as hers, nearly a decade later.

It worked out as hoped and planned. It was in Paris that Kylian became Mbappé, in Paris that the boy who pointed excitedly at the giant screen where the cameras picked him out sitting on the bench of Monaco in a Champions League game left his teenage years behind him for good. It was in Paris that his de rigueur 'crossed arms, thumbs up' goal celebration became a personal trademark, something more than an affectionate nod to his younger brother Ethan, who'd adopted the posture after beating him at PlayStation and daring him to copy him in a real game. Kylian had used it for the first time after scoring against Borussia Dortmund for ASM in the Champions League, in the spring of 2017. From now on, in the real world, a world far, far away from the family's Bondy Arcadia, the pose would be used to promote branded merchandise and inspire publicity cutouts displayed at sponsors' events.

In this, Kylian was a natural, but not as is commonly understood; what I mean by this is that he took to his new status without missing a beat, as if to the manner born. He mutated into 'KMB', the public figure, as if there was no distinction between the person and the persona. In some ways, there wasn't. The education he'd been given and the guidance he'd received from his parents, coupled with his own desire and singlemindedness, had prepared him to take every step in his rise to superstardom in his stride, as if it were meant to happen, as if it were more than the accomplishment of a dream shared by thousands of other young boys and girls – a destiny. The devil-may-care nonchalance he displayed on the pitch was an extension of his character; but a character is also a role to be played. Discerning the two became ever more difficult as years went by.

It is something I have often been told when researching this book. 'Kylian has not changed.' 'Kylian is the same as he ever was.' They may well be right. Some of the people I spoke to had known him well enough. They had dealt with the Mbappé family at various stages of Kylian's career. They had played alongside the prodigy and the World Cup winner. Others had come across him on a photoshoot or at a sponsor's event, or given advice on commercial deals; brief as their encounters were, their insights were often more revealing than the guarded comments I heard from people whose interests were still attached to his own.

Those I did not speak to include the player himself and his immediate family, though they were the first I approached through mutual friends or, perhaps more accurately, mutual acquaintances. Friendship is not a common currency in elite football. Does Kylian Mbappé have any friends? I couldn't say. I haven't met any. The ones I've heard of do not sound much like friends to me. Ousmane Dembélé, his fellow Bleu, is said to be one, but the way Mbappé has spoken about him doesn't suggest the two players are exceptionally close. When asked by *Le Parisien* about the chances of his 'friend' winning the 2025 Ballon d'Or, after Dembélé's goals had propelled PSG to their first Champions League title, all he had to say was: 'We shouldn't rule anyone out; all the players can receive the award, maybe even a goalkeeper. The last one I thought would go to Vinicius Jr, but in the end, it went to Rodri. If I had told you three months ago, you would have said, "What the hell are you talking about?"' Yes, Kylian, even a keeper, like the immense Lev Yashin, who won the award in 1963.

Friends. French comedian, actor and PSG fan Jamel Debbouze claimed to be one in a nauseating interview with *La Tribune du Dimanche*. 'I was very close to Nicolas Anelka, "Zizou Christ" and Kylian Mbappé,' he emoted. 'I even spent [COVID] lockdown with Kylian and his family, the craziest of moments.' Debbouze was 'profoundly moved by their family connection in adversity'. 'Of course, they put [on] a brave face,' he continued, 'but I saw the child in Kylian. As they have money, they shouldn't be pitied. But as to me, when I meet a human being and I see the child in them, I cannot not be moved.' Debbouze was promoting his football-themed feature film *Mercato* at the time.

Friends. Mbappé has team-mates, some of whom he gets on well with, some of whom he's clashed with, like keeper Mike Maignan, who didn't spare him in the dressing-room dissection of France's 1–3 loss to Italy in September 2024. He has advisors who value and admire him and get their share in the end. He has an entourage, bodyguards, gophers and hangers-on. He has, thank goodness, an extended family to lean on. They wouldn't speak. They let it be known politely and did not put any obstacles in my way, for which I am grateful; but they too went through the dark mirror of celebrity a long time ago.

*

The football was thrilling at times. Throughout those seven years with PSG, Mbappé scored and scored, and scored again. Some of his goals took the breath away, literally so in the case of the poor defenders who tried and failed to hang on to his coat tails, until there had been enough of these goals, and for so long, that we took for granted that breathtaking goals was what he dealt in, when he did not. Watching these goals again, they all seem to follow similar patterns. There is the burst of speed on the counter, often from the halfway line, defenders drifting behind like autumn leaves caught in a contrary wind, the face-off with the keeper left for dead, dinked or nutmegged. There is the ball received on the wing at speed, the dribble inside, the shot across the goal, opposite corner – goodbye. There is the opportunistic poacher's finish – there have been plenty of those – scored inside the six yards, the surest indicator of an attacking player's focus and game-reading ability. More often than not, especially in the first three years of Mbappé's stay at PSG, the instigator of those goals was Neymar, whom Kylian once called 'the greatest passer in world football, even better than Messi', and who supplied him with what the French call *un caviar* – an unmissable chance – on 26 occasions in the 141 games they played together.

The 'howitzers' from distance, the 'gravity-defying' volleys are a rarity in his repertoire, even if we all remember his gorgeous scissor-kick against Argentina in the 2022 World Cup final, the most balletic of his hundreds of goals, perhaps the one goal he will be remembered for, but which is not representative of his art for that. He was, he is a spectacular player, but not in the way he scores, in the way he plays.

The only books in which numbers hold an absolute value are treaties on arithmetic. In team sports, figures are not commensurate with greatness, a quality which is both elusive and self-evident; not even in games which consist of a series of duels, like baseball or cricket, in which some exceptional talents have been able to lead their sides to consistent success, as Martin Crowe and Richard Hadlee did with a modest New Zealand XI, for example; and even less so in football, which is why Diego Maradona's four blessed years with Napoli at the end of the 1980s have acquired mythical status: no-one had ever done anything comparable at that level in the history of the sport, and no-one will ever do so again.

Yet those figures are prodigious in Kylian Mbappé's case, so much so that he is routinely described as a 'great' player on the strength of them and that, until recently, excitable commentators have argued that he was – or would become – the 'greatest' of his age. At the start of the 2025–26 season, with his twenty-seventh birthday still four months away, Mbappé had already scored more goals for club (331) and country (50) than either Michel Platini (313 and 41), who was forced to retire at 31, or Diego Maradona (311 and 34), whose playing career spanned more than two decades. Two more seasons at Real Madrid should probably be enough for the Frenchman to go past Johann Cruyff (400 and 33). George Best, with 209 goals for Manchester United and Northern Ireland when he turned his back on football for the first time, aged 28, was distanced a while ago.

Platini, Maradona, Cruyff, Best, Mbappé. *Cherchez l'intrus,* the French would say. Seek the odd one out, as something doesn't feel right in that list. The place of the first four in football's pantheon is beyond doubt, but despite the goals, despite the titles, of which he's won more than any of them already, the fifth may never join them – and his seven seasons at Paris Saint-Germain partly explain why. He had great success there; but success is not everything.

It was in Paris that Mbappé spent what should have been the best years of his footballing life; and, from a statistical point of view, they were. He now sits at the top of the club's list of most prolific goalscorers, with 256 goals to his credit, scored at a rate of 0.83 goals per game, 56 goals ahead of club legend Edinson Cavani, with Parc des Princes god Zlatan Ibrahimović a further 50 goals behind. He was Ligue 1's Golden Boot in six of his seven seasons with PSG, was voted L1's 'Player of the Year' on five occasions, collected six L1 and four Coupes de France winners' medals. The sore point is PSG's failure to win the Champions League when he was at the club, only to do it as soon as he'd joined Real Madrid; but he still took part in two semi-finals and one final of the competition.

Moreover, to blame PSG's repeated stumbles in Europe on Mbappé's incapacity to weigh-in on the game as a world-beater like him should do (something I've heard from a few people) shows, at best, selective memory at work. It is true that he disappointed in PSG's run to the final in 2019–20, failing to score in any of the knockout games; but on the other two occasions the club reached the semi-finals, in 2020–21 and 2023–24, he delivered what was hoped of him. It was his hat-trick at the Camp Nou on 16 February 2021 – final score, 4–1 to the visitors – which turned the tide in the Parisians' favour in the round of 16. Two months later, he made a decisive impact in PSG's 3–2 win over Bayern in the Allianz Arena, scoring a double which effectively took his team to the semi-final – where a calf injury prevented him playing any part in the return leg against Manchester City. In 2023–24, having already scored three of his club's goals against Real Sociedad in the round of 16, he inspired PSG's improbable 4–1 victory in the Camp Nou, scoring two goals that night, when the Parisians had been beaten by Barcelona 3–2 in the first leg of the quarter-final. These were not the contributions of a mere passenger.

Why, then, is there so little love left for him at the club he gave his best years to?

10

Je t'aime, moi non plus: the PSG years – 2

It didn't take long for the relationship between Mbappé and PSG to sour. Two years were enough for the first aftertaste of vinegar. It never was more than a marriage of convenience, at least for the player, whose endgame was clear. This does not mean it was an unhappy one to begin with. The pawn had to reach the eighth rank to be promoted to a more powerful piece; Paris was a square on the seventh, so one more move, and it would be Madrid.

The first public cracks appeared in May 2019, when Mbappé, having just received the 'Ligue 1 Player of the Season' trophy from fellow footballers – he'd scored 39 goals and provided 18 assists in 43 games for the French champions – dropped a carefully phrased verbal bomb which he must have known would make the headlines in Spain as well as in France. 'I feel the time has come for me to have more responsibilities,' he said. 'Maybe here in Paris – I'd be happy with that – or maybe somewhere else for a new project.' It was a typically Kylian-ish statement, in which the barb was wrapped in cellophane rather than cotton, visible to all; and it stung.

A generous interpretation of Mbappé's words was that things had to change within the team and within the club if the huge disappointment of going out of the Champions League at the hands of Marcus Rashford, Ole Gunnar Solskjaer and Manchester United in the round of 16 after a 2–0 win at Old Trafford, was not to be repeated ad infinitum. If that were the case, who the dig was intended for was not clear. The Parisians had won their sixth title of the Qatari era at a canter, sixteen points ahead of Lille, in manager Thomas Tuchel's first season at the club. Perhaps it was the recruitment Kylian thought had been insufficient, with 40-year-old keeper Gianluigi Buffon the only addition of note to the squad in the summer of 2018. Perhaps, and more probably, it was the role he was asked to fill in the side that season, when PSG's number 9 Edinson Cavani missed nineteen games through injury and Tuchel deployed Mbappé as a centre-forward rather than on the right wing, where Kylian was convinced he would be at his best. The German coach's favoured 3–4–3 formation, a tactical set-up which Mbappé had close to no experience with for club or country, did not suit his natural attributes, or so the player felt, who loved nothing more than having space to run into.

Not everyone read it that way. My friend Julien Cazarre, a comedian who was one of the main attractions in France's most popular football radio show, RMC's *L'After*, told me it was at this point he realised that everything was not quite as he'd believed regarding France's golden boy. I do not mention Julien gratuitously here. His brand of humour grates with some, but very few people know as much as he does about PSG, a club he has followed since childhood, well before the Qatar flag was raised at the Parc, and whose games he still attends in the *tribunes populaires* though 'celebrities' far less famous than he is sit as close to Nasser Al-Khelaifi in the presidential box as they can. To him, it was all about Kylian's status within the team and the club and, in particular, his own position in the pecking order relative to Neymar. Mbappé's first two seasons at PSG had been everything the club could have hoped for when they signed the 18-year-old, with a return of 60 goals and 35 assists in 89 games. He still had three years to go on his contract, now worth €20.8 million per year before tax, and about to rise by another two million for the 2019–20 season. He dovetailed beautifully with Neymar and gave every indication he was enjoying that partnership. He also thrived on Ángel Di María's selfless service. Yet that wasn't enough. Kylian wanted to be the main man, the solution, and he felt that he could contribute more if he was deployed in his favoured position on the right wing.

Unai Emery shared that view, and deployed him there in 31 of the 44 games he took charge of in Kylian's inaugural season at PSG; but the year after that, Thomas Tuchel did not. Tuchel preferred to call on Ángel Di María and, five times, on left-footed Julian Draxler. Mbappé played in the centre-forward position in 32 of his 41 games for the German coach in 2018–19. The pattern would be repeated in 2019–20. The player's dissatisfaction with his manager's choices may have been one of the reasons why that campaign was also marked by disciplinary problems, with two straight red cards punishing outbursts against Nîmes in September 2018 and in the French Cup final on 27 April 2019 – a costlier moment of petulance, as ten-man PSG were to lose the match to Rennes on penalties, after Kylian had scored a hat-trick against his old club Monaco a week beforehand.

The 'change' Kylian said was needed was also a not-too-subtle allusion to the off-pitch behaviour of some of his team-mates, Italian midfielder Marco Verratti and Neymar chief among them. Verratti, almost unknown when he joined PSG from Pescara in 2012, had proved one of the club's more inspired signings, providing bite, drive and vision in midfield, but it was no secret that he struggled to contain his love of good food and craving for tobacco in the off-season (and sometimes beyond). Neymar, carrying on from what he'd been doing while at Barcelona, never missed a chance to fly back to his home country and party, hard. He followed PSG's catastrophic second leg of their round of 16 Champions League tie against Manchester United from the stands, having just flown back from Brazil, where he'd managed to attend the carnivals of Salvador de Bahia and Rio in the space of a single week.

The irony of Kylian's transparent dig at the lifestyle of his teammates and its impact on the club's performances was not lost on everyone, as he'd never been the hardest trainer himself, be it at Clairefontaine or Monaco, something which had exasperated some of his early coaches and did delay his integration in ASM's first team. He never changed in that respect. Much later, when his departure from PSG had become a certainty, his manager Luis Enrique was filmed for a Spanish fly-on-the-wall documentary tearing into his star attacker during a video analysis session. 'You said you liked Michael Jordan?' Luis Enrique exploded. '[Jordan] grabbed his teammates by the balls and defended like a son of a bitch. You have to set that example as a player and as a person.'

PSG fans took note of Mbappé's *petite phrase*. They also took sides. Mbappé, a national hero after France's 2018 triumph in Russia, was seen as the clean-living, humble-but-confident, level-headed-but-ambitious young man who was speaking out for the greater good of the club. Neymar was a genius, true, but of the uncontrollable kind, always one night out away from injury, the most expensive player in the world who had ended up costing more than money.

Mbappé's entourage and family did nothing to discourage that perception. Several press room *habitués* told me how Kylian's mother Fayza, in particular, regularly attended media events around PSG and Les Bleus. Mbappé's thinly veiled warning was typical of his communication style, of which damning with faint praise was a characteristic trait. To the uninitiated, it could pass as courtesy and fairness, a desire to speak honestly checked by respect and plain good manners. This is certainly the way the supporters heard it to start with.

Those supporters had never lionised their Qatari owners and their president Nasser Al-Khelaifi as, for example, Chelsea fans celebrated Roman Abramovich's reign over their club, waving wads of cash at their rivals, singing along to 'Kalinka' in the pre-match build-up and deploying their (club-approved) banner 'The Roman Empire' at Stamford Bridge, even after Putin's army invaded Ukraine in February 2022. They did not don approximate versions of Arabian robes as a few Newcastle fans did at St James' Park after the Saudi takeover of their club. There are plenty of reminders of the emirate's influence and power in the Parc des Princes, such as the advertisements for the Qatari-owned companies and institutions which flash on the stadium's perimeter boards, but there are no Qatar flags on display in the stands, and Al-Khelaifi's name has not been sung there as Sheikh Mansour's was at the Etihad on the rare occasions he attended a Manchester City home game. Yes, we'll take your money and be grateful for it, but, deep down, we don't really care. When Qatar was rumoured to be preparing an exit from PSG after having hosted the 2022 World Cup, there was no gnashing of teeth in the Parc. *We don't really care.* If Kylian Mbappé had a problem with his club's owners, it had to be those owners' fault. *You've used us to serve your political agenda, now we're quits.*

This pantomime war was fought against the background of the 'big question': how long would Mbappé, and PSG, resist the call of Real Madrid? Even then, in the late spring of 2019, when a 20-year-old Mbappé was three seasons away from the end of his contract, the concern was that he would not see it through. PSG kept failing in almost comical fashion in the Champions League, the one competition which mattered the most, the catwalk test for those players itching to tread the Ballon d'Or red carpet. It marked the beginning of the most drawn-out parting of ways in the history of football, which spread over five years of bickering, skirmishes and low blows, to end with a bitter conclusion, which was still being fought in the courts as these lines were written.

Real Madrid made their move in the summer of 2021 with an opening offer of €160 million, when Mbappé had one year left on his contract with PSG. The Parisian club had no intention of letting go of the 22-year-old. 'We will never sell him,' Al-Khelaifi had said as the COVID-hit 2020–21 season was drawing to a close, another campaign in which his club had flattered to deceive, winning both domestic cups, but relinquishing their league title by a single point to Lille Olympique and losing both legs of their Champions League semi-final against Manchester City. Mbappé had flourished and topped PSG's goalscoring charts for the third time in a row, with forty-two goals to his credit in all competitions, his best return since arriving from Monaco four years previously. This constituted a remarkable achievement, given that his main purveyor of chances, Neymar, had hobbled from injury to injury throughout. Manager Mauricio Pochettino, in his first season at the club after Thomas Tuchel had been prised away by Chelsea, could only call on the Brazilian in eighteen out of thirty-eight Ligue 1 games.

Al-Khelaifi promised that things would be different this time. Mbappé had asked for things to change? They had. Most of the summer recruits had come on free transfers, but what recruits they were, a mixture of the old and the new, of potential and exceptional achievement. Some were in their early twenties, like keeper Gigi Donnarumma and full-backs Nuno Mendes and Ashraf Hakimi, three of the future heroes of the 2024–25 victorious Champions League campaign. Two others had long passed 30, but nobody cared too much about that, as they were Sergio Ramos and Lionel Messi, fifteen La Liga titles and eight Champions Leagues between them, plus the small matter of six Ballons d'Or for the 34-year-old Argentinian. How could Mbappé miss out on the chance of playing alongside one of the game's greatest-ever players? On 11 August, as the recruits were presented to the media, with rumours of Real Madrid intensifying efforts to get Kylian making headlines in Spain and France, Al-Khelaifi sent the clearest message possible to his player: 'Mbappé has said he wanted a competitive team. There is now no team more competitive than this one.

'He has no excuse to do anything other than stay.'

But Mbappé was not looking for excuses. He was looking for a way out; or, at least, not doing anything to discourage Real's pursuit. French media reported that the player had 'made his mind up' and would go, which felt logical. In the Mbappé project, all clubs bar Real were stepping stones, including PSG; but he did not in the end. He chose to sit on his hands for another season. Come January 2022, he would be able to negotiate with the Madridese, with PSG unable to do anything about it. To get him, Real would have to pay a huge signing-on fee and a salary well in excess of the €26.6 million he was now entitled to in Paris. In the meantime, he would discover what it was like to wear the same shirt as Leo Messi as part of the most scintillating attacking trio European football had to offer – at least on paper, and when Neymar was fit, that is. Whichever way you looked at it, Mbappé would win in the end.

It worked on many levels. The constant speculation as to what the next move of France's star striker would be, in a World Cup year as well, didn't have a visible impact on the quality of his performances. Mbappé's numbers were again unmatched in France, with 39 goals and a prodigious 26 assists in all competitions to add to his record. Half of Messi's 22 assists in Ligue 1 featured Kylian in the role of a finisher. Messi could play with Mbappé. Mbappé could play with Neymar. That Messi could play with Neymar, well, everyone knew already, as everyone had seen the two of them combine in Barcelona. The problems started when Mauricio Pochettino tried to have all three of them lining up together. He had to find a system in which seven outfield players could do the work of ten when out of possession, as none of the trio was known for their defensive ability or, more to the point, for their appetite to defend.

The Argentine coach tried various formations to address the imbalance of his team, mostly alternating between 4–3–3 and 4–2–3–1, but could not find a lasting, effective solution to what was a problem no coach in the world could solve, unless it was by doing away with one or two of his 'undroppable' stars. Neymar was cast in the role of villain by many, including by members of Mbappé's entourage who grumbled about the Brazilian's chaotic lifestyle and its impact on the team's overall discipline and performances. Others, like Cazarre, and like me as well, felt it was too easy to turn the party animal into a scapegoat. What we saw was that Neymar missed far too many games, but he never hid when he could play. If he looked far more affected by his team's setbacks than his fellow players did, it is because he was. The footballer mocked for his on-field histrionics was a terrible actor. The thought crossed my mind that Neymar would always be a child, whereas you had to wonder whether Mbappé had ever been allowed to be one. Messi remained a mystery, perhaps even to himself.

If that season constituted a progress of sorts for the Brazilian, who missed four fewer L1 games because of injury than in 2020–21, he still sat out sixteen of those. He appeared in less than two-thirds of the 180 league games PSG took part in during his five years in the French capital. Moreover, things did not improve when he was on the pitch. By February 2022, fans and media had noticed that PSG won more of their matches when only one or two of the *trois fantastiques* were fielded together from the outset. Pochettino's team still reclaimed their L1 title fifteen points ahead of Marseille, but it was the same old song about 'The One That Really Matters'.

To the delight of editors hungry for narratives and controversy, PSG were drawn against Real Madrid in the round of 16, and for 168 of the 190 minutes of the tie, it looked as if that exasperating European monkey would be shaken off the Parisians' backs. Then Karim Benzema, who would go on to win the Ballon d'Or, completed his hat-trick at the Santiago Bernabéu to send Real Madrid through. The heroics of the first leg were forgotten, when Mbappé, assisted by Neymar, had scored in added time to make it 1–0 to PSG after Thibaut Courtois had saved a Messi penalty. Kylian scored in Madrid as well, Neymar the creator once again, making it 2–0 over the two legs. As away goals were still a thing in UEFA competitions at the time, Real now had to put three past Donnarumma in little over half an hour. They did. PSG went to pieces. It dawned on them that they were about to knock the thirteen-times European champions out of the tournament, and that was enough to make them fall apart; that, and the conviction in the Real Madrid ranks that winning on that stage was their God-given right.

The French media which covered the 'Will he? Won't he?' saga ad nauseam throughout the spring of 2022 were now convinced that Kylian Mbappé's time in Paris was up. What they didn't know was that Mbappé's family, his mother Fayza in particular, had never stopped talking to Nasser Al-Khelaifi. She had travelled to Doha on 22 April to meet the PSG president in the office of the Qatari capital's tennis club. The discussion had focused on the financial details of a possible extension to her son's contract, which had little over two months to run. Fayza did not commit to anything other than holding a further meeting – but in Paris this time, and in the presence of Kylian. Real Madrid, meanwhile, still believed they would snap up their target as soon as his Parisian deal expired.

The Mbappés held the upper hand in those negotiations. The Qataris were desperate to hold on to the footballer who was bound to be one of the main attractions at their forthcoming World Cup. France, the holders, had secured qualification in October of the previous year by trouncing Kazakhstan 8–0 in the Parc des Princes, with Kylian scoring the second quadruple of his career (the first had come for the Parisians against Lyon in October 2018). It had been sixty-four years since another French international, Just Fontaine, had scored four goals for Les Bleus in an official game, against West Germany at the 1958 World Cup. For Qatar, losing Mbappé meant losing face at the worst possible time; conversely, retaining him against all odds would demonstrate PSG's ambition and power. Money was never going to be an object for a country which had spent in excess of $220 billion to build the infrastructure needed to host the World Cup.

The crucial meeting was held on 2 May in the sitting-room of PSG president Nasser Al-Khelaifi's apartment on the Avenue de Malakoff, three days after Mbappé had scored twice and assisted a goal in PSG's 3–3 draw at RC Strasbourg. The speculation was clearly not affecting the player's efficiency: Kylian had scored twelve times in his last nine Ligue 1 matches when he sat down to discuss his future with Al-Khelaifi. Mbappé's mind was not quite made up when he left after a five-hour conversation; but he promised he would make a decision before the playing season was over. PSG were hopeful but not quite certain they'd win their *mano a mano* with Real. Hadn't Kylian been spotted having a late lunch with his PSG team-mate Ashraf Hakimi in one of Madrid's best restaurants less than a week after the meeting at NAK's apartment? That we know so much about what should have been confidential exchanges should not be a surprise: the media which covered the story most extensively, RMC radio and daily newspapers *L'Équipe* and *Le Parisien*, were briefed in detail by both camps throughout.

On 19 May, PSG were informed of Mbappé's decision to agree to a two-year extension to his contract, with the option of an extra year, two days before the last round of the Ligue 1 season, when the club would celebrate the tenth champion's title in its history. It was not a subdued affair. A rostrum was erected on the pitch of the Parc des Princes, from which Al-Khelaifi and Mbappé soaked up the applause of an ecstatic crowd. In typical PSG fashion, the ceremony was staged *before* the game kicked off, as if the day's visitors, FC Metz, were just extras in the Mbappé show, which they were. They capitulated 5–0, with the hero of the day scoring a hat-trick in the space of twenty-six minutes, to make sure he would top L1's goalscoring charts for another season, three goals ahead of Monaco's Wissam Ben Yedder.

The official line was that Kylian felt there was 'unfinished business' at PSG – that elusive Champions League title, of course – and that the 'change' he had been calling for was being implemented. Luís Campos, the man who had been instrumental in kick-starting Kylian's career in Monaco, and one of the very rare outsiders the family trusted and turned to for advice, was about to be named PSG's sporting director. Family friends such as comedians and fanatical PSG supporters Thomas Ngijol and Jamel Debbouze had weighed-in, and so had former French president Nicolas Sarkozy, another habitué of the Parc des Princes, whose uncomfortably close relationship with Al-Khelaifi and Qatar is discussed elsewhere in this book. 'I didn't say "no" to Real,' Mbappé told journalists, Al-Khelaifi nodding by his side. 'I said "yes" to France and to a new project by Paris.' Kylian was 'the happiest he's ever been', according to *Le Parisien*, who followed the player when he spent a few days at the Cannes Festival before joining the French squad for Euro 2021. He was accompanied on that trip, as on so many others, by Brice Tchaga, a celebrity 'capillary artist' (hairstylist) who shared his Cameroonian roots and had made a career (and a fortune) out of his association with famous French footballers. Tchaga, who struck up a friendship with Mbappé when he was at AS Monaco and has also become close to his younger brother Ethan since, would later jet to the Qatar World Cup to look after his clients.

Listening to club and player, it was as if financial considerations had been secondary for both parties. They had not. Fayza, now officially in charge of Kylian's interests, including his image rights, took a leading role in the discussions in that respect, when she hadn't been allowed to in previous negotiations as she did not hold an agent's Fifa licence. Wilfrid had receded into the background by this stage. The couple had separated on amicable terms over a year previously, with Fayza asserting her authority on all matters pertaining to her son's career, bar its purely sporting aspects, which remained her former partner's prerogative. They still pulled in the same direction, however. As far as the Mbappés were concerned, as the plan was to move to Madrid anyway, they might as well try their luck and ask for the moon, which they did. Fayza later told French TV programme *Envoyé Spécial*: 'I do not feel guilt or shame. If we could have taken ten billion, we would have. It's *le système* that demands it.'

What *le système* demanded was a gross salary of €72 million per year, just under three times what he earned previously, plus a colossal signing-on fee (presented as a 'loyalty bonus') of €125 million which would make Mbappé one of the best-paid athletes in the world. The Mbappés were calling PSG's bluff. PSG went all-in, which means that PSG folded and agreed to everything.

And a short drive away from the Parc des Princes, another man was celebrating the news: French president Emmanuel Macron.

11

The president's man

Macron hugging Kylian after the 2022 World Cup final, Doha.

Général Charles de Gaulle was not the kind of statesman who would normally be associated with football. He could be imagined on horseback, yes; in shorts, cleats and stockings, perhaps not. Yet he'd played the game himself when studying at a Jesuit school in Belgium, shortly before entering Saint-Cyr, the French equivalent of West Point or Sandhurst. *Le Grand Charles*'s elevated idea of his office precluded him from showing too much enthusiasm for the favourite sport of the French proletariat; but he still turned up at the odd match, including three French Cup finals, and it is at the last of these, in 1967, that he uttered one of his best-known one-liners. The Lyon defender Hector Maison booted the ball into touch with such force that it landed in the presidential box or, more accurately, in the presidential lap. De Gaulle instantly rose and threw the ball back to the player, adding: 'I really have to do everything myself in this country.'

De Gaulle also understood what sport could and should do to extend France's influence beyond its borders, what he called its *rayonnement*, or 'radiance', and was stung by the catastrophic showing of the French delegation at the 1964 Tokyo Olympic Games, winning a solitary gold. Things were not much more glorious in football, with the national team failing to capitalise on its third place at the 1958 World Cup and missing out on the 1962 tournament as well as on the 1964 European Championships. French clubs fared even worse. The exploits of Stade de Reims, twice a European Cup finalist in the late 1950s, fast receded from memory, like half-remembered dreams. De Gaulle, while remaining at arm's length as he believed a president should, decided that the State should intervene.

On one hand, centres of excellence for elite athletes would be created and financed with taxpayers' money; on the other, so would facilities which could be used by those taxpayers for free or at very little cost to themselves. This transformational project proved a huge success and directly led, for example, to the creation of the Institut National du Football which opened its doors in Vichy in 1972 and later morphed into Clairefontaine.

De Gaulle's successors followed his example. They were supportive, but kept their distance, something which suited their tastes and personalities. Georges Pompidou, who was passionate about contemporary art in general and contemporary music in particular, did not forget sports altogether and greenlighted the construction of the Parc des Princes, where it is true he only ventured when protocol demanded it, as when he turned up for Olympique de Marseille's 2–1 win over Bastia in the French Cup final in 1972.

France's next president, the suave, handsome technocrat Valéry Giscard d'Estaing, showed more willing, if only for political ends. His aristocratic name had been a late and not entirely legitimate addition to the family tree; but 'VGE' looked and sounded the part. He owned a medieval château in the Auvergne as well as a magnificent *grand bourgeois* townhouse in the 16th arrondissement of Paris. To ingratiate himself to voters who found him 'distant' and 'cold', Giscard multiplied what would now be called 'media stunts', playing the accordion, 'the poor man's piano', on television (to a backing tape, which nobody was aware of at the time), inviting himself for dinner at the home of 'ordinary French people' and doing nothing to dispel persistent rumours about his frequent infidelities to wife Anne-Aymone, as the French, at least back then, liked to have a bit of a rogue in the Elysée Palace. He played football, too, at least for the cameras. Well, he did once – in 1973, as the Finance Minister was readying himself for the presidential election to come.

The occasion was an impromptu game between the shopkeepers of Chamalières, the small *auvergnat* town of which he'd been mayor since 1967, and the local councillors, with the stork-legged 6 ft 3, 47-year-old looking stiff and awkward, as if he'd been liquefied and poured into a Subbuteo figurine mould. With his team trailing 1–2 late in the game, Giscard, having patted down his Bobby Charlton combover, toe-poked a spot-kick to earn his team a draw, then spoke to journalists in the dressing-room, the only time, I think, a future president of the Republic addressed the nation bare-chested. Once this was done, VGE reverted to type and was never seen in shorts and stockings ever again.

Neither was François Mitterrand, ambiguous in this respect as he was in so many others: a tennis player and golfer by inclination, bourgeois proclivities which didn't sit well with his aim to install a Socialist – himself – in the Elysée for the first time in history. So Mitterrand, a man who read *L'Équipe* every day, looking at the cycling results first, stopped frequenting courts and fairways, at least in public. As for the football, he turned up where and when he was expected to, but did not venture beyond the necessary. Michel Platini and his team-mates were not invited to the presidential palace when France won their first international trophy, and on home soil, at Euro 1984. Mitterrand's interest in the game was genuine, however. It was not just by obligation that he sometimes paid a visit to AJ Auxerre's manager Guy Roux; but he had entered his seventh decade by the time he finally became president, a mature man who felt more at ease in the company of the writers of the past than of the sports people of today. There were no comments from François Mitterrand when France failed to qualify for the 1994 World Cup in ludicrous circumstances or when Eric Cantona kung-fu'ed a racist fan at Selhurst Park two years later. All of this changed when Jacques Chirac succeeded the cancer-ridden socialist president in 1995.

Sport was low in Chirac's list of interests, with one exception. Since boyhood, the young Jacques had been a regular visitor to Paris's Musée Guimet, the National Museum of Asian Arts, and developed a passion for all things Japanese, including sumo. He would stay up late to catch the big tournaments broadcast by Japanese network NHK (which, as a presidential perk, the Elysée could access via a satellite feed) and could apparently recite the names of all of the *yokozuna* who'd been awarded sumo's supreme title since its inception in 1909. He could also quote many of Basho's *haiku* by heart; whereas he struggled with the names of France's international footballers who won the world title in his first presidential term. Chirac being Chirac, this did not prevent him from milking their success for all it was worth. 'He didn't like sport,' Guy Roux remembered, 'but he liked champions', athletes as well as heads of state and captains of industry.

No French president had invited sports people to the Elysée before he did, starting with the French Olympic medallists who'd just come back from a successful 1994 Atlanta Games. He also invited himself into the dressing-room of Les Bleus to take part in the post-match celebrations after their 3–1 win over Brazil on 12 July 1998; planted a kiss on Fabien Barthez's shaven head as Laurent Blanc was accustomed to do before every game (unaware of the significance of the gesture, which was of a very private nature); and paraded in front of the cameras clad in an ill-fitting blue jersey bearing number 23, as there were only 22 players in Aimé Jacquet's squad (and the significance of that number escaped nobody). As a politician blessed with an uncommon human touch, Chirac was forgiven this blatant act of *récuperation*. Jacques will be Jacques, and that was all.

The same could not necessarily be said of those who succeeded him at the Elysée, even if all three were genuine football fans. Nicolas Sarkozy's links with Qatar and PSG, which deserve to be the subject of a book by themselves, are better left alone here, as the disgraced president, already sentenced to a prison term for accepting funding from Libyan dictator Muammar Gaddafi, may have to face justice again for his role in the award of the 2022 World Cup to Qatar. The portly François Hollande, a fan of modest FC Rouen since he was a child, had played a bit himself, been a spectator at the 1998 World Cup final (seated next to Christian Karembeu's supermodel wife Adriana, true), and didn't disgrace himself in the numerous public kickabouts he took part in before, during and after his single presidential mandate.

Then came Emmanuel Macron, who tied the presidential car to the Les Bleus bandwagon as no other French politician had done before him, bar Bernard Tapie. In fairness to Macron, he did not discover football when it became politically convenient for him to do so; but he certainly hasn't moderated his public displays of 'passion' for it since he became president. Everyone knows that his loyalty lies with Olympique de Marseille. He reveres Basile Boli, the defender who headed in OM's winning goal in the 1993 UEFA Champions League final, when 'Manu' was a 15-year-old schoolboy studying in his home town Amiens, over 800 kilometres away from the Stade Vélodrome. That love hasn't dimmed with time. One of the most memorable scenes in *Les Coulisses d'une victoire*, the documentary which tracked him over the seven months preceding his success in the 2017 presidential election, showed him watching OM getting a proper drubbing – at home – against AS Monaco, the final score 4–1 to the Monégasques. 'Oh merde!' he exclaimed, to the horror of his wife Brigitte. 'For the second time! For fuck's sake!' (Monaco had also put four goals past Marseille when the two clubs had met in the principality two-and-a-half months previously). So that much is true: Emmanuel Macron is no Valéry Giscard d'Estaing when it comes to football, even if, as a player, he is not much better than his predecessor.

What he is good at, however, even if the act has worn a bit thin as years have gone by, is exploiting every opportunity football gives him to express his love for the *patrie* and those who have represented it so well on a football field since he took office, none more so than – Kylian Mbappé, who else? Mbappé who, fortunately, only appeared for a couple of minutes for Monaco in the two games which had upset the presidential candidate so much.

The player's first of at least half a dozen visits to the Elysée, some public, some private, took place on 21 February 2018, on the occasion of the state reception given for the freshly elected president of Liberia and 1995 Ballon d'Or winner George Weah. Other football figures such as Fifa president Gianni Infantino, African Football Confederation president Ahmad Ahmad and Chelsea's former striker Didier Drogba also sat down for lunch at the palace. The discussions – held in English – were meant to revolve around the use of sport as a tool for development in Africa, a subject which the 19-year-old Mbappé said was 'close to his heart'. His presence did not go unnoticed, to the extent that Weah was only mentioned *en passant* in most of the reports on the occasion, which focused on what the impeccably attired teenager told the journalists on the steps of the presidential residence afterwards. 'I will devote all my energy to help as much as possible,' he said with a smile in which there was not a trace of irony. 'Current projects were mentioned. It will happen in the near future. I cannot say much more for the time being, but I will invest myself in this project as best I can.' The words he chose – *thématiques* for 'topics', for example – and the tone in which he answered reporters, with the fluency and the suavity of a consummate politician, made quite the impression on the French public who watched the news on television that evening.

Mbappé wasn't a world champion yet. His transfer from ASM to PSG on 31 August 2017, only hours before the closure of the transfer window, had attracted attention outside of the football world and the specialist media because of the colossal amount of money involved in the operation: Monaco would receive €180 million, and the player would be paid a salary of €10 million – after tax – per season. The Parisian club, which had just disbursed a world record €222 million for Barcelona's Brazilian star Neymar, had to use an unusual trick to avoid breaking French and European financial fair-play regulations. Mbappé would be loaned to PSG for one season, after which the French champions would exercise their option to buy the player outright, deferring their outlay for a year for accounting purposes. A farcical clause had been added to the loan-to-buy agreement: the transfer could only be annulled if the serial French champions were relegated to Ligue 2. This had been talked and written about; but Mbappé, to the general public, remained a footballer who happened to be extremely good at what he did and was rewarded accordingly; and that was that. That evening at the Elysée turned him into a public figure, the smartly dressed kid from the *banlieue* who looked perfectly at ease among heads of state and spoke better French (and far more engagingly) than quite a few of the palace's habitual guests.

Kylian did not have to wait long to visit Emmanuel again; but this time it was with his France team-mates, on 16 July 2018, twenty-four hours after they had beaten Croatia 4–2 in Moscow's Luzhniki Stadium to become world champions for a second time, twenty years after Jacques Chirac had gatecrashed Zidane and Deschamps's victory party in the Stade de France dressing-room. France's best player and most prolific goalscorer – alongside Mbappé, who also scored on four occasions – had been Antoine Griezmann, just as he had been at the 2016 Euros; yet the Atlético de Madrid forward was not the most talked-about player of Les Bleus. The world had been waiting for the proof that Kylian, not yet 20, could do for his national team what he had done over the past couple of years for Monaco and Paris Saint-Germain; and he provided that proof in Russia. It seemed apt that the new global superstar should put the cherry on the French gâteau in the final, scoring their fourth goal shortly past the hour, with a low, right-footed strike from outside the box.

The jacket-less Macron had jumped out of his seat in the presidential box when Mario Mandžukić beat his own keeper to give France the advantage, probably the last time he was photographed beaming in the company of Vladimir Putin. Now back in Paris, the fan-president was waiting for the world champions to pay him the now-traditional visit to 55, rue du Faubourg-Saint-Honoré, right opposite Pierre Cardin's flagship Parisian store; but he didn't intend to wait too long. The coach transporting players and staff from Roissy airport had to park outside the Elysée bang in time for the arrival of the footballers and their welcome by the president to be broadcast live on the *Journal de 20 heures*, the most-watched news programme on

French television. This was easier said than done, as the coach was meant to make its way from the Place de l'Étoile down the Champs-Elysées, where an estimated 300,000 celebrating fans had gathered to cheer the world champions. Progress would be painfully slow, far too slow to respect the presidential timetable; yet, right on the stroke of 8 pm, captain Hugo Lloris and his team walked through the gates of the Elysée Palace.

How this miracle was accomplished was revealed a few months later in an investigation by the satirical weekly *Le Canard enchaîné*. One of Macron's personal security officers, Alexandre Benalla, who also served as deputy chief of staff in the presidential office, had been tasked with accompanying the players. The official reason for his presence in the procession was that he would guarantee the safekeeping of the players' luggage. The truth is that it was he who imposed a very fast pace on the convoy, much to the disappointment of supporters who only caught a brief glimpse of their heroes. They were to be disappointed again a couple of hours later. It had become customary for successful French athletes, rugby players, footballers and Olympians to salute the crowd from the balcony of the Hôtel de Crillon when they returned from global competitions. The fans made their way from *Les Champs* to the Place de la Concorde, hoping that, this time, Les Bleus would not just whizz past. Well – they did not even show up. They stayed the whole evening at the Elysée Palace, where they were served sandwiches, posed with Macron for selfies, sang an impromptu 'La Marseillaise' (as well as Gloria Gaynor's disco hit 'I Will Survive', the national team's unofficial anthem since 1998) and, in Paul Pogba's case, helped Macron's wife Brigitte lift the golden trophy for the cameras. Not everyone was enthused by the Elysée's hijacking act; but it had set the tone for what would happen over the next seven years, with

Macron's interest shifting more and more towards Mbappé rather than the team as time passed.*

It is possible to view Macron's private and public courting of Mbappé with unadulterated cynicism, to present it as a transparent attempt to 'connect' with the young voters who worship the footballer – and, at the same time, to use him as a political tool when the occasion presents itself. However, there is also genuine interest at play here, not just self-interest – and from both sides of this unusual relationship. Macron's admiration for the young man who is almost exactly twenty-one years his junior (Kylian was born on 20 December, 'Manu' on the 21st), is sincere, even if the language he uses to express it can sound clumsy, pompous, even meretricious, as in an interview he gave *L'Équipe* at the beginning of 2022. '[Mbappé] keeps his distance from the excesses which, sometimes, go with celebrity,' he said. 'He is the incarnation of calmness and of tranquil ambition, his eyes turned to the stars, but his head on his shoulders. He has chosen [to embrace] the risk which goes with commitment, for [COVID] vaccination, against violence, in communion with the emotions of the nation. Kylian Mbappé has a rare awareness of his role, the weight of his words,

---

* There is an almost surreal postscript to what would become part of '*l'affaire Benalla*'. On the very day Macron's security officer instructed the driver of the France coach to speed down Paris's most famous avenue, an investigation into 'violence, usurpation of the functions of a police officer and using signs reserved for public authorities' was launched by the public prosecutor: Benalla had been identified as the mystery man, dressed as a policeman, who'd been filmed beating up a protester and grabbing a young woman by the neck during a May Day demonstration two-and-a-half months previously. Macron's aide was dismissed twenty-four hours later and sentenced to a three-year jail term in 2021.

the power of his actions. He has demonstrated the qualities of the greatest: lucidity, courage, resistance.'

For once, the word 'fulsome' can be used here as it is meant to be used. There is too much cream in that sauce, too much sugar in the coulis. The hyperbolic vocabulary and the arch grammatical constructions betray the humanities student who tried hard but was not quite good enough to pass the entrance exam of the École Normale Supérieure. Yet Macron didn't have to force himself to heap praise on Mbappé the way he did, and whether he also did it for political gain is somehow immaterial. He meant it. He does like that young, well-spoken, rocket-heeled young man; and the wonderful thing about it is that it also serves his purposes.

To start with, Mbappé seemed flattered by the attention his president showed him. As he, ever the diplomat, put it to *Paris Match* magazine in 2021, 'it is always a pleasure to be able to talk to the president and to tell myself that he's following me, that he is acknowledging my work and the way I put myself at the service of my country or of my club'. He was also amused by Macron's tongue-in-cheek announcement on a YouTube show hosted by two French influencers, 'McFly' and 'Carlito', also in 2021, that Mbappé would leave Paris Saint-Germain in a matter of weeks. 'I'm in charge of his career,' the president explained. Kylian would not go to Real Madrid but to Marseille. When Macron's hosts expressed, or, more likely, feigned surprise at this revelation, their guest took out his mobile and speed-dialled Mbappé's number, his phone on speaker mode. The president, using the formal *vous* to address the player, asked him to confirm the move. 'Impossible,' Mbappé retorted, 'impossible to go to Marseille. It's not in our DNA.' Cue guffaws from all concerned.

Toe-curling as the exchange was, it at least showed that Mbappé was a willing participant in Macron's stunt. It was for a good cause, after all – the president was goofing around with B-list YouTubers to make young French people aware of the necessity to get their COVID jabs, when France was among the most 'vaccine-sceptic' countries in Western Europe. The video was streamed six million times in twenty-four hours, with the views counter now going past the twenty million mark. McFly and Carlito were rewarded with an official invitation to the Elysée. Macron didn't quite shake off his Jupiter-like image because of the jokes he cracked in a YouTube video; but his skit was generally well-received by his target audience. At least he'd tried. Marine Le Pen and Jean-Luc Mélenchon wouldn't have.

It is hard to gauge whether Macron and Mbappé are linked by something more than a community of interest. The courtesy and expressions of respect are genuine enough, but the warmth which was on show in the early stages of their rapport, when the teenager from the *banlieue* was thrilled to dine in the gold-panelled salons of the presidential palace, has dimmed somewhat, certainly since Macron overplayed his hand by inviting himself onto the field after the 2022 World Cup final, where he spent what felt like an eternity 'consoling' its loser. Mbappé had just delivered one of the greatest performances in French football history, only to end on the defeated side against Lionel Messi and Emiliano Martinez's Argentina. Had Kingsley Coman and Aurélien Tchouaméni not failed to score their spot-kicks in the penalty shoot-out, Kylian's hat-trick may even have enabled him to take the place of Zinédine Zidane and his two headers in the 1998 World Cup final at the very top of French football's pantheon. And here he was, head bowed, hands on his knees, perhaps trying to make sense of what had just happened, perhaps lost in the kind of numbness that athletes experience in defeat, drained, exhausted, hollowed out by the effort and the enormity of his disappointment.

But Macron couldn't help himself. I believe that, for once, it was not – not just – the presence of the cameras and the irresistible urge to place himself at the centre of things which made him run down the steps from the presidential box and step onto the Lusail Stadium pitch. Rather, it was the fan making the most of the privileges of the head of state. Four-and-a-half years earlier, in Moscow, he'd hugged Kylian and planted a kiss on his head when presenting him with the Silver Ball awarded by Fifa's Technical Committee to the second-best player of the tournament. In truth, all of France wanted to plant a kiss on Kylian's forehead that afternoon. But this time, in defeat, it looked and felt excruciating. Macron didn't stop there. He invited himself into the dressing-room of Les Bleus and delivered a short speech (filmed on a smartphone and uploaded on his Twitter account within hours of the final whistle), concluded by the traditional presidential valediction, '*Vive la République! Vive la France!*'. What France's manager Didier Deschamps and his disconsolate players made of it, they kept to themselves.

Things have not been quite the same between 'Manu' and 'Kyky' since, not that the president was done with the player. Mbappé did not stop enjoying the hospitality of the Elysée. In February 2024, he took his seat at a state dinner given in the honour of the emir of Qatar, Sheikh Tamim bin Hamad Al Thani, alongside his then-employer, PSG president, beIN Sport supremo and Qatari minister without a portfolio Nasser Al-Khelaifi. Like his predecessor Nicolas Sarkozy before him, Macron had attempted to convince the footballer that he should remain a while longer in Ligue 1, twice – with success in 2022, when Mbappé extended his deal with PSG to 2025, but in vain two years later, when the player decided to run down his contract and join Real Madrid at long last. In May 2024, Macron also tried to sweet-talk Real's president Florentino Perez into letting his new recruit take part in the Paris Olympics, using the celebration of Fifa's 120th anniversary as a pretext to invite Perez to yet another lunch at the Elysée. Such is the hold Kylian exercises on his most powerful admirer.

It could never be a relationship of equals – which is not to say that the player has a lesser hand in that game, only that he must play it carefully. Mbappé's willingness to engage with Macron went further than what is customary in French sport, where athletes are expected to keep their beliefs and convictions to themselves; but it still stopped well short of a personal endorsement. The player always took great care to refer to '*le président*', not to 'Emmanuel Macron': to the function, not to the man. The distance he kept from Macron was not just out of respect for the presidential institution, but also the fruit of caution: there is no place for political controversy in a global superstar's handbook. By all means help orphaned children and succour the victims of war; but do not mention who or what is responsible for their ordeal. Confrontation has no place in the Mbappé project.

Mbappé, however, has not shied away from speaking out about more delicate subjects on occasion, especially to address the issue of police violence towards young brown and black men of the *banlieue*. He did it in 2020, following the publication of a video showing the brutal beating of Parisian rap producer Michel Zecler in his recording studio by four police officers. He did it again in 2023, when a 17-year-old French–Algerian boy named Nahel Merzouk was shot at point blank range and killed in Nanterre at a vehicle check. 'I feel bad for my France,' he said. Then came the legislative elections called early – to everyone's astonishment – by Macron in the late spring of 2024, when polls indicated that the extreme-right Rassemblement

National had an outside chance of commanding enough seats in the Lower House of the French Parliament to become a party of national government.'

The first round of the elections would take place bang in the middle of the European Championships. Mbappé had been French captain for just over a year by then, and was called to appear in his team's first press conference of the tournament on the eve of their game against Austria. He hadn't prepared a statement; but he had prepared himself for the questions that he knew would be put to him about the political situation back at home. His team-mate Marcus Thuram had already said 'we have to fight to make sure the Rassemblement National doesn't win' a few days earlier. It was known that conversations had taken place in the French dressing-room, with a large majority of the players, most of whom came from ethnic minority backgrounds, agreeing that they had to take a stance. Kylian would be their spokesperson. He didn't disappoint them.

'I think we are at a crucial time in the history of our country,' he said. 'The situation is unprecedented; this is why I want to speak to all of the French nation and to the young generation, which can make the difference. I call on the young to go out and vote. We see that extremists ['*les extrêmes*'] are at the gates of power. We have a chance to choose the future of our country. We need to identify with the values of tolerance, diversity and respect. I hope we'll still be proud to wear this jersey on 7 July [the date of the second, decisive round of the elections]. The situation is more important than tomorrow's game.

'I do not want to represent a country which doesn't correspond to our values.'

This will have been music to Macron's ears. Unlike Jules Koundé or Ibrahima Konaté, two other Les Bleus who'd expressed themselves publicly about the forthcoming election, Mbappé had not mentioned Marine le Pen's Rassemblement National by name. He'd spoken about *les extrêmes*, which could also refer to Jean-Luc Mélenchon's extreme-left La France Insoumise. The message he'd delivered was unambiguous but delivered in terms which a majority of French voters could and did agree with in the end. Participation was markedly higher than usual, almost 20 per cent up on the 2022 election, with record numbers of young voters turning up at the polling stations. The Rassemblement National won fewer seats than the Nouveau Front Populaire left-wing coalition and the Macron-supporting Ensemble movement.

France somehow reached the semi-finals of the Euros, in no small part thanks to the generosity of their opponents, with Austria and Belgium both beaten by an own goal to nil. Mbappé himself was a shadow of the player who'd lit up the 2022 World Cup, his sole contribution of note a penalty in a drab 1–1 draw with Poland. To be frank, nobody cared that much. France had been a caricature of itself and did not deserve better. Most of us French had more pressing concerns and were just relieved that we were OK – for the time being. Most of us were also grateful that a young man from Bondy had spoken as he did.

Emmanuel Macron had stayed at home this time. There were no comforting words for France's golden boy at full-time on the pitch of the Allianz Arena, there was no address to the defeated heroes in the dressing-room, only a few lines expressing the president's and the nation's gratitude on the Elysée's Twitter account. It's true that Macron had more reasons than most to feel thankful.

12

Je t'aime, moi non plus: the PSG years – 3

Shortly before the 2022 World Cup took place in Qatar, a strange rumour started circulating among French football journalists. Kylian Mbappé had been shocked by reports of the enslavement and brutal exploitation of the migrant workers called in to build the infrastructure the emirate needed to host the tournament. He had granted an interview – to whom, nobody knew or could say – in which he shared his concerns about the World Cup, which PSG had 'killed' as soon as they'd seen a transcript. None of us reported this, yet it became a staple of post-match conversations, our version of the vanishing hitchhiker's urban myth. Everyone knew someone who knew someone, and so on. I did. I also had some idea of where the rumour had originated – or at least, who had been among the first to spread it, and the person I had in mind had a direct line to the player's family. That 'interview' was never published, and I doubt that it ever took place; but what I do not doubt is that the rumour was part of the 'communication war' between Mbappé and his club, which his contract extension appeared to have had little effect on. It quickly became clear that the picture of unity presented on 19 May by Mbappé and Al-Khelaifi to the fans assembled in the Parc des Princes did not reflect the true nature of their relationship. The couple made too much of an effort to reassure everyone that they got along famously.

That relationship was further dented when French investigative website Mediapart revealed in October 2022 that PSG had employed a company called Digital Big Brother (DBB) between 2018 and 2020. DBB's mission was to create a 'troll army' which – or so Mediapart asserted, and PSG denied ('we never contracted with an agency in order to harm individuals and institutions') – created multiple Twitter accounts to post insulting, derogatory and even defamatory tweets targeting individuals or media (of which Mediapart was one, and *L'Équipe* another) the club was having problems with. France midfielder Adrien Rabiot, never the most pliable of characters, was singled out for special treatment. An abusive Rennes supporter whom Neymar had pushed, rather than punched, in the face at the end of PSG's defeat to the Breton club in the 2018–19 French Cup was also targeted, as was, much more disturbingly, a young woman who'd accused the Brazilian striker of rape (Neymar denied the accusations, and no charges were brought). Kylian himself wasn't spared when he suggested at the end of the 2018–19 season that his future might lie away from Paris. And, as had been the case all along, both camps were still briefing French journalists about each other, not always in flattering terms.

Kylian's performances were barely affected by the constant flow of speculation and hearsay, at least as far as his numbers were concerned. He topped Ligue 1's goalscoring table in both of his last two seasons in Paris, and ended up PSG's most prolific player in the Champions League during those two years, though he failed to score in the ties against Bayern Munich and Borussia Dortmund which saw the Parisian club exit that competition in the round of 16 and the semi-final. Things were more complicated in the dressing-room, where many of his team-mates found it harder and harder to accept Mbappé's desire to be the 'main man' and expectation to be treated as such, especially once Lionel Messi had decided to join Inter Miami and Neymar, constantly hampered by fitness problems, was sold to Saudi government-owned club Al-Hilal for €90 million. Two of the other 'big beasts' of the dressing-room also left at the same time, Sergio Ramos and Marco Verratti.

Things came to a head in August 2023, in the wake of the departure of the two superstars. New manager Luis Enrique, who'd taken over from Christophe Galtier in the summer, asked his players to choose their captain for the season to come. Mbappé put his name forward, only to be beaten by the incumbent, Brazilian central defender Marquinhos, now in his eleventh year at the club. Mbappé asked for a second vote to take place, a request that did not go down well with his team-mates, who complied nevertheless. The result of the second ballot must have come as a shock to the would-be captain, who only came fourth out of four in the popularity contest, behind Marquinhos, vice-captain Presnel Kimpembe, one of the rare products of the club's academy to have made it to the first team, and Portuguese defender Danilo Pereira. Coming second to the irreproachable Marquinhos was much easier to accept than being relegated to the role of 'fourth captain' behind two players who were not considered automatic starters. That stung, especially since Didier Deschamps had chosen Kylian to wear the armband for Les Bleus in March of that year, a decision which, it must be said, was not universally welcomed within the national team, where Antoine Griezmann was the favourite of many.

As nothing which happens at PSG stays within PSG for long, the detail of the vote was passed on to the media. Christophe Dugarry, a world champion with France in 1998, did not mince his words on RMC Radio. 'PSG players prefer to have Danilo as captain rather than Mbappé,' he said. 'This is a huge rejection for Mbappé, who did everything he could to become captain of the French national team, and also wanted to be captain of PSG. Mbappé always wants to be the number one, the leader, the goal scorer, the penalty taker and the free-kick taker. That's what he's like. He is formatted for that.'

Then, as it was bound to do, the question of his future rose again as he entered the final stretch of his de facto two-year contract – as an extension to 30 June 2025 had never been more than an option which only Mbappé himself could activate. The same PSG fans – a majority – who had sided with the player in his previous entanglements with the club's hierarchy were not so sure of what to think anymore. Mbappé's decision to remain at the club in 2022 had come as a wonderful surprise to them, which they saw as clear proof of the player's deep attachment to their colours. So why would he want to go away now? But he did. The first sign of it had been Mbappé's refusal to activate the optional clause which would have given him an extra season at the club, or at least increased his sell-on value should both parties agree to an amicable parting of the ways. PSG felt they'd been played by their star asset and reacted accordingly. The player received a three-page letter in which he was asked, or rather ordered, to inform the club of his final decision by 31 July. That order was ignored.

Mbappé, though fit, was kept out of the squad which flew out to Japan for a pre-season tour in the summer of 2023. Luis Enrique also benched him for the opening game of the new season, a drab 0–0 draw at home against FC Lorient; after which sporting imperatives forced his return to the fold. As ever, what was happening off the field seemed to have no impact on how Kylian performed on it. He scored seven goals in the four Ligue 1 games which followed his reintegration.

Come February 2024, the question was no longer whether Mbappé would go or not (he would), but when he would announce it. According to Spanish sources, an agreement with Real Madrid had been reached a month previously (though French sources reported that the Mbappé clan felt that some important details of the deal still needed to be ironed out).

Then the *Athletic*'s transfer specialist David Ornstein revealed that Kylian himself had told Nasser Al-Khelaifi on the eve of the round of 16 Champions League game against Real Sociedad (in which he scored, as per usual) that come 30 June, he'd no longer be a PSG player. There were still over three months of the season to go. PSG were top of Ligue 1 (which they would win), had qualified for the quarter-finals of the Coupe de France (ditto), and were well on course to do the same in the Champions League (where they would fall to Dortmund in the semis, but not before they'd beaten ten-man Barcelona 4–1 in Barcelona, Mbappé scoring twice, to get there).

Agreeing to a 'free' move to Real Madrid meant losing out on an even more generous new contract from PSG, which would have seen Mbappé's yearly gross salary jump to €250 million, over eight times more than what the Spanish club were offering him. This is not to say that, in this case, financial considerations were set aside in order to fulfil a childhood dream. The nature of the deal Real put on the table guaranteed that the player would not have to sacrifice tens of millions of earnings. To start with, he was to receive a signing-on fee of €143 million, spread over the five years of his contract; but this was not the key factor. The project had always been about control over every aspect of his career. By staying at PSG, Mbappé would have had to forfeit a large chunk of his image rights; but in Madrid, he was to keep 80 per cent of them, more than any other player had ever been granted in the history of the club. He would have the final say on personal endorsements, which, unlike other superstars like Leo Messi, who advertised everything from potato crisps to Pugliese wines and dubious NFT ventures, he and his advisers kept to a minimum. His existing commercial deals were estimated to add €58 million to his income per year at the time, with Nike, his sponsor since 2006, contributing €20 million on their own. His arrival in Madrid would boost the club's shirt sales by 300 per cent according to internal sources, and Kylian would be entitled to a sizeable percentage of that income.

These were bitter months, which were to turn ugly. The official announcement came on 10 May through a four-minute video posted on Mbappé's personal social network accounts, in which, his customary fluency undiminished by the absence of a teleprompter, he thanked all the players and staff who'd helped him 'grow as a player and grow as a man' and name-checked all of his five managers, but not the man who'd brought him there, his chairman Nasser Al-Khelaifi. 'I didn't think it would be as difficult as this to leave France, to leave my country,' he said. 'But I felt I needed this, I needed a new challenge after this [season]. More than anything, I want to thank the supporters. I know I am not the most demonstrative of players. I know I haven't always lived up to the love you gave me for seven years, but I never cheated, I always wanted to perform.' His valediction was not *adieu*, but *au revoir*.

There was no official homage to the departing player in the game which followed the announcement, a disappointing 1–3 home defeat to Toulouse in which Mbappé, in his last appearance at the Parc des Princes in a PSG shirt, wearing the captain's armband in the absence of Marquinhos, scored the 256th and final goal of his Parisian career.

Genuine emotion was in short supply. The stadium announcer asked the crowd to sing Kylian's name, which it did, though there was no spontaneous reprise of the song which the PSG Ultras had welcomed him with on his return from the 2022 World Cup a year-and-a-half previously. Some scattered boos were heard in the stands at the whistle; but they had more to do with the team's mediocre showing on the day than with the departing star. There was a walk round the pitch with his team-mates, carrying the L1 trophy which had been presented to them that afternoon. Then it was all over. It had been over for a while already. Mbappé, now an undesirable in the eyes of the club's hierarchy, was left out of the squad which won the two concluding matches of the season.

Meanwhile, lawyers were hard at work.

Though Mbappé was the only party who could decide whether to activate the option for a one-year extension or not, his choice still had contractual and financial implications. PSG used these to justify withholding his salary for the month of April, as they also would for the two months which followed. They also cancelled a bonus payment which was due in February. That loyalty bonus would have rewarded his acceptance of a contract extension to June 2025 and was reported to be worth €80–€90 million. The player and his advisers hoped that Real Madrid would step in to make up any shortfall; they also believed that, regardless of what the Spanish club would agree to, PSG still owed Kylian a considerable amount of money, and turned to every single organisation they thought would advance their cause, with some success. In September 2024, the legal department of the French League, the LFP, formally asked PSG to pay what Mbappé was asking for. Its appeal commission concurred. PSG ignored these recommendations and chose to file a complaint against LFP instead.

I confess I laughed when I heard the news: the dog was threatening to bite its own tail. This was the same LFP in which Nasser Al-Khelaifi wielded feudal-like power through his close ally and president of the organisation Vincent Labrune. To give a flavour of their working relationship, Labrune, despite his past role as chairman of PSG's arch-enemy Marseille, had encouraged everyone to support the Parisians in their Champions League endeavours. Imagine for a second the Premier League's CEO Richard Masters asking everyone in English football to rally around Manchester City when they were chasing their first European title if you can. It was a neat encapsulation of the toxic paradox at the very heart of French league football, crushed by PSG on one hand, incapable of survival without them on the other, bound to fealty and subservience just to see the dawn of another day.

In parallel, Kylian's lawyer Delphine Verheyden had also filed complaints with the French FA, which refused to exert pressure on the club (earning a rebuke from the French players trade union UNFP in the process), UEFA and, somehow, the French Ministry of Sports to force PSG to cough up. This contradicted a statement Kylian had made back in January 2024 that, 'thanks to the agreement I reached with [Nasser Al-Khelaifi] last summer, whatever my decision [on staying at the PSG or not] will be, we have managed to protect the parties involved as a whole and to preserve the club's serenity for the challenges to come. That's what matters the most.' PSG sources used the same word, 'serenity', to describe the ongoing discussions and assured that 'everything was about to be settled'. It may be one day; but the litigation was still ongoing at the time of writing.

That grubby affair wormed on to 10 April 2025 when, in a press conference organised in a Paris hotel located close to the Eiffel Tower, the Mbappé legal team, his 'rock' Delphine Verheyden flanked by three of her colleagues, announced that they had obtained a garnishment order (a preventative seizure of funds on the PSG accounts, prior to a ruling on the litigation) for €55,416,668 from a Parisian court. One of Mbappé's lawyers, *maître* Thomas Clay, tore into PSG. 'The club respects nothing in this case,' he said. 'Neither the work contract, nor the law, nor the decisions of French justice. That is why, yesterday, we pleaded in front of the judicial tribunal of Paris to be allowed to seize PSG's bank accounts.' That sum corresponded to the third tranche of Kylian's signing-on fee for his last contract (€36.66 million) and unpaid salaries for the months of April, May and June 2024 (€18.75 million).

A judge cancelled the garnishment order on 26 May but refrained from expressing an opinion on the rights and wrongs of either party. He acknowledged that PSG's refusal to pay what the Mbappé clan insisted was the player's due was not an act of grandstanding and considered that the club had ample means to produce the funds, should another court rule in the footballer's favour. Consequently, there was no need for the original order. Neither side commented on that decision. That skirmish was over, the battle could go on. A criminal complaint was filed by Mbappé against PSG in June 2025, in which he accused his club of 'moral harassment' and having tried to 'extort' his signature when the extension of his contract was discussed a year previously. That complaint was withdrawn two weeks later.

When this legal tug-of-war will end is anyone's guess, as neither side seems intent on giving an inch. On 17 November 2025, the litigation took another unexpected turn when the Conseil de Prud'hommes de Paris, the Paris labour court, heard that Mbappé's counsels had revised their original claim of €55 million and were now asking for almost five times that amount, €243 million to be precise, reprising their allegations of 'moral harassment' and adding 'unfair implementation of a contract' and 'concealed employment' to the charges levied at Kylian's former employer. Delphine Verheyden said her client was 'determined' to see the matter through, even if she assured that she had done everything in her power not to have the case brought to the court in the first place and PSG were to blame for the escalation.

PSG countered with their own, even more extravagant claim, suing Mbappé for €440 million for 'reputational damage' and 'loss of transfer opportunity', as the club would have expected a huge fee from Real Madrid had their player exercised the one-year option included in the contract signed in the late spring of 2022, as he'd promised he would; or so they argued in front of astonished councillors, all of them trade unionists, none of them versed in football affairs, who'd never heard such colossal sums bandied about in their court. Neither had they ever seen such a crowd gather in the room set aside for the hearing on the fourth floor of the Prud'hommes' 10th arrondissement headquarters. All of the fifty-plus seats set aside for the general public had been filled before the session had started. People sat on the floor to listen to the 'armadas of lawyers' (*Le Figaro dixit*) delegated by the club (five) and the player (four, including Verheyden who unceremoniously shooed away the onlookers who'd sat in the front row). 'I can't do anything about the lack of room,' the president of the Conseil Marie-Anne Kovrig said in her opening statement. 'This is going to take a long time, so we'll try to keep as calm as possible.' *Bonne chance, Madame la présidente.*

In fact, it took the court just under a month to reach a decision which vindicated the player in every respect. On 16 December 2025, PSG was ordered to pay the third tranche of Mbappé's signing-on fee (€36.6 million), his wages for the months of April, May and June 2024 (€17.2 million), paid holidays and 'ethical bonus' for the same period

(€3.35m); as well as an extra €5,000 in court expenses. The club must also publish the text of the decision on the home page of its website. Kylian's legal representatives could afford a little smugness. *Maître* Thomas Clay, who had assisted the ever-present Delphine Verheyden on this dossier, explained to RMC listeners that PSG 'had managed to impose a narrative which was now hitting them [in the face] like a boomerang'. 'Why hadn't they paid?', he asked. 'Because of pride. They had not accepted that their jewel could go to Real Madrid.'

However, just like hikers discover new hills to climb on the horizon every time they reach a summit, Verheyden and Clay's work is not quite done yet, and neither is Marie-Anne Kovrig's. Come the new year, the judgement of the Paris prud'hommes still had not been officially published yet. Once it is, PSG will have one month to lodge an appeal. Given how fiercely they fought their corner so far, it is unlikely they'll retreat and call it a day that time.

As of 1 January 2026, Kylian Mbappé had scored 73 goals in 83 matches for Real Madrid, including 16 successful penalty kicks, that's 0.88 goals per game, compared to 0.83 while at PSG. Real's failures in the 2024–25 Champions League, where Arsenal saw them off with ease in the quarter-finals, and Gianni Infantino's souped-up Fifa Club World Cup, in which PSG, of all clubs, swatted them away 4–0 in the semis, may have impacted the Merengue fans' ambivalent judgement on their recruit at first, but the numbers were impressive, especially since goals are shared more evenly in Madrid than in Paris. There is Vinicius Jr to contend with, who found the net 22 times to Kylian's 44 in 2024–25 (and Vinicius Jr only takes penalty kicks when Kylian is unavailable or declines to do so, which is not often). Jude Bellingham, Rodrygo and Federico Valverde also registered double figures in that season. The debate as to whether Mbappé had stepped up to the plate in Madrid or not was over. The few remaining doubters, if there were any left, were silenced in spectacular fashion when, on the evening of 26 November 2025, Kylian scored all four of his side's goals in a hair-raising 4–3 win at Olympiacos in the UEFA Champions League, all of them in open play. Only three other players had netted a quadruple in Europe in Real's history before him, and what players they were: Alfredo Di Stéfano, Ferenc Puskás (both of them twice) and, the last to achieve this feat, Cristiano Ronaldo, in an 8–0 obliteration of Malmö FF back in December 2015. Spanish commentators were no longer discussing the worth of Mbappé's contribution to Real's performances, but wondering whether his team was now over-dependent on his brilliance.

Mbappé was no longer the 'shrimp' of AS Monaco or the impish winger of his early PSG years. He looked stockier, though his main attribute, pace, seemed unimpaired by the muscle mass he put on. He was not quite as popular in France as he once had been. A recent poll suggested that over half of the national team's supporters thought he should be relieved of the captaincy; but how many of those were disgruntled PSG fans was not specified. He scored in the six matches he played with Les Bleus since June 2025, including a double in the 4–0 win over Ukraine which sealed France's qualification for the 2026 World Cup on 13 November, and with 55 goals to his credit at this point in time, might have beaten Olivier Giroud's record of 57 when you read this. Yet the PSG page hasn't been turned for good. When *L'Équipe* secured a one-to-one interview with him at the tail end of summer 2025, a large part of it was dedicated to the fight his legal team was still involved in, with no side intent on giving away an inch to the other. That sleeping dog wouldn't lie any time soon.

'It is my responsibility by right, it is labour legislation,' he said. 'The procedure gave the impression that I wanted to harm PSG. I signed an employment contract. I just wanted to get paid. I have nothing against PSG, I love this club, I have friends there. But it's the only way to get what I'm owed, something I've earned by the sweat of my brow. Whether you like it or not, it's still a job.'

Not everything he said held up to scrutiny. 'I already knew that I [wouldn't] get paid when I was at PSG,' he said, which was correct. 'When the money doesn't come in, you see it,' he continued. 'I could have made a fuss while I was there, but I told myself it wasn't worth it', which wasn't quite the story we were told then. 'But when you see that you don't get paid, after a while, you have to react.

'I have friends in the team and those who know me know that friendship is important to me.' But hadn't those 'friends' placed him fourth out of four when he asked to be their captain? 'You can't spit on a team where your friends are, even if it wasn't PSG. My story ended and I left with no regrets. Even the things I did wrong are part of my story. When I played there, we were very close [to success], we reached two semi-finals and a final. We didn't win and my time is up. Real Madrid is calling me; it's always been my dream; I could have gone earlier.' Perhaps he should have.

*

It would be harsh to describe Mbappé's seven seasons at PSG as a box ticked on the project's roadmap and nothing else, the last-but-one step to Madrid and, he hoped, greatness. He gave the club what may have been the best years of his footballing life and was richly rewarded in return. Yet the acrimony of his protracted move to Spain cannot but taint what happened, all the more so since his future departure had been a constant thread in his Parisian back story. Looking back, what he left behind him is nowhere near the legacy his phenomenal statistics would suggest. His place in the record books is safe, his place in the hearts of PSG's supporters less so. There were moments of adulation, as when he chose to remain in Paris in 2022, but admiration and gratitude were, particularly in the later years, tinged with a degree of reluctance, even indifference. The Portuguese striker Pedro Pauleta spent two fewer seasons at the Parc than Mbappé, scored 147 fewer goals than the French record-holder, but retains such an aura that, seventeen years after his departure from the club, most stadium-going PSG fans would put him higher up in the pantheon of 'legends' of their club; they'd do the same for Zlatan Ibrahimović. Older supporters would add names such as David Ginola, George Weah and Rai to that list.

Perhaps it is because of the nature of Mbappé's game. He spared himself on the pitch, didn't track back or press as, say, Thierry Henry did with Arsenal when the game demanded it. The three straight red cards he collected at PSG might hint at a player who was not afraid to 'mix it' and assert his physical supremacy. Such an interpretation would be misleading. In each case, Mbappé had reacted to what he felt were personal affronts. They punished his petulance, not his over-eagerness to fight for a common cause.

Perhaps it is because there was no palpable connection between the habitual match-winner and most of the players who helped him shine. Even the connection that was evident with Neymar during the first two years they played together in Paris dimmed and turned into an ambiguous association of individual interests. Neymar remained the provider of many of his goals, but there was no longer a sense of genuine complicity in the way they combined. Even the club's press officer Yann Guerin admitted that there had been 'highs and lows' between the two, when, in a game against Montpellier in September 2021, a lip-reader noticed that Kylian had called his striking partner a *clochard* ('tramp') in an exchange with midfielder Idrissa Gueye after Neymar had failed to pass him the ball for what should have been a certain goal. Mbappé being Mbappé and Neymar being Neymar, the story made headlines in *L'Équipe* and *Le Parisien* and etched another scratch in a picture of togetherness only the most naive of observers believed was drawn from life.

Perhaps it is because the strongest emotional links are born in moments of hardship, and PSG didn't do hardship: it did disappointment, which isn't the same thing at all. They were expected to win just as Kylian was expected to score. The worst that could happen to them was to finish second in the League and go out in the knockout rounds of the Champions League, which they did seven times out of seven when Mbappé was at the club. Where was the jeopardy, where was the actual drama? A penalty shootout loss to Rennes in the 2019 French Cup final was as bad as it got. Losing a round of 16 Champions League tie to Manchester United after having won 2–0 at Old Trafford (Mbappé scored the second of those goals) was not a tragedy, but an embarrassment. The Parc des Princes did not stage tragedies, but farces and soap operas.

The constant media attention got to him too. No story was small enough to be ignored by the press pack which followed the Parisian circus wherever it went. As years went by, and whatever was left of the innocence of the teenager had been eroded by the need to protect himself and his family, Mbappé became more remote and caught up in his own performance. He craved attention, as attention was a compliment paid to his prowess, but detested what came with it.

Madrid would test him even more. Madrid – and Stockholm.

13

Stockholm

Kylian and his bodyguard snapped in Stockholm in 2024.

Stars of our age live in a panopticon where a semblance of privacy can only be achieved by fooling the surveillance system which is constantly trained on them. They never escape their prison for good: run they must, then run some more. Camouflage can work. When filming Jonathan Glazer's *Under The Skin,* in which her role demanded that she picked up random men in the streets of Glasgow, men who had no idea that cameras and microphones were recording their every word and every move, Scarlett Johansson discovered that wearing a dark wig (and, it must be said, driving a lorry on the banks of the Clyde) hid her identity so well that not one of her passengers even told her she *looked* like Scarlett Johansson. Novelist William Boyd has recounted how David Bowie used a characteristically elegant trick to escape undue attention in New York City. 'As I arrived I saw Bowie stepping out of a yellow cab and paying the driver,' Boyd wrote. 'Greeting him and vaguely surprised to see him in this form of transport I asked him if he ever had any problems moving around the city. Not at all, he said, he happily used cabs and subways. 'I just carry one of these,' he said, and held up a Greek newspaper. People think: that's David Bowie, surely? Then they see the Greek newspaper – no, can't be, just some Greek guy who looks like him.'

Yet the most effective of strategies may well be the simplest: to accept the curiosity of strangers as a tribute to pay for wealth and fame. Spanish international Juan Mata, whom I visited regularly in London and Manchester when he was at the peak of his football career, was one of these easy-going celebrities. While in the capital, he'd chosen to rent a flat in a new development overlooking the Thames, where his neighbours were mostly younger middle-class professionals who had no idea that they shared their tower block with a European and World Champion. Juan did his shopping himself, took the Tube, visited galleries, went to concerts, sat on the terraces of cafés and restaurants on his own or with his girlfriend Evelina – but never a bodyguard. Later, in Manchester, he'd walk down Deansgate to his father's tapas restaurant and share a glass of *tinto* with friends in full view of the crowd. Fans who recognised him said hello, gave a silent thumbs-up sign or asked – in my experience, always politely – for a selfie, which he would grant with good grace, always thanking whoever had come to his table or stopped him in the street. This required kindness and patience, two qualities which Juan possesses in abundance; the reward was that, most of the time, he was left alone and earned a reputation in London as in Manchester for being courteous and approachable which, not so paradoxically, protected him from unwanted attention.

It wasn't so for Kylian. It couldn't be, when his ambition demanded he should be the centre of attention in everything he did as a footballer and a public figure. Juan's honours roll is every bit as impressive as Kylian's in terms of titles won, if not in goals scored for club and country. Yet they are two individuals separated by a common profession, and not just because one did not quite possess the talent to be another Zinédine Zidane, while the other's prodigious gifts made it legitimate for him to dream of rivalling Cristiano Ronaldo. At 37, Juan, now playing for Melbourne Victory after spending a year in the Japanese league, still trains as hard as he did when trying to break into the first team at Valencia; but 'being the best' never really mattered to him; 'being the best he could be' was enough. The money on offer in Japan and Australia bears no relation to the fortune he could have amassed in the Gulf; but he couldn't care less about it. He dreamt of discovering two countries which fascinated him and has done so, thanks to football. He and Kylian never truly lived in the same world. Juan strove to preserve ordinariness, and if that meant being less visible or underrated (though not underappreciated), so be it. In fact, so much the better. He played alongside geniuses – Xavi, Iniesta – whom he knew he could not emulate, and satisfied himself with sitting with the first violins when others conducted or played the lead part of the concerto. Not so Kylian, for whom, from the very start, only the very top would be high enough. Kylian the champion must be on show, all of the time; so Kylian the young man had no choice but hide as best he could.

He was largely successful in that respect. The French media which could not get enough of him and chronicled the minutest details of his *je t'aime, moi non plus* seven-year-long marriage with PSG, drew the line at his private life, of which barely anything was known outside of the close relationship he enjoyed with his parents, his mother Fayza in particular. What little was published was anodyne – Kylian was en route to the Cannes Festival, he'd appeared at a charity event in Paris, he'd been seen in a plush Madrid restaurant, he still played Fifa with younger brother Ethan. Speculation as to whether he may or may not be in a relationship with a Spanish trans glamour model was as far as it went, and even that story was treated with what could pass for delicacy in the tabloid press.

Then, on 14 October 2024 it all changed. The Swedish dailies *Aftonbladet* and *Expressen* published reports which, if substantiated, would not just destroy his career, but his life as a whole. An unnamed young woman had reported to police that she had been raped in a

Stockholm hotel. According to local media, the main suspect of the investigation was Kylian Mbappé.

Mbappé, who was fit and had played for Real Madrid against Villareal on 5 October, would have been expected to join the French national team who were due to face Israel and Belgium in the forthcoming international break. Didier Deschamps decided otherwise and chose not to call on his captain for these UEFA Nations League fixtures (he was also to leave him aside for the two matches which followed, in November), explaining that he was acting 'in the player's best interest'. Kylian had plenty on his mind at the time. His bitter dispute about pay and bonuses with PSG dragged on. He was acclimatising to a new life in Spain and had yet to find his mark at Real. He had missed out on the Madridese derby against Atlético in late September because of a slight muscular injury. Resting him for two fairly inconsequential games did make sense, even if Carlo Ancelotti had felt differently and fielded his striker in Real's next game anyway; but not everyone took the French manager at his word. Mbappé had had a problematic year with Les Bleus. He'd been ineffective at the European Championships, scoring only once in five games before future winners Spain stopped a lacklustre France in the semi-finals. He'd looked well below par and, indeed, strangely unconcerned in a stinging 1–3 defeat inflicted by Italy at the Parc des Princes in the Nations League in September. His apparent lack of commitment hadn't escaped his team-mates. When it became known that Mike Maignan had torn into some of the 'leaders' of Les Bleus in the dressing-room after that defeat, no-one was in much doubt about the identity of the keeper's main target. Perhaps it was time for Kylian to have a breather. He had only been rested four times in France's previous forty games.

Be that as it may, with time on his hands, Mbappé chose to charter a private jet and flew from Madrid to Stockholm for a short break. His plane landed in Sweden on the afternoon of Wednesday 9 October, carrying him and two of the closest members of his entourage, his private bodyguard 'Jeremy' and his personal assistant 'Yaëlle' (their family names have been kept private). Jeremy, the former employee of a security firm which provided services for PSG, had looked after Kylian since 2018. Yaëlle, now 35 years old, the daughter of a sports educator, had come across the player and his mother Fayza when she was working for a hotel chain in Monaco, a role in which she frequently came in contact with ASM players. First hired as Kylian's private chef in 2016, she soon gained the family's trust to become the player's personal assistant, taking care of all his arrangements, from travel, restaurant and hotel bookings to public engagements, keeping his diary, checking all security details,* as well as serving as

---

* Kylian's security details have attracted the attention of the French media after it was revealed in September 2025 that a 56-year-old former UN Blue Helmet and division commander of the Compagnies Républicaines de Sécurité, only known as 'M.S.', had been summoned to appear in front of the disciplinary committee of the national police inspectorate because of a payment made by the player. The charges, 'undeclared work' and 'tax evasion', related to a cheque for €60,300 he received from Kylian in June 2023, which had been spotted by the French anti-money-laundering agency Tracfin and which 'M.S.' had not included in his tax return. Four other police officers had received €30,000 each from the French international. These payments had been made shortly before Kylian made a well-publicised trip to Cameroon in which these officers ensured his security. 'M.S.', nicknamed 'Momo' and 'La République' by the footballers he protects, was and remains a familiar and much-liked figure among Les Bleus, whom he has watched over since 2011. As Kylian's father Wilfrid testified, the family of 'M.S.' have private, long-standing connections with the Mbappés and the Lamaris. Could the €60,300 be considered a 'gift', as Kylian insisted, or did they constitute compensation for work done outside of his official obligations? The disciplinary commission failed to reach a verdict, and 'M.S.' will be travelling with the French national team to the 2026 World Cup. 'M.S.' had been assisted in the hearing by Marie-Alix Canu-Bernard.

the unbreachable rampart which sheltered the young superstar from unwanted solicitations. Kylian judged her 'untransferable'. Her 24/7 role had only become public knowledge a month before she travelled to Stockholm with her charge, when she gave her first – and, to date, last – interview, to *L'Équipe*.

'I felt a lot of guilt at the beginning,' she told them. 'I felt I was spending my time saying "no" to other people. But in the end, I understood it was my role. I take [my role] as a protector at heart. He can't do it himself. Someone else has to do it. [If] people are always very kind, most of the time, it's because they want something [from him].'

The trio were joined by one of Mbappé's former Parisian teammates, Nordi Mukiele, then of Bayer Leverkusen, now a defender for Sunderland, and made their way to one of Stockholm's best-known night spots, the 'V', an upstairs nightclub which VIPs can book outright when they wish to let their hair down away from the *hoi polloi*. Mukiele was said to have suggested Stockholm as a destination, as he had connections there. According to Swedish media, Kylian and his retinue were celebrating the birthday of an acquaintance and were joined by 'twenty to thirty' guests, mostly young women, who all had to leave their mobile phones behind. A ping-pong table had been set up, on which Kylian hit a few balls with an unknown partner between visits to the bar and the dancefloor.

I write this, and ask myself: the devil might be in the detail, but what kind of devil are we looking for in detail of this kind? What Mbappé was up to that night, who cares? He played table tennis? Big deal. Good luck to him. But the devil, here, is that, despite the protection provided by his entourage and the absence of mobile phones, the detail would soon be public knowledge. Kylian Mbappé had nowhere to hide. The Swedish tabloids got wind of his presence in their capital and despatched paparazzi who quickly found out where the group was staying – the Bank Hotel on Arsenalgatan ('Arsenal Street'), a short stroll away from the Royal Palace. Mbappé was snapped shortly past midnight leaving a French restaurant, Chez Jolie, making his way for the second night in a row to the 'V' club, where the same space had been booked for him and his entourage, with guests – seemingly handpicked by the nightclub's owner – joining them until the small hours of Thursday morning.

If the accounts printed in French and Swedish media are to be believed, when the time came to go back to the Bank Hotel, a young woman followed the player's car in another vehicle and joined him in his hotel room. Several hours later, on Friday, she went to a hospital to have alleged physical lesions recorded by medical staff. She was heard by police on the Saturday and filed an official complaint for sexual violence and rape, which the press got hold of. There has been no suggestion that the alleged victim, whose name remains unknown, received any kind of financial reward from the media – or even talked to journalists herself. By that time, Mbappé's private jet had already left Stockholm and taken him to Corsica for the weekend.

Aftonbladet and *Expressen*, who are believed to have had access to the complaint, had no hesitation naming the player as the man who was suspected to have committed the alleged crime (Swedish police, accompanied by a forensic unit, had visited the Bank Hotel on Monday morning, looking for CCTV footage and DNA evidence), and doubled down on their version of the story when the Mbappé camp angrily denied that it had any foundation whatsoever. Swedish prosecutor Maria Shirakova confirmed that an investigation had been opened but refused to reveal the identity of the suspect. Kylian himself was furious. 'FAKE NEWS!', he thundered on his X account on Monday afternoon, when the *Aftonbladet* journalists were still polishing their article. 'It's becoming so predictable, on the eve of a hearing as if by chance.'

Few people would have understood what he meant. Mbappé was referring to a meeting of the appeal committee of the French League, convened for Tuesday, which was to confirm (or repeal) a prior injunction against PSG, who had been ordered to pay the €55 million the player claimed he was still owed in salary and bonuses. He didn't know what would be published in Sweden yet, but was aware of the 'rape' rumours getting propagated out of control on the internet. *Cui bono*? It had to be PSG. Had they not employed a troll army to insult and defame some of their own players in the past?

To the surprise of many PR experts, who would have advised caution and restraint in such cases, Kylian's legal team went for the jugular. There was no 'Kylian Mbappé denies the baseless allegations made against him, will cooperate with the investigation and welcomes this opportunity to establish his innocence' spiel in this case, as tends to be the rule when footballers find themselves accused of sexual offences. They used the most forceful language imaginable in the circumstances and took the unusual step of going to the media themselves, as the 'scandal' threatened to spin out of control. Mbappé's main communications advisor Patricia Goldman immediately sent a statement to the Reuters news agency. 'A new slanderous rumour is starting to ignite the web,' it read. 'These accusations are totally false and irresponsible, and their propagation is unacceptable. Kylian Mbappé will under no circumstances tolerate his integrity, reputation and honour being sullied by unfounded insinuations.'

French newspapers had immediately sent reporters to Stockholm, who attempted to track Mbappé's movements since he'd arrived in the Swedish capital as if they were documenting the assassination of John F. Kennedy, pestered the owners of the V nightclub and Chez

Jolie (who batted their questions away), and wrote thousands and thousands of words (maps included) on the ifs, the buts and the maybes of the affair.

The lawyer chosen to spearhead Kylian's fightback was one of the 'big beasts' of the French criminal legal scene, Marie-Alix Canu-Bernard, who specialised in 'sensitive' cases. Her most notorious client had been Islamist terrorist Amedy Coulibaly, whom she defended before he murdered French policewoman Clarissa Jean-Philippe and was shot dead in the siege of a Parisian Jewish kosher supermarket in January 2015. Four people had died at the hands of the hostage-taker before the police intervened. More to the point, she had also assisted a former employee of the French Football Federation who had lodged a complaint for sexual harassment within the organisation.

Canu-Bernard spoke to *Le Parisien* and invited herself to the studios of BFM-TV, the television partner of RMC, the radio station known for its football coverage and its appetite for sensational stories, the more salacious the better. She reminded readers, listeners and viewers that Swedish authorities hadn't even got in touch with the alleged suspect; in other words, that the stories which were being published the world over were based on nothing but wild presumptions and a couple of local press reports. 'We will sue for calumnious denunciation,' she said. 'The only thing we know about this affair is that we know nothing. [Kylian] knows what he has done and, especially, what he hasn't done. All we know is that a complaint for rape has been filed in Stockholm. I'm perfectly able to file a complaint against the Pope. Anyone can file a complaint against anyone. We don't know who made it. Kylian Mbappé has no idea of what it's all about. He doesn't understand what is going on and is amazed by the scale this story has taken.'

Like her client, Canu-Bernard also felt that the timing of the story was suspicious. 'I am not a conspiracy theorist,' she said. 'But what is certain is that he's been the target of a smear campaign for months and months. It's undeniable.' Her finger was pointed at PSG. Alluding to the 'troll factory' PSG was alleged to have used in the past, she added that 'a number of players were subjected to a form of harassment from the club. It's up to the French justice system to do its job; but there *is* a smear campaign against Kylian Mbappé'. French manager Didier Deschamps concurred, albeit in a very Didier Deschamps way. While refusing to be drawn into the speculation ('Kylian is big enough to answer for himself'), he added: 'I feel like some people want to blame him for everything.'

Expressen stood by their reporting. Their crime editor Katrin Krantz led the counter-attack. 'What I want to say is that we're 100% certain that Mbappé is suspected of rape,' she said, 'without a shadow of a doubt. Of course, we don't know whether he's guilty or not. It's up to the police and the prosecutor to investigate. But we're certain [of what we've printed].'

The observers who believed that the aggressive stance taken by Mbappé's team would backfire were proved wrong. Swedish prosecutor Maria Shirakova published a statement on 12 December. 'My assessment is that the evidence is not sufficient to proceed and the investigation is therefore closed,' she announced. 'I have concluded, based on what has emerged in the case, that new evidence, including interrogations of the person in question [Kylian Mbappé, whose name she never mentioned in public], would not change the evidence situation right now.' The lawyer of the alleged victim, whose identity was never revealed, responded to the closure of the case in two words. 'No comment.'

*

So nothing happened in the end, because nobody knew whether something had happened or not; or even if something had happened, what that something was. *Aftonbladet* and *Expressen* moved on to other celebrity stories. The Mbappé team decided against filing a lawsuit against them in the end. They'd never written that Kylian was guilty of anything in any case, only that an investigation had been launched, in which he was the prime suspect. Chasing them in the courts would only revive interest in an episode which Mbappé wanted to put behind him for good. It would cause renewed hurt and risked tainting the player's image some more – the image which mattered so much to him and to the 'project' as a whole that it had been decided to fight back as Canu-Bernard had.

There are no lessons to be learnt from Stockholm; but despite this, Stockholm revealed much about Mbappé that was hitherto unknown – not what he had done while in Sweden, but what it was like to be Mbappé, and the lengths to which he and his family would go to protect his privacy and exert complete control over every aspect of his life. *Nothing should and could happen to Kylian.* Canu-Bernard had perhaps said more than she intended when she talked to BFM TV, though barely anyone took notice of her words.

'What I can tell you,' she said, 'is that his family has set up security measures which are such that things like these [the alleged rape] cannot happen. I will not go into details, but, except in moments of strictest intimacy, he is never alone. He doesn't go out alone. He doesn't come home alone. There is always somebody around. [He is] aware of the risks which he is constantly exposed to and because of that, he and the people who are closest to him are in a constant state of hyper-vigilance.'

Things like these cannot happen. He is never alone. There is always somebody around.

A few months later, when he was the guest of the Canal+ show *Clique,* Mbappé opened up about how he had to tread 'a fine line between paranoia and vigilance'. 'Some people wish you ill, but not everyone,' he said. 'We all build our lives differently. As to me, I did it thinking that football was my whole life. Maybe I'm wrong . . . maybe I'm right? Only time will tell, or God, when the moment comes. [But] when you choose things, the result is easy to accept.' Even if it means you are never alone, and that to escape the public panopticon, Kylian and his family had created their own.

14

La vie en bleu: Capitaine Kylian

Antoine Griezmann and Kylian Mbappé with the 2018 World Cup Trophy.

No photographs are more emblematic of the 1966 World Cup than those John Varley of the *Daily Mirror* took on the Wembley pitch on 30 July, the day England beat Germany 4–2 in the final. One of them in particular, reproduced tens, perhaps hundreds of thousands of times since, of captain Bobby Moore lifting the Jules Rimet trophy, held aloft by Geoff Hurst and Ray Wilson, remains *the* image of the tournament. But why? It did not capture an incident which collective memory transformed into the defining moment of the competition, like Diego Maradona's Hand of God in 1986 or Zinédine Zidane's headbutt on Marco Materazzi two decades later. What it did instead was to fix a moment of triumph for all eternity in such a way that a whole mythology could be built around it: Varley did for Bobby Moore what the paintings of Jacques-Louis David did for Napoleon. For once, it is correct to say that he immortalised his subject, which was not the England team, but its skipper, the handsome, blond West Ham defender who, more than any other footballer before or since, came to embody the virtues the English wanted to believe best characterised their national character: calm in the face of danger, fairness, grit and humility; the kind of man

Jack Hawkins portrayed in countless war films glorifying Britain's stand against Nazi Germany.

We are here in the realm of fancy, a fancy that tells us more about those who harbour it than about the man on whom they projected their fantasies. Bobby Moore was not only the England captain who led his team to a World Cup victory; Bobby Moore was the England captain who all others should aspire to emulate. Because of this, captaincy itself changed in nature to become a national obsession, and whom it should be bestowed on a matter for passionate debate. The principal tenet of this belief system is: England needs a leader and fails when it cannot call on one. The armband should not be desecrated as it was in June 2003, when Sven-Göran Eriksson let it be worn by four different players in a single friendly game against Serbia and Montenegro, when Michael Owen, Emile Heskey, Phil Neville and Jamie Carragher passed it around between them as if it had no more value than a shinpad or a protein shake. A Swede could not be expected to understand this, as foreigners have a very different idea of captaincy and perhaps even nationhood; in fact, they do not care much for it, not as much as we English do.

This is poppycock. Other nations may not fetishise the function to the same extent, maybe; but the idea that captaincy and who should hold it is a minor concern for them is absurd. Paraguay had José Luis Chilavert, the Ivory Coast Didier Drogba, West Germany Franz Beckenbauer. France had Roger Marche, Michel Platini and Didier Deschamps. France had Hugo Lloris, who retained the role for ten years; and now, France has Kylian Mbappé. Should anyone think that giving him the role was a mere detail in a country where such things do not really matter should think again. Just ask Kylian.

*

At the age of 23, and with only 18 caps to his name, Hugo Lloris was one of the youngest captains the French national team had known when new *sélectionneur* Laurent Blanc chose him to lead Les Bleus in a friendly against England at Wembley, on 17 November 2010. Nearly six months had passed since the disaster of Knysna, when Raymond Domenech's players had gone on strike during the 2010 World Cup, refusing to leave the team bus for a training session after *L'Équipe* revealed that Nicolas Anelka had told his manager 'to go fuck himself up the arse' during half-time in France's second group game, against Mexico. André-Pierre Gignac took the place of Anelka (who was excluded from the team twenty-four hours later by the French FA), France conceded two goals to *La Tri* in the second half, and no-one was shocked when their exit from the tournament was confirmed in the next game, a 2–1 defeat to the South African hosts. The deafening chorus of vuvuzelas sounded like the whole world was having a laugh at the expense of the shambolic French. The unmourned Domenech was dismissed for serious misconduct and Laurent Blanc brought in, who decided that the quiet Lloris should be his first captain, a role he wished to test several other players for before making a permanent appointment. Alou Diarra, Steve Mandanda, Samir Nasri, Florent Malouda, Philippe Mexès and Eric Abidal also wore the armband before Lloris was confirmed as the skipper of Les Bleus just before Euro 2012, which he remained until announcing his retirement from international football in January 2023.

The soft-spoken Lloris took charge of a team that did not just need to regain the place at the top of the footballing table it had occupied since 1998, but also to reconnect with supporters and, beyond, with a whole nation that had felt betrayed by the Knysna debacle. It was a remarkable appointment in more ways than one. France is unlike Spain, where the three players who skippered La Roja on most occasions were all glovemen: Iker Casillas, Andoni Zubizarreta and Luis Arconada. Les Bleus had had goalkeeping captains before – nine, to be precise – but all of these, bar Alex Thépot in the early 1930s, had been chosen on an ad hoc basis, when the incumbent was unavailable because of suspension or injury. Lloris's background and character also made him an unlikely candidate for the position.

The Nice-born keeper shared the immigrant roots of many of Laurent Blanc's men, with this difference: his father Luc, whose family came from Spain, earned a very comfortable living as a Monte Carlo-based banker, and so did his late mother Christine, a lawyer of Italian heritage who died when her eldest son was only 21. Hugo had not been told that she was suffering from terminal cancer; despite the shock, he insisted on playing for Nice two days after her death. Yet his upper-middle class upbringing did not put a wedge between him and his less privileged team-mates. He was not 'one of the boys' and preferred to keep himself to himself; but neither was he a loner or a sulker. Those who wished to confide in him or sought his support found a willing ear. He did not seek the limelight, quite the opposite in fact. 'The less people talk about me, the happier I feel,' he said. He rarely raised his voice within the dressing-room (Yohan Cabaye said: 'He is the kind of captain who only says something when he needs to') but proved an articulate if uncontroversial speaker when called upon to answer the media's questions. He also happened to be one of the very best in the world in his position, France's unsurpable number one, a deceivingly tough competitor who led by example and commanded respect and even affection in the dressing-room, with France as with Tottenham, who he skippered for eight seasons, reaching a Champions League final and serving four different managers during that period. You do not end your career with 145 caps, a French record, and captain your country 121 times, another record, if you do not possess qualities way beyond the ordinary.

But time caught up with Lloris, as it must. The 2022 World Cup finalist was still capable of brilliant performances, but not as consistently as the winner of four years previously, when he was one of four Frenchmen – the others were Raphaël Varane, Antoine Griezmann and Kylian Mbappé – selected by Fifa's technical committee to feature in their 2018 Team of the Tournament. The problem for Didier Deschamps was not so much replacing him as a keeper, as Steve Mandanda and Mike Maignan, and, later, Lucas Chevalier were more than able successors, but as a captain, the role Lloris had fulfilled with such success for over a decade.

Only a few days after France's defeat to Argentina on penalties in Qatar, Lloris himself had suggested that Mbappé would be a logical choice. 'A passing of the baton has taken place between a generation that has reached the last phase of its cycle and a new generation that is led by Kylian,' he said. '[He] has shown strong leadership, even more so in the [World Cup] final.' Happily for Kylian, Deschamps concurred, and, on 21 March 2023, three days before France were to face the Netherlands to kick-start their qualifying campaign for the 2024 Euros, confirmed that the PSG striker would succeed the Tottenham keeper as the skipper of the French national team on a permanent basis.

Considered from the outside, Deschamps had done nothing more than validate the obvious. On 18 December 2022, Mbappé, the tournament's Golden Boot with eight goals, had become the second player in history to score a treble in a World Cup final, after Geoff Hurst in 1966. He had been an automatic choice at the tip of France's attack since exploding on the stage in thrilling fashion at the 2018

World Cup and had only missed four of the national team's previous thirty-two matches, either because he had been rested for a game of little consequence or was hampered by injury. He had finished fourth in the traditional end-of-year *Journal du Dimanche* poll of the country's favourite personalities, behind singer Jean-Jacques Goldman, astronaut Thomas Pesquet and *Lupin* actor Omar Sy. He was still only 24, on course to beat all-time goalscoring records for both club and country. The ease with which he dealt with the press, both in French and English (Spanish would come later), or that he did not look out of place when President Macron invited him to the Elysée Palace, showed he could be expected to fulfil the public duties of a French captain with eloquence and dignity; and he hankered after the role. All of France's best players, those whom the rest of the world recognised as 'great' beyond dispute, had captained their national side. Raymond Kopa, Michel Platini, Zinédine Zidane, Thierry Henry; a few lesser ones too; but this was the company Kylian wanted to keep and must join if he were to be recognised as the greatest of them all.

Yet Deschamps's choice provoked contrasting reactions among those who follow football more closely than the average French fans, whose interest see-saws between major competitions to such an extent you sometimes wonder whether they care at all. One of the reporters who attended the Deschamps press conference at which the official announcement was made asked a question that occupied many a mind at the time. Wasn't Mbappé too *égoïste*, too selfish, to be a captain?

Deschamps bristled almost imperceptibly but quickly contained himself. 'Mbappé selfish? This is the image you have . . . ,' he said, leaving the unfinished sentence lingering in the air for a couple of seconds. 'Kylian can do individual things on the pitch, that's part of [the game of] a striker like him. He can afford it, when others . . .

less so. But to do that is not selfishness or anything like that. I have no doubts about that. He doesn't have to change. He has this ability to be captain. If I make this choice, it's not to please him. This debate takes up space because being captain of Les Bleus is a responsibility. Kylian, when he's on the pitch, thinks about what he has to do on the pitch. It happens naturally in the dressing-room. I don't even have any advice to give him – he knows.'

I don't have any advice to give him – he knows.

That was quite the endorsement from Deschamps, the outstanding captain of the 1998 World Cup and the 2000 European champions, whom Aimé Jacquet picked for his leadership qualities as much as for his footballing intelligence and his ability to control the midfield with the minimum of fuss. Deschamps knew that his choice had not met with unanimous approval in his own dressing-room. Some of his players felt ambivalent towards Kylian. They knew what they owed to his talent, but they also questioned his reluctance to track back and his commitment in training, neither of which had ever been Kylian's forte. As long as he produced the goods, fine; as long as the individual project was in line with the collective project, no problem; but should the lines diverge, the ambivalence would soon turn to hostility, as it did later. They did not quite buy the smooth persona which the young man was so adept at projecting in his dealings with the media. More than anything, they found it hard to swallow that Mbappé should have been chosen ahead of a player who, to most if not everyone, incarnated every virtue a captain should possess: Antoine Griezmann, whose dedication to the cause of Les Bleus was absolute. I should make a confession here: I felt the same myself. 'Grizou' was 32, still young enough to take France to Euro 2024 and make his farewell at the 2026 World Cup. No-one deserved it more than he did. He had been France's best player at every major tournament he took part in, the outstanding footballer of the 2016 Euros and, I would argue, of the 2018 and 2022 World Cups too. As Mbappé himself put it, Griezmann would remain 'one of the most important, if not the most important player of the Deschamps era'. I would have no hesitation to rank him alongside Platini and Zidane among the greatest France has ever produced; yes, ahead of Mbappé, who has time on his side to join him, but hasn't yet.

He is the yin to Mbappé's yang. Everything Griezmann achieved, he had to fight for. Nike didn't offer him a sponsorship deal in his third year at primary school. He was deemed too small and too fragile by a couple of French clubs (looking at you, Lyon and Montpellier) who let him go before his voice had broken. The Institut National du Football did not beckon, as no coach thought highly enough of him to put his name forward for the admission tests. He was rescued by a Real Sociedad scout who saw him by chance play at a youth tournament and convinced his parents to let their boy take part in a one-week trial. Usually, triers who 'make it' get the popular vote. But Griezmann is unique among 'triers' in that it's not the lack of talent, or skill, which made him one. It is that, in his mind, his personal achievements have always come second to the achievements of the team he'd fought to be in. He was too good to be a trier, yet a trier he was and he remains. It is one of the many paradoxes which Griezmann managed to reconcile throughout his career, but which affected the perception and judgement of others.

Here is another of those paradoxes. The two managers with whom he'll always be associated, Deschamps and Diego Simeone, place tactical discipline and combativeness at the very top of footballing virtues. Yet Griezmann, the most agile of minds to go with the nimblest of feet, never rebelled against their rule, when others would have felt it stifled their creativity. More than that: he found joy in playing an attritional style which he admitted – with a smile, as usual – was *on est chiants à regarder* ('a pain in the arse to watch'). If there was joy to be found, and none was obviously at hand, he'd bring it to the table himself. And he was tough as nails: his record of playing eighty-four consecutive games for France between August 2017 and November 2023 will never be broken. Find me a footballer who was better suited to set the example for others as a captain.

Denying Griezmann the captaincy which he so richly desired could also push him towards retirement when he still had much to offer, as was obvious by his ongoing contributions to Atlético de Madrid. The attacker who finished with the Golden Boot at Euro 2016, as a right-winger, and the Silver Boot at the 2018 World Cup, as a second striker, agreed to sacrifice himself for his team's sake at Qatar 2022. At his manager's command, he reinvented himself as a deep-lying midfielder whose vision, skill and hunger took France to the final. Even that was not enough.

When Mbappé's turn came to comment on the mission he'd been entrusted with, shortly after Deschamps had held his press conference, he delivered a masterclass in communication which addressed the main issue head-on: that his elevation meant that Griezmann would be denied the prize he coveted and many felt he merited more than Kylian did. 'I spoke with Antoine, as he was disappointed,' he said. 'It was understandable. I told him that I would have had the same reaction. He is 32. He has been one of the best, if not the best player of the Deschamps era. I told him that I was not his line manager. He is esteemed and loved by the group. We must benefit from his experience. We'll be side to side, we'll go forward, hand in hand.' The words were chosen with great care, tact and skill and delivered with some emotion, yet without undue emphasis. Whether

Griezmann would readily accept the hand of the man, seven years his junior, who could have waited a couple more seasons to take the armband, was a different matter. Then there was this sentence: 'He [Griezmann] has been one of the best.' Why use the past? Wasn't he still?

Kylian's first words as a French captain were overwhelmingly well-received, however. The best communicators are not those who speak the most fluently, but those who are just as good at reading the room. He knew the tune his audience wanted to hear and pitched his address accordingly: when it comes to this, Mbappé has a near-perfect ear. Who could dislike the portrait he drew of the captain he aspired to be? 'The door should not be shut to anyone,' he said. 'Everyone is free to express themselves in this group: that's what the France team is. It belongs to no-one [in particular].'

There were 'fundamentals' which no captain could disrespect. He intended to be a leader who would be 'open to the others', who 'had no desire to decide, to impose' as 'when everyone has his place, great things can be achieved'. Yes, he believed that others listened to him when he spoke, but 'the collective' came first; there should be no discrepancy between the aspirations of his team-mates and his own.

Rather less convincingly, though his tone was unchanged and his fluency unaffected, he said that he hadn't thought about the captaincy in the months which had followed the 2022 World Cup and the announcement of Lloris's retirement. He'd only broached the subject with Deschamps over the last few days. He felt very happy – of course he did – but, once the initial moment of elation passed, he realised this was a 'new responsibility', which may not change the way he played, but would probably have an impact on the way he behaved towards others. He would have to make himself more available and attentive to them than he had done in the past.

You may read this and think there is nothing remarkable about those words. They were what could be expected from a very intelligent young man put in the examinee's chair in front of the media and public opinion, who knew which buttons to press to pass his *viva* with the compliments of the jury; and that is also true; just as it is true that he could not do otherwise, and did it like a master of his craft.

His first nine months in the captain's role were the smoothest of cruises. France sailed through its qualifiers for Euro 2024 like a perfectly rigged clipper gliding on a placid sea. True, save for the Netherlands, the opposition was not of the highest calibre: Ireland, Greece and poor ten-man Gibraltar, who shipped *fourteen* goals when visiting the Nice Allianz Riviera in November, Kylian helping himself to three goals on that occasion. Still, to finish that qualification campaign with a record of 22 points out of a possible 24 and a goal difference of +26 was more than satisfactory. Mbappé, playing on his favoured left wing, with Kolo Muani, Olivier Giroud and Marcus Thuram being rotated at centre-forward, topped the group's goalscoring charts. Antoine Griezmann, no longer used by Deschamps in the holding role which had suited him so well in Qatar, only contributed a couple of goals and a handful of assists, but remained a fixture in the team as an attacking midfielder or a second striker. All was for the best in the best of all possible worlds, the only blemish on a near-flawless picture a 1–2 defeat to Germany in September; but Kylian sat on the bench at the Westfalenstadion for that friendly, preserving his unbeaten record throughout his first year in the role. Irony of ironies, Antoine Griezmann had worn the armband that evening in Dortmund, the only time France had tasted defeat since the 2022 World Cup final.

Euro 2024 would make for a very different story.

*

It would have been impossible for Kylian, the international footballer, not to be affected by what happened to Kylian, the club player, whose tumultuous, fractious and sometimes sordid divorce with PSG was being consummated as France prepared for a European Championship which fans, pundits and bookmakers all thought they had an excellent chance to win. I have written about this episode at length elsewhere in this book but chose to leave its impact on Mbappé's trajectory with the French national team aside, as this impact can only be understood in the context of how he was chosen by Didier Deschamps to lead it. Now is the time to try and understand it, and how it is still felt two years down the line, as France is readying for another World Cup.

Things didn't start well for Kylian at the Euros, a competition he had approached by telling the press that he 'wanted to leave [his] mark on it'. He suffered a broken nose after colliding with Austrian defender Kevin Danso in France's first game of the tournament, a workmanlike, uninspiring 1–0 win, and had to sit out Les Bleus' next engagement, another workmanlike, uninspiring performance against a Dutch team they'd scored six goals against in the qualifiers; 0–0 this time, not one of the good ones. Fitted with a black mask which he said made him see things 'as through 3-D glasses', Kylian rejoined the team to score a penalty in the 1–1 draw with Poland which ensured progress to the round of 16. There, a Jan Vertonghen own goal was enough to give France victory over Belgium and a place in the quarter-finals. So far, so underwhelming, so workmanlike and uninspiring – but Deschamps's side was still in contention, even more so after a hard-fought, cagey victory on penalties against Portugal in the quarters. Vision-impaired Mbappé, who seemed well short of full fitness, had exerted minimal influence on the game and was subbed by Deschamps after the first period of extra-time, which was already too late according to one of the manager's fellow 1998 World Cup winners, Emmanuel Petit. 'Up until now,' Petit said, 'he [Mbappé] hasn't been worthy to be a captain. He hasn't been up to the [required] standard since the beginning of this Euro.' We would hear this again, and not just from Arsenal's former midfielder.

Whatever Petit thought, France were in the semi-finals of a major tournament once again. It is not unknown for sides which have struggled to find their rhythm in the early phase of a global competition to go on and win it. Beat Spain in the semi-final, and all would be forgiven. With the team doctor's blessing, Kylian decided to do away with his mask to face the Spaniards and, for a while, seemed liberated. It was his perfectly weighted, perfectly swung cross which led to Kolo Muani heading in the opening goal in the ninth minute of the match, the only goal Les Bleus scored in open play in the tournament. But then he faded, quickly; Spain came back and took the lead through, first, Lamine Yamal, in stunning fashion, then Dani Olmo in under five minutes of the first half. Kylian had a glorious chance to change the course of the game when, with four minutes to go, he found himself in his favourite position, running at full pace, sent through on the left wing on a counter, with plenty of space to attack and conquer. He cut inside Spain's centre-back Dani Vivian as he had cut inside hundreds of other centre-backs before, but his right-foot shot flew yards above Unai Simon's goal. To make things worse, Olivier Giroud was unmarked at the penalty spot, not that passing the ball to him had been on Mbappé's mind: this was the kind of glorious chance he'd turned into goals so many times before.

I have watched the video of that miss at least a dozen times, not to dissect what went wrong in the execution of the shot, but to try and make sense of Mbappé's reaction after he saw the ball sail into the stands. It wasn't rage. It wasn't the universal hands on the head gesture which players and fans alike use to express disbelief, not until a few seconds afterwards anyway. There was what looked like a quick glance at the giant screen, as if he wanted to make sure that what had happened was not some bad dream. The expression was that of a child who's been caught doing something he shouldn't and wondering if retribution is coming – not fear, just *zut alors*. He had just wasted what would probably be France's last chance to draw level with the Spaniards yet barely showed any emotion when he must have been furious at himself. He was. 'The competition was a failure,' he said immediately after the game. 'At the end of the day, football is simple: either you're good, or you're not. I wasn't.'

Some pointed the finger at Deschamps rather than at his captain. *L'Équipe* castigated the manager's flawed 'plan', which over-relied on Mbappé and made him the sole focal point of France's attack. It was bound to backfire if Kylian failed to reproduce at the Euros the kind of form he'd shown through most of the season with PSG. In six games, France only scored twice themselves, once from the penalty spot, and owed their positive results against Austria and Belgium to own goals by the opposition. Mbappé made for a better target, however, and some media outdid themselves in making the hero of Qatar 2022 the villain of Euro 2024. Later in the year, French daily *Sud Ouest* felt justified to chronicle what it called the eight stages of the player's 'descent into hell', starting from his 'tug-of-war' with PSG in the summer of 2023, with Euro 2024 'which Mbappé went through like a ghost' the centrepiece of Kylian's *annus horribilis*. Ridiculously over-the-top as this attack was, it was symptomatic of how much French public opinion towards its favourite son had shifted over the past year-and-a-half.

And there was something else: come the final whistle at Berlin's Olympiastadion, Europe was not talking about Kylian Mbappé, the predicted star of the European Championships, but about a slender boy born in Barcelona eight-and-a-half years after Kylian had come into the world in Paris: Lamine Yamal, the author of Spain's astonishing equaliser in the semi-final, now the youngest-ever goalscorer at a European Championship, at the age of 16 years and 362 days. A future Ballon d'Or winner, no doubt. Now, who had we heard being talked about like this in the past?

The issue of Mbappé's captaincy had never really gone away for good, only been 'put in parentheses', as the French say, and the disappointment of Euro 2024 provided a perfect excuse for radio phone-in shows and clickbait journalists to make it a hot topic again. The tall poppy syndrome was to blame in part for this: France is no better than most of its neighbours in this respect, and so much pent-up rancour and jealousy had been building up in the hearts and minds of the *kylianophobes* that they were not going to miss that golden chance to open the floodgates of their resentment. Mbappé's body language and on-field demeanour, his lack of apparent concern when things went wrong (beyond displays of petulance towards his team-mates), his studied goal celebrations, aimed at the nearest camera rather than at the exultant crowd, did not help redress the perception that here was an athlete who treated football as an individual sport and was therefore unsuited for the role of a team leader. Who was serving whom? To this must be added the bitterness felt towards the schemer who had supposedly managed to talk, if not blackmail, Didier Deschamps into picking him rather than Griezmann for the captaincy of Les Bleus. This was absurd. Nothing of the kind had happened.

Yet his accusers seized their chance to pile on him. Following a triumphant presentation in a sold-out Santiago Bernabéu stadium on 16 July of that same year, in which Mbappé addressed the Madridese *socios* in excellent Spanish, his first few months as a Real Madrid player had not been exceptional by his standards, but still represented a solid start in a team where goals were bound to be shared more widely than in Paris, with Rodrygo, Vinicius Jr and Jude Bellingham rather than Gonçalo Ramos, Kolo Muani and Bradley Barcola as his attacking partners. He had to wait until his fourth game to open his account with the Merengue, then scored in the three which followed – and would finish that 'difficult' season with 44 goals, exactly the same number he'd scored in his last season at PSG, and a first Pichichi award. No other striker had ever been as prolific in his first season at Real, not even Cristiano and Ronaldo Fenômeno. His critics preferred to single out a rare poor performance in the catastrophic clásico which Real lost 0–4 to Barcelona in late October (he'd score a hat-trick when it was Real's turn to visit Barça seven months later) and a couple of missed penalties against Liverpool and Athletic at the end of the year. Old stories resurfaced. We were told that Deschamps's choosing Mbappé rather than Griezmann for the captaincy had 'set the French dressing-room on fire', and soured Griezmann's relationship with Deschamps to such an extent that it explained why the Atlético player had announced his international retirement at the end of September.

It hadn't been a clean break, more of a stress fracture which had worsened over a year to become yet another subject of polarisation within the French support. It didn't help that Kylian looked and sounded on the defensive when questioned by a Canal+ interviewer over the circumstances of his elevation. 'In any case, [Griezmann] would have been a perfectly legitimate [captain],' he said. 'I remember the conversation with [Deschamps]. He told me: "how would you feel if you were captain of the French national team?" I answered that it would not change my life. [It would be] an immense honour. I'd be super happy if you gave me [the armband]. If you don't, you don't. But that was twisted into: "if he hadn't given it to Kylian, Kylian would have turned everything upside down".' The mask slipped a bit more. 'I do not wear the same armband as Hugo,' he said. 'People ask a lot from me. Hugo [Lloris] was a very good guy, a very good captain, but I feel that when it's about me, people expect me to do a different job.' This was true. For Lloris, the number 1 referred to what was printed on the back of his shirt; for Mbappé, it was what he was meant to be; it was what he wanted to be as well.

Then there was Stockholm.

15
Mbappé power

Kylian scoring his second goal in the 2022 World Cup final.

Mbappé's exile from Les Bleus could not last. If his natural talent didn't suffice already, his excellent form for Real Madrid after a tricky few months in the late autumn and early winter of 2024 demanded his inclusion in Deschamps's first squad of 2025. There had been eight goals for him in nine La Liga games since the turn of the year, and another four in a spectacular double-header against Manchester City to take his club to the knockout phase of the Champions League. The damage done to his image and reputation by the Stockholm affair would never be completely repaired, but, in legal terms at least, that case now belonged to the past. The quarters of the Nations League beckoned, against an opponent which evoked one of the sweetest of memories for him: Croatia, the antagonist of the 2018 World Cup title match, when Kylian became only the second teenager to score in the final of the competition, the first since Pelé in 1958. His right to be included to Deschamps's squad was not questioned seriously by anyone; but his confirmation as captain was, after a four-game hiatus during which Aurélien Tchouaméni (twice), N'Golo Kanté and Ibrahima Konaté had deputised in that role.

Former French international Jérôme Rothen, who played under

Deschamps at AS Monaco in the early 2000s, led the charge from the RMC broadcasting studio, only a few hours after Kylian's re-appointment had been confirmed by the France manager, who did not wish to elaborate about the conversation he'd had with his returning skipper. 'Unlike some others, I can remember things,' was Rothen's opening gambit. The 'others', here, included Deschamps, who, according to the player-turned-footballing shock-jock, 'had a selective memory'. He accused Mbappé of questioning the French manager's leadership on several occasions, not least just before a 2–0 win over Belgium in September 2024, when *L'Équipe* said that the France captain had launched into a dressing-room tirade in which he deplored that his team 'was not doing enough work on tactics'. Rothen did not question the authenticity of the quote and interpreted it as a direct attack on Deschamps's competence, which the manager, though hurt, had chosen to forget about. Rothen was warming to his subject by then. 'I'd question his status as captain,' he said. 'For the sake of France's image, and to go and win the World Cup [in America] with a real boss on the pitch, sorry, but Kylian had done so much wrong that he did not deserve to be given back the armband straight away.' Neither Deschamps nor Mbappé responded publicly to the comments of Rothen and others, sticking to the 'don't explain, don't complain' strategy they'd adopted whenever the media had suggested a cooling in their relationship.

Did the opinion of a presenter really matter that much? It did in France, where Rothen's employer, RMC, leads the prevailing discourse on all things football and stirs controversy to drive up listeners and the number of interactions on social networks; and if there is no ready controversy to get excited about, they will make one up. Should you think that, say, certain broadcasters do something similar in England, think again. I should know. RMC were one of my employers for nearly fifteen years, until I could not take any more of the cacophony and torrent of nonsense they were pouring into their listeners' ears from dawn until long after dusk, when some things were said on air which made me want to rip the headphones off and smash them underfoot. Again, does it matter? Of course it does. France is a country of many voices, but RMC's chosen strategy is to shout louder than anyone else, be it about sport or politics, where it positions itself as a 'counter power' (to what is unclear), when it is in fact a key enabler of populist figures and opinions, mostly from the Le Pen hard and extreme-right, but also from the Mélenchon Insoumise left, who take turns to tear into each other, something which must appeal to many of their compatriots, given how the radio station's audience share keeps on rising. So, if the amount of criticism that comes Mbappé's way in his own country appears ridiculous to you, remember where most of it originates, and that it is not just a handful of lunatics and abusers screaming into the digital void who should be held responsible for it.

Don't let's pretend that Mbappé was welcomed with bunches of lilies, words of gratitude and a Kylian-shaped cake when he rejoined Les Bleus at Clairefontaine in March 2025 before their Nations League two-legged quarter-final against Croatia. The tensions within the dressing-room had not been invented; they had been amplified to a ridiculous degree but were no less real for that. However, listening to colleagues who spend their working life covering Les Bleus, and all have their mole, or moles, in the dressing-room, those tensions were mere ripples on fairly placid waters compared to the chaos, fear and loathing of the Domenech era. Mbappé's unique status, which he'd earned, and personality, which was unlikely to change at this stage, could be the source of antagonism, if mostly of the unspoken kind.

Michel Platini too got on other people's nerves when he reigned over French football, and so did Zinédine Zidane, Didier Deschamps and Thierry Henry. Dare we discuss how 'popular' Lothar Matthäus was within the West Germany side which won the Italian Mondiale in 1990? It could not be otherwise in a sport in which winning is the only thing, and where team-mates are also direct competitors. Kylian himself had gone past that stage almost from the outset. He had no competitors to speak of: the French team consisted of Mbappé plus ten others. Some could resent this; some probably did and do; but only in defeat would they question him, as what he brought to the communal table went beyond goals and assists. He was the only one in this group of players who felt powerful enough to stand up and defend his rights, and their rights, when he considered them to be under attack. They owed him, big time.

Knysna had changed the whole dynamic between the French Football Federation, the FFF, and the players who were called on to represent their country. The administrators' failure to keep the rebels in check in South Africa and the appalling mudslinging which followed did not result in structural changes at the top of the French game. The FFF chairman Jean-Pierre Escalettes resigned on 28 June, less than a week after France's elimination at the group stage, but what ensued was not a full inquest into the dysfunctions of the federation and how they played their part in the debacle, but an internecine 'war of the clans' within the administration, in which the figureheads of the various factions, all of whom had held key positions before, jostled to protect their interests and further their personal ambitions. The man who was chosen to succeed Escalettes was Noël Le Graët, a 68-year-old Breton businessman and former head of the French league who had sat on the FFF board for so long that he was already there when Eric Cantona was ejected from the national team for calling then-manager Henri Michel a 'bag of shit', some twenty years previously. He was also serving as vice-chair when he put his name forward for the election. Le Graët only vacated the presidency in 2023, after lurid media reports about his behaviour, towards women in particular, made his position untenable. He denied the allegations, and the formal investigations into his conduct were later dropped.

Back in 2010, however, Le Graët had earned enough credit in his management of the FFF finances, bringing in Nike as one of Les Bleus' main commercial partners among other achievements, to build the support needed to be given the presidency. It was he too who, that same year, re-drafted the FFF's image rights policy and drew a new collective agreement which defined the 'rights and obligations' of national team players on international duty. The terms of the twenty-six-page document would have been unacceptable in any other branch of business and, more to the point, in any other context. As of 2010, all French internationals would have to surrender their image rights associated with the national team from their debut until – wait for it – five years after they retired from the game, regardless of how many caps, or how few, they had collected during that period. In the case of Mbappé, who signed the charter in 2017, this meant he would probably be tied to the agreement until he was 40. Players would receive a compensation of €25,000 per game played, and tough luck for those who weren't selected: the FFF could still use their name and likeness for nothing. Le Graët knew that there would be no rebellion this time. What had happened in South Africa ensured that the footballers who had 'disgraced' their country would acquiesce and sign on the dotted line. One Knysna was enough.

It normally fell to the national team captain to serve as a conduit between his team-mates and the administration in negotiations of this kind, except that in this case, normality had gone out the window, and of negotiations, there were none. Laurent Blanc had taken Raymond Domenech's place but had yet to pick a permanent skipper, and once he did, in 2012, it was already too late for Hugo Lloris, a Knysna veteran, to instigate a discussion on the subject, unless he wished to be presented as another troublemaker. The rules remained unchanged when Mbappé was first called to Les Bleus in 2017 and would still be in place today if Kylian had not decided to stage his own strike in the spring of 2022, as France prepared to face the Ivory Coast and South Africa in two friendlies.

Tuesday 22 March 2022 had been set aside in the national team's calendar to accommodate the various duties its players must fulfil towards its sponsors: Volkswagen, Uber Eats, Orange, Xbox, Coca-Cola and Konami. Kylian did not turn up, causing consternation among the FFF suits. This was no fit of pique, but a decision taken after a long period of fruitless discussions with the France management. A statement drafted by his legal advisor Delphine Verheyden and sent to Agence France-Presse insisted that Mbappé's decision to sit out the planned sponsor events was 'in no way a rebellion' but aimed 'to re-state his expectations and move the lines'. The Mbappé camp had attempted to broach the subject with the FFF 'for over three years'; they also reminded the general public that all of Kylian's appearance bonuses with Les Bleus had been donated to charities ever since his very first call-up. It was not all about money. 'The terms of this agreement no longer allow for the development of the image of football in a way that respects the values that the institution can uphold, but also those specific to each player on the team.' It was also about ethics, and control.

Noël Le Graët tried hard to convince supporters and media that this did not constitute 'an affair of state' or even a 'tug of war'. Bumps in the road of that kind were all 'part of life', he said. Discussions would be held, *mais oui*, and he was certain that Kylian would be on the pitch of the Stade Vélodrome when France played the Ivory Coast in Marseilles. He wasn't. The reason given for his absence was a slight nose and ear infection, from which he recovered in time to be included in the side which beat South Africa 5–0 in Lille four days later, Mbappé scoring two and assisting Mattéo Guendouzi's first goal in a French shirt. Delphine Verheyden had spoken at length of what was at stake on the eve of that game via a column in *L'Équipe* in which she proposed that the FFF's agreement with its players should be re-negotiated at regular intervals, before each World Cup, for example.

'The world of 2022 has nothing to do with the world after Knysna,' she wrote. A key part of her message was that 'players [must be] in harmony with the advertisements they participate in', and that 'the messages a player wants to convey can become inaudible, or even completely contradictory'. The 'player', here, was clearly Mbappé, who was far more discerning (and therefore far more valuable) than any of his France team-mates when it came to picking the right kind of sponsor: that is, a sponsor whose image would reflect positively on his own and 'whose values [he] shared'. Kylian's relationship with the organic food brand Good Goût ('help children grow by teaching them the joy of eating healthily') sat uneasily alongside the FFF's choice of Uber Eats and Coca-Cola as long-term partners. Therefore, the French federation should add a 'conscience clause' to its standard agreement, which would give players the right to opt out of advertising campaigns they disapproved of and, beyond, to exert collective oversight of its commercial endorsements. Verheyden also pointed out that the media landscape had been radically transformed since the agreement had been drafted in 2010, the year in which

Instagram was launched in Sweden and Twitter added 100 million subscribers to its platform. Footballers should be able to choose who they speak to, not be forced to answer 'all questions from all media without exception' when on international duty, as was specified in the existing arrangement, which also did not take into consideration the extra demands put on the squad's most marketable players; no prizes given for guessing who was referred to here.

The dialogue Noël Le Graët had promised to instigate did not take place. The FFF announced that it refused to review the agreement, and Kylian responded by announcing he would not show up at a photoshoot staged at Clairefontaine on 20 September, two days before France were due to face Austria in the UEFA Nations League. Mbappé and his advisors sent another statement to Agence France-Presse, in which they 'regretted that no agreement had been found, as requested, in the run-up to the World Cup'. Within hours, following last-minute talks with Mbappé, Deschamps and French captain Hugo Lloris, the FFF conceded defeat. Discussions would start to draw up a new collective charter. France could now concentrate on the task at hand: defending their world title in Qatar. True, those talks lingered on for the best part of a year, but, come September 2023, the FFF announced that 'a new agreement [had] been reached between the players of the French national team and the French Football Federation', which reflected 'a shared vision between the players and the Federation regarding the values of the French national team' and would 'allow for a balanced and clear relationship regarding the management of image rights for the team and its players by establishing a concerted framework for the development and monitoring of the implementation of the agreement'.

This was not 'player power' in action. This was Mbappé power. A 23-year-old had made the FFF blink when his team-mates, most of whom were his seniors, had shown no desire to shake up the status quo. None of them had publicly expressed support for Kylian when he had made his stand or celebrated his victory in a battle they had chosen not to fight themselves; but all of them knew what they owed him. Given his fame and status, Mbappé stood to benefit from the new agreement more than they did, but did this really matter when they too were to gain from it? He had shown courage and determination, while managing to keep public opinion onside throughout. He had acted like the captain he wasn't yet. He had also proved that the individual project could fit within a collective one, off the pitch as on it.

Kylian's critics have never needed much encouragement to seize upon his rare fallow periods to question his standing in world football, going as far as to say that the magnitude of his contributions was part of the Mbappé conundrum. His desire to be at the centre of everything unbalanced the teams he was part of, which came to over-rely on his talent and his efficiency in front of the goal. In tight, hard-fought matches, his refusal to assist in defensive work outweighed his influence in attack. What better illustration of this could there be than PSG's win in the 2024–25 Champions League? The door on which the Parisians had been knocking ever more desperately in the seven seasons he spent at the club, topping the goal charts in every single one, had finally been broken through. Why? Because (they said) Mbappé had gone and PSG had played like a team. To add to their schadenfreude, PSG had destroyed Kylian's Real Madrid 4–0 in the semi-finals of FIFA's new and certainly not improved Club World Cup little over a month after their European triumph. Mbappé, who was suffering from gastric flu, had missed the first three games of the absurd end-of-season tournament, and played less than half-an-hour of the round of 16 and quarter-final meetings with Juventus and Borussia Dortmund (against whom he still scored a late goal which confirmed Real's qualification). The game against PSG passed him by like it passed by all of Xabi Alonso's men, his defenders in particular. The Parisians pounced on comical mistakes by the likes of Antonio Rüdiger to kill the game almost as soon as it had started, racing to a 3–0 lead in the first twenty-five minutes – though 'racing' may not be the *mot juste*, as playing at a canter was enough to destroy the Madridese. Mbappé bore no responsibility whatsoever for the debacle, but the temptation to conclude that his former club was better without him – that it could not have improved as spectacularly as it did if he'd still been around – proved too strong for some. Look at Barcola, Dembélé, Doué, Kvaratskhelia: these guys give everything, they track back, they snap into tackles and run and run, they do all the things Mbappé thought were unworthy of his special talent, and they can score as well.

But that is PSG, the club which Mbappé left under a cloud, a storm in fact, and where he is seen by a significant number of fans through the prisms of rancour and partisanship. France is a different matter altogether. One thing you will not hear is that the French national team is better without Kylian Mbappé. The 2026 World Cup qualifiers which took place in the autumn of 2025 provided another illustration of his importance. He scored in the first three, against Ukraine, Iceland and Azerbaijan, which France won, but an ankle injury forced him to miss the return fixture against the Icelanders, which ended in a draw. Les Bleus had been far from convincing when facing Azerbaijan and were heading for a scoreline of 0–0 at the break when Mbappé took things into his own hands. With seconds of additional time left on the clock, he picked up the ball 40 yards away from the visitors' goal and embarked on a solo run which saw him go past four defenders, driving with the ball in the tightest of spaces with exquisite control, à la Messi, before slotting the ball in the back of the net with his right foot, very much à la Mbappé this time. France went on to win comfortably, with Mbappé assisting their second goal. *Quod erat demonstrandum.*

Kylian must play, Kylian will play, and, as a result, will soon overtake Olivier Giroud at the top of the list of France's most prolific goalscorers. It may be as early as the 2026 World Cup, when, injuries permitting, he will arrive as the tenth centurion in the history of Les Bleus; given his young age and his excellent fitness record up until now, Hugo Lloris's 145 caps will be the next milestone in his sights. Yet these prodigious numbers do not quite register as they ought to, as tends to happen when exceptional players make a habit of turning the extraordinary into the ordinary, and anything but the extraordinary is deemed a failure. In Kylian's case – certainly in France – you'll often hear people qualifying his achievements by adding 'but so many of his goals have been penalties', or 'it's not that difficult to score so many goals when you play the likes of Gibraltar in qualifiers', or 'just look at how many he's had in friendlies'. Well, let's do this and wring the neck of a few canards; haters of statistics, please look away now.

Penalties, first. What is true is that 13 of Mbappé's 55 goals for France so far have come from the spot, a 23 per cent proportion. Of the top 10 France goalscorers, only Antoine Griezmann, with 20.5 per cent (9 out of a total of 44 goals) comes close in this regard. Perhaps surprisingly, given his mastery of dead-ball situations, Michel Platini only scored 9.7 per cent of his 41 goals from 12 yards; but Jean-François Larios was France's appointed penalty-taker in the early 1980s, before *Platoche* added this responsibility to the captaincy in 1982: the equaliser the French captain scored in Les Bleus's legendary

World Cup semi-final against West Germany in Sevilla was the very first time he'd scored that way. It is hardly Kylian's fault that he has excelled in this exercise since taking on the role of executioner for good – from Griezmann, as it happens – in March 2022, in a 5–0 win over South Africa. He hasn't missed one of the ten he's attempted since, including two in the Qatar World Cup final. Why his excellence in the exercise which presents elite footballers with the greatest test of their nerves should be held against him is a mystery. Nobody would dream of belittling the contribution of France's greatest player of the 1950s and 1960s, Raymond Kopa, because a third of his 18 goals for the national team were scored from the spot. If Cristiano Ronaldo had not missed ten of the thirty-two penalty kicks he has taken for Portugal for twenty years now, spot kicks would account for almost exactly the same share of his international goals: 22.4 per cent, a mere 0.2 per cent differential. The figures are similar in the case of Lionel Messi, one of only three players to score four penalties in a single World Cup, in 2022 (Eusébio in 1966 and Rob Rensenbrink in 1978 are the other two): 21.9 per cent, and without taking his five failures into account.

Next, the Gibraltars of this world. Let's accept that there is no great merit in sharks feeding on sprats, and that there are plenty more of those in the Fifa waters today than there were a few decades ago: only 116 countries took part in the qualification stage for the 1990 World Cup, whereas 211 were eligible to compete in the 2026 edition. And yes, Mbappé scored a hat-trick against Gibraltar in November 2023 and a quadruple against Kazakhstan two years earlier; but the surprise is that those goal gluts against third- and fourth-tier footballing nations have been the exception for him. Looking more closely at his statistics, I found that only 12 of his 55 goals for Les Bleus to date were scored against sides which were outside of Fifa's top 100 at the time of the encounter, like Moldova, Luxembourg or Azerbaijan. The two countries which have suffered the most at the hands, or, rather, the feet of Mbappé are the Netherlands (six goals conceded) and Argentina (five, all of them in the knockout phase or the final of a World Cup); so much for his reputation as a flat-track bully.

Moreover, Kylian has scored a higher share of his international goals in official competitions than any of the other players who make up the top five of France's greatest goalscorers. Goals in friendlies only account for 18.9 per cent of his tally to date, compared to 33 per cent for Thierry Henry, 34 per cent for Antoine Griezmann and Michel Platini, and a whopping 50.1 per cent for the current record-holder Olivier Giroud. The obvious conclusion should be that the proliferation of international fixtures and the greater likelihood of facing no-hopers in European and World qualifiers have played no role whatsoever in Mbappé raking in numbers which, at least mathematically, make him of one of international football's most lethal strikers ever. But this is not the conclusion reached by everyone else; the reluctance to give him his due remains widely shared in his home country, where these figures, when they're known, do not weigh much compared to the growing narrative of a footballer who sees the national team as a stage on which he and he alone should shine, wearing the armband, taking penalties, exerting more control in the dressing-room than any other French skipper since Michel Platini. Another World Cup title may change this. Didn't Lionel Messi have to lead Argentina to victory in 2022 to be, at long last, talked about in the same breath as Diego Maradona at home?

16

La débâcle

Kylian visiting Stade Malherbe Caen, February 2025.

One of the most unusual aspects of the Mbappé project is how, from the outset, the player and his family chose to bypass channels which everyone else is compelled to use when working in football, starting with agents. This had brought them many benefits, starting with a larger cut of the player's earnings; this also meant that all of the major decisions taken since the very beginning of Kylian's career were taken without outsiders weighing-in in favour of choices which might have been more suitable to their own interests than to the player's or his family's. There is a downside to this fiercely defended independence, however: the temptation to believe that, since it had worked wonders in most respects so far, this methodology could be applied to the management of all of Mbappé's affairs. What happened with his acquisition of Stade Malherbe Caen at the end of the summer of 2024 would suggest this is not always the case.

Mbappé was not the first player to invest in a football club, even if most footballers wait until their career is over to do so, like Paolo Maldini did with Miami FC; Ronaldo Fenômeno with first, Real Valladolid, then Cruzeiro; and Gary Neville with Salford City, among dozens of others. Some did it for sentimental reasons, to repay a debt they owed a club which had played a key part in their development or which held a special place in the community they grew up in; this is how the Galicians Juan Mata, Santi Cazorla and Michu bought shares in Real Oviedo to save it from bankruptcy, for example. For others, it was more out of a desire to be part of a project for which they felt a particular affinity, as Hector Bellerin, still an Arsenal player at the time, did when becoming the second-largest stakeholder in Forest Green Rovers, the 'greenest' club in European football. Then there are those who see a business opportunity and jump in to exploit it, of which David Beckham's *ex nihilo* creation of MLS franchise Inter Miami is a textbook example. Mbappé's acquisition of Stade Malherbe Caen in July 2024 largely fits in the latter category, though, as we've seen, there was a former connection with the Normandy club. Back in 2012, when Kylian was in his second year at France's national academy of Clairefontaine, he'd nearly signed an *accord de non-sollicitation* – the first step towards being offered a professional contract – with SM Caen after a rave report submitted by David Lasry, the club's chief scout for the Île-de-France region. Caen's relegation to the second tier of the French football pyramid put paid to this plan, and Kylian went to AS Monaco instead.

But this was twelve years previously. All of the staff and executives who the Mbappé family had spoken to at the time had left the club by then. The American private equity fund Oaktree Capital Management had taken control of 80 per cent of its capital in 2020 after being called in by local businessman Pierre-Antoine Capton; but, four years later, Oaktree had far bigger fish to fry. In May 2024, they'd repossessed Italian giants Internazionale after the Chinese owners of the Milan club had failed to repay a €400 million loan provided by the Americans. Oaktree wished to concentrate on the side which was about to win the 20th Serie A title in its history; and despite its lowly status, SM Caen was also an expensive ship to run, with losses which would rise to €8.5 million in the 2023–24 season, over half of its total income. Oaktree's desire to part with Caen was not a secret. This is where Kylian Mbappé stepped in.

He used Coalition Capital, the investment subsidiary of his company Interconnected Ventures, to purchase Oaktree's stake in the club in a cash deal which French media reported to be worth a minimum of €15 million, with some sources putting the figure as high as €20 million. However, the accounts of the 2024 tax year filed by Coalition Capital in March 2025 suggest that the acquisition of SM Caen by the company was financed by a loan of €13 million from an unspecified source. Up to that year, Coalition Capital had been a dormant vehicle, registering a loss of just €20 for 2023. Still, if this were to be correct, €13 million represented a hefty sum for a club which had a long way to go to be profitable and would require substantial investment to make it competitive again.

There was no official statement from the player himself, Coalition Capital's CEO Ziad Hammoud obliging with the niceties de rigueur in such circumstances. 'As the lead investor in this project, we are very excited to continue the development of Stade Malherbe Caen, alongside [minority shareholder] PAC Invest,' the former beIN executive said. 'Our shared vision with the club of sporting excellence and community engagement is at the heart of our approach. We are determined to create an environment where young talents can flourish and where the club can defend its identity with strength and ambition.'

The move came as a surprise to observers. It was not so much the bare fact that a 25-year-old footballer should become the owner of a struggling Ligue 2 club; it was more that it should have cost him the equivalent of a year's net salary at his new club, Real Madrid.

SM Caen, despite being the sole professional club of some stature in a radius of 50 kilometres – as the crow flies – had never established itself as a contender of the first rank in French football. Its highest-ever finish was a fifth place in Ligue 1 in the 1991–92 campaign, after which Caen had been stuck in the proverbial yo-yo-ing lift between the top two divisions. Ligue 2, where it had remained stuck in the five years before Mbappé walked in, seemed its natural habitat. A community club? Without a doubt. The attendance figures were among the best in the division, and Caen had gained an enviable reputation for offering a warm, welcoming environment to both players and fans, who'd created one of the very first *association de supporters* in the country, back in 1936. A challenger? Unlikely. Money was in short supply at the Stade Michel d'Ornano; but not ambition if the new management team was to be believed. There was talk of a quick return to Ligue 1. There was talk of playing in Europe, which Caen had never done before, unless taking part in the 1992 Intertoto Cup counted for something. Those were the days.

The daydreaming was short-lived, at least among the fans. See-sawing results unnerved the new owners in the autumn, when Caen also lost their most influential player to injury, midfielder Yann M'Vila, a regular in Laurent Blanc's France team in the early 2010s. Three consecutive defeats in the run-up to Christmas cost manager Nicolas Seube his job, when Caen still had an outside chance of promotion; but Seube was a survivor of the previous regime and had been expected to be shown the door sooner rather than later; so off he went. The management team put in place by the Mbappés held on to the hope of an immediate return to Ligue 1, and chose a little-known Portuguese coach, Bruno Baltazar, to replace the outgoing manager. Baltazar, whose modest CV included a short stint as Sabri Lamouchi's assistant at Nottingham Forest in the late 2010s, failed to redress the situation. As one Caen insider told me, he was 'a decent coach, but also the wrong man at the wrong place at the wrong time' and would only last a few months. By the time the season had reached the halfway stage, Caen were sixteenth out of eighteen, and the first hostile banners had appeared in the d'Ornano arena. *'Mbappé, le SMC n'est pas ton jouet'* ('Mbappé, SMC is not your toy'). On 24 January 2025, a group of twenty supporters wearing balaclavas staged a pitch invasion at the end of yet another home defeat, this time to Guingamp.

It was not the results, awful as they were, which rankled most with fans known for a sense of humour derived from their fleeting relationship with success. It was the decisions taken by the management, an absentee owner – Kylian has visited the club only once since he acquired it – and a president, Ziad Hammoud. Hammoud had no qualification for the job other than the family's trust, admitted he knew very little about football and struggled to explain his strategy on the rare occasions he could be persuaded to travel from London or Paris to Normandy and face the media. He waited until 16 December 2024 to address the fans properly for the first time, to express some regrets on a local radio station about what he called 'a certain lack of cohesion at the beginning', which manifested itself in, among other things, the absence of a recruitment team and of a chief financial officer, shortcomings he promised would be addressed in the near future. Then it got worse. Caen kept losing and found itself dropping to the bottom of the league table. A relegation to the third tier, the *National*, was no longer a hypothetical scenario, but a likely outcome of the worst season SMC had known in over four decades.

Come February, on the eve of a crucial home game against Dunkerque, Hammoud admitted that the club 'had fallen well short of [its owners'] ambitions' and called for a 'sacred union' of all those who cared about SMC. 'There are still thirteen games to go, and a quite a few points to get,' he said. 'The season is not over.' The fans responded to his call. The drums kept beating throughout the match in a packed d'Ornano stadium, even after Caen's Billal Brahimi was sent off for an outrageous chest-high tackle in the first half, even after Dunkerque took the lead via a comical mix-up in Caen's box, and even after the visitors were allowed to score a second by an obliging defence just before the hour. The season was over.

Ten days later, on 20 February, an Astrojet Cessna Citation Latitude chartered by the player landed at Caen's Carpiquet airport. Kylian, who had scored a Champions League hat-trick against Manchester City in Madrid the previous evening, was driven to the d'Ornano stadium to meet with the club's newly appointed manager Michel Der Zakarian and his players, who'd only been told of his coming a couple of hours before his arrival. It was the first time the club's owner had paid them a visit. The media who had gathered for a scheduled press conference with Der Zakarian could hardly believe their luck. Fans alerted by social media posts also made their way to the stadium. Kylian did not try to evade either.

'I wanted to come much earlier,' he told the journalists. 'To be in contact with the players, the staff, the employees, so that people would know how much it means to me to be here. And in the current situation, it felt even more natural to be here today. I met a group of players who are not at all resigned [to their fate] and are motivated by the idea of staying up. I think that, given the quality of the squad, with the support of the fans and everyone showing solidarity, we can achieve something great. This week could be pivotal for the rest of the season.' SM Caen's captain Romain Thomas expressed a similar wish. 'Seeing him is always important,' he said. 'I hope this will be a wake-up call [for us]. He's showing he's here. I hope this will trigger [a reaction].'

It did not. I am writing this on 19 April 2025, as Caen's relegation to the *National* was confirmed with three games to go, following a twentieth defeat in thirty-one games, to Martigues this time. Martigues, who were also fighting for survival, but who had at least the excuse of coming from the third tier and of having one of the league's lowest budgets; Martigues, who struggle to bring 2,000 spectators to their Stade Françis Turcan, when Caen had close to a full house of 19,000 fans to cheer them that evening. What they saw was a capitulation. Caen lost 3–0. More banners were unfurled. *'Direction, joueurs: tous coupables, tous dehors'* ('Management, players: all guilty, all out') read one of them. Michel Der Zakarian, the coach the Mbappés had turned to at the eleventh hour, after Baltazar was sacked in February, said much the same thing. 'It is everyone's fault.'

Many of these players wanted 'out' anyway, a friend who knows some of them told me, something which agents who deal with Ligue 2 clubs confirmed. Wages would have to go down in the *National*, where professionals train and play with and against semi-pros and amateurs. Some of Caen's players were earning €20,000 a month or more and would not accept the unavoidable pay cut, now that SMC would no longer receive its share of Ligue 2's broadcasting rights and existing sponsors would re-negotiate the terms of their contracts. 'They've given up on Caen.' Why was that? 'Because nobody there knows what they're doing,' was his answer. 'It is a ghost club.'

Yet someone would have to pick up the bills. Selling players would only go so far, as the most valuable of them had been sold already, some of them by Oaktree, who cashed in some key assets just before the Mbappés officially took charge. Burnley had paid €4 million for Beninese international Andréas Hountondji, the scorer of 14 Ligue 2 goals in the 2023–24 season. A fellow Championship club, Coventry City, had acquired Belgium U21 striker Norman Bassette for €2.7

million. Another U21 international, French striker Tidiam Gomis, had been allowed to join RB Leipzig for €1 million in February 2025, about a third of what his value was supposed to be. Foreign clubs knew how delicate Caen's financial situation was and took advantage of it in what was now a buyer's market. The list went on. To compound the weakening of the squad, most of the recruits brought in by the Mbappés were not match-fit when they arrived at the club, and soon fell victim to the climate of morosity, and worse, which surrounded their new team.

Kylian himself made no public comment after his club was relegated. Others did. Patrice Garande, SMC's head coach from 2012 to 2018, was scathing in his appraisal of his former club's management. 'When you don't work, or you work badly,' he said, 'and you make people believe that [you will be doing great things], well, in the end, the club sinks. It's not just shameful in sporting terms. The way the season was run, that's what makes me angry, that's what is shameful.' The fans were no more forgiving. The president of Caen's main Ultras group, the Malherbe Normandy Kop, Christophe Vaucelle lamented 'a succession of dubious decisions, the sacking of former manager Nicolas Seube in particular, which led to a worsening of the situation'. 'The Mbappé clan arrived late on the scene, [but] has its share of responsibility in this failure,' he added. The failure stung all the more because the new regime had promised far more than it could deliver, and because supporters, perhaps dazzled by the identity of their new owner, had bought into those promises to the extent the club broke its record of season-ticket holders before a ball had been kicked, with over 10,000 locals signing up for what they'd been told would be a triumphant ride back to Ligue 1.

The Mbappé clan's biggest mistake had been to believe that it could let things take care of themselves. Caen was rudderless. No-one was quite sure who was supposed to do what. The family, as ever, placed its trust in a small group of individuals who were already part of its entourage, which is how Hammoud, who had no previous experience whatsoever in that field, found himself named president of the club, and why Kylian's former headmaster at Clairefontaine, 64-year-old Gérard Prêcheur, who'd never worked as a sports director before, found himself working in that role, only to quit it 'for personal reasons' six months later. Prêcheur's previous three appointments had been to coach the women's sides of Olympique Lyonnais, Chinese club Jiangsu Suning and Paris Saint-Germain. His last managerial involvement in men's football, with modest FC Valence, dated back to 1992. Yet this was the man who had been put in charge of overseeing the club's strategy in an unforgiving environment he'd never really been a part of.

Other Ligue 2 clubs watched the crisis deepen into a catastrophe with a mixture of disbelief – that nothing was done to stop the rot – and schadenfreude – that a direct rival had believed it could fly that close to the sun and had paid the price for it. A couple of L2 executives I spoke to pointed the finger squarely at Kylian's mother Fayza, criticising her 'arrogance' and 'ignorance' of their business. These were the comments of people who'd spent their working lives in lower division football, had made up their minds as to the 'folly' of the Mbappés' project and predicted its failure from the outset; but these were also the comments of *men* who, by default, adopted a hostile attitude towards outsiders who thought they could beat the system at its own game, outsiders whose chief strategist happened to be a woman – far from a detail in the deeply misogynistic environment of men's football. Fayza was their idea of the 'difficult woman', as, to them, all women who aspire to make a place for themselves in football and are prepared to fight for it are deemed to be 'difficult' anyway. It is not a specifically French trait. In 2026, of the 211 football associations which compose Fifa, only seven have a female president, and of the 96 football clubs which make up the so-called 'Big Five' European leagues, just one, Olympique Lyonnais, is owned by a woman, Michelle Kang. In these men's eyes, if Caen were to fail, it would be down to the influence Fayza wielded on her son, down to the queen of clubs in the pack.

This is not to say the Mbappés were not guilty of hubris in this particular case. The crux of the plan made sense, if its execution was ill-thought, or not thought through at all. Kylian had money to invest and wished to invest it in football. SM Caen was and remains a club with genuine potential. But, on one hand, he'd paid far too much for a loss-making venture whose financial situation was unlikely to improve in the short term, while, on the other, his resources were limited compared to entities such as Oaktree, which were now acquiring clubs at an increasing rate throughout Europe. Those investment funds, most of them based in the USA, managed billions of dollars of assets and were able to sink huge sums into the transfer market to progress on the field and see their asset grow in value accordingly. They could afford to take risks on the way. Mbappé could not, not to the same extent. Moreover, French football was experiencing an economic meltdown which, by the time this book is published, might well have caused several top-flight clubs to cease functioning as professional entities, as Bordeaux did when they were relegated to amateur status in the fourth division in the summer of 2024. If this could happen to Bordeaux, the 2008–09 French Champions and 2012–13 French Cup winners, the club of Tigana, Zidane and Lizarazu, this could also happen to Caen, twice Ligue 2 champions and nothing else besides.

*

Things have not improved since Caen's relegation to the *National*, despite continued investment from Coalition Capital. Stade Malherbe's annual budget of €12 million for the 2025–26 season made it the division's top spender ahead of former Ligue 1 clubs Valenciennes FC and Dijon Football Côte d'Or, and therefore a clear favourite for promotion. That hope had almost vanished before autumn was over, with Caen stuttering in mid-table, well off the pace set by leaders Rouen. No fewer than twenty first-team players had been sold or let go, and new manager Maxime d'Ornano, perhaps the only coach in the world whose team plays in a stadium bearing a name identical to his own, was coming under growing criticism from an impatient fan base. The discontent took an unusual twist when Normandy rapper Orelsan, a.k.a. Aurélien Cotentin, the bestselling recording artist in France in 2021 and 2022, who sometimes performs wearing a SM Caen shirt, name-checked Kylian and his family in 'La petite voix', one of the tracks on his fifth album, *La Fuite en avant*, released on the day, 7 November 2025, Caen failed to beat modest Paris 13 Atletico at the d'Ornano stadium and dropped into the bottom half of the table. '*Yes, you're going to sink your city like the Mbappés,*' he rapped.

Only a few hours after the record had been made available online, Kylian took to X to react. That post didn't read like it had been composed by his comms team. 'You're welcome to "save" the city you love so much, Orelsan,' it read. 'PS: the dude has done nothing but implore us to let him get a 1% [stake in SM Caen] without paying for it because he hasn't got a penny but so he can have the nice image of the little guy from Normandy.' Discussions had indeed taken place between the Mbappé family and the 'French Eminem' (he is white), who was keen to take a symbolic place on the board of the club. The musician's huge popularity in the Caen region would have been an asset to the Mbappés as they tried to reassure fans that they were in this for the long haul, but the conversation led to nothing. The prospect looks grim. As this book went to press, the news came from Stade Malherbe that a euphemistically called 'job protection plan', the second one in five years, would be activated with immediate effect and result in another thirteen jobs being lost in the club's administrative structure.

In late December 2025, with Caen in tenth place in the National league and showing no sign of rising higher, the Mbappés replaced d'Ornano with former Arsenal and Manchester City left-back Gaël Clichy, whose sole managerial experience so far had been to sit next to Thierry Henry when he looked after France's Olympic team at the 2024 Paris Games. By then, Caen had already been kicked out of the French Cup 2–3 by Bayeux, a team playing three divisions below them. An apoplectic d'Ornano said that his team had 'cheated with football'. Angry fans tried to force their way into their dressing-room, fortunately without success. Another group of Caen ultras waited for the team bus at the Stade Malherbe. Local police had to intervene, with one arrest made at the stadium.

The project had failed, for once.

17

The Ballon d'Or and beyond

Kylian at the 2021 Ballon d'Or awards ceremony, about to present the women's trophy to Barcelona player Alexia Putellas.

At 15 kilograms, the trophy weighs nearly three times as much as the World Cup, but unlike the World Cup trophy, it is not made of pure gold, only gold-plated brass on a socle of natural pyrite, crafted in the ateliers of Mellerio, the rue de la Paix jeweller whose creations once adorned the ill-fated neck of Marie Antoinette. It costs *France Football* magazine, which created the award in 1956, €13,000 to have it made each year, though to some, it is worthless, as it is a mere charade, an overblown commercial operation staged for the benefit of sponsors, big clubs and *France Football* themselves. Why should a bunch of arbitrarily selected journalists feel entitled to single out an individual when football is a team sport, and trophies – real trophies, not end-of-term badges and lollipops – cannot be won on one's own? Moreover, those journalists are probably bribed or pressured into voting for whomever it is in the interests of the organisers to win that year; and, finally, without fail, someone else should have been given the award.

The same criticisms are heard every autumn as the ceremony draws near. We at *France Football* have long been immune to them. I write 'we', as, when required, I assisted *France Football*'s small

Ballon d'Or team from 2005 (winner: Ronaldinho, ahead of Frank Lampard and Steven Gerrard) for almost two decades. Though I was never admitted to the inner sanctum of the Committee, which consisted of our editor, the senior writer who'd been designated as his *aide-de-camp* for that campaign, and no-one else, I can vouch for the integrity of the process, which we went to ridiculous lengths to protect. The secrecy which surrounds the counting of votes is such that, in 2024, it was only hours before the ceremony took place at the Théâtre du Châtelet that Real Madrid, who had made all their plane and hotel arrangements, pulled out and released a surreal statement in which they deplored the 'lack of respect' shown by the 'Ballon d'Or-UEFA' (UEFA does not have and has never had anything to do with the award) to their star Vinicius Jr, who finished second in the vote behind Euros winner and English champion Rodri of Manchester City. 'Real Madrid does not go where it is not respected,' they thundered. If they only knew.

My own role consisted of finding suitable jury members for various exotic locations and establishing contact with English clubs whose players were in contention, which was the rule rather than the exception during that period. Should the eventual winner be one of them, I'd serve as a liaison officer, as happened in 2008, when I spent a surreal few days with two colleagues of mine in the company of Cristiano Ronaldo and his agent Jorge Mendes in Manchester. We had all taken different routes to rendezvous there to avoid raising suspicion. It was only when we were in situ that we were allowed to unseal the envelope containing our instructions, jumped in a car and headed for the player's residence somewhere off a dark country lane in the Alderley Edge footballers' belt.

My abiding memory of our stay is our then-editor Denis Chaumier showing the trophy to an emotional Ronaldo for the first time, and how broken-hearted the young man was when he was told that he couldn't display it in his trophy room yet: we had to bring his Ballon d'Or back to Paris. It would only be his for good when the official presentation took place in early December. The scale of his disappointment showed us how deeply he cared. According to Denis, it was the kind of reaction he had come to expect from all of the laureates after years of taking care of the award, with the exception of one: Kevin Keegan (1978, 1979), who cannot remember where he stored his two trophies, which may be the most Keeganesque thing about one of football's oddest characters.

Michael Owen (2001) mounted his on a revolving pedestal at the centre of the memorabilia room of his Chester home. It is lit from multiple angles, illuminated like a Brancusi bronze would be in a Bond Street gallery. 'This is something no-one can ever take away from me,' he said when showing me around. 'That one year, I was judged to be the best footballer in the world.' Winners of the Champions League or even the World Cup are custodians who, like boxing champs whose belt is up for grabs at every fight, will relinquish their title one day. Ballon d'Or winners and Olympic champions have this in common: the award is theirs to keep for life and, beyond life, in history. Igor Ivanovich Belanov (1986), the striker of Valeriy Lobanovskyi's luminous Dynamo Kyiv side of the 1980s, enlisted in the Ukrainian army at the age of 62 after the Russian invasion and takes his trophy to the trenches on the front line to inspire his fellow soldiers. George Best (1968) made £167,250 from the trophy he auctioned in 2003 when he owned nothing else which could be sold, but was overjoyed when, two years later, I told him that a replica would be presented to him in Paris on the occasion of the fiftieth Ballon d'Or award ceremony, for which I would be his chaperone. I still have the official invitation I couldn't hand out to him as, only a few days after we met in Chelsea, he was admitted to Cromwell Hospital, where he died of multiple organ failure four weeks later. An empty seat was left at the table where he should have sat with Bobby Charlton and Denis Law, Eusébio and Giacinto Facchetti, my friend and colleague Jean-Michel Brochen and I acting as starstruck hosts and translators. All of them, our childhood heroes, are now gone. Of all the great nights I owe football, this will always remain the most memorable, the most precious, and the saddest. The Ballon d'Or matters. Kylian Mbappé agrees. The 'project' will not be completed until his name is engraved on the trophy.

In 2018, still a few months shy of his twentieth birthday, but already a world champion and the top goalscorer for the national team as well as in Ligue 1 that calendar year, Kylian confessed he had hopes to improve on the seventh place he'd been given in the previous season's poll. 'I have put all the ingredients [*sic*] on my side to win it,' he said. 'I've done everything I could do, until the day the voting closed. Whatever happens, I will have no regrets. That's the objective, year after year – to progress, to go as high as possible every single time.' He was well aware of the criteria which members of the panel take into account when they make their choices: they do not just pick a winner, but rank the five players they think have been the most deserving of the award. Results are paramount. As 2018 had been a World Cup year, Mbappé stood an outside chance, as, on the French side, did that tournament's Silver Boot Antoine Griezmann and its outstanding defender Raphaël Varane, also a Champions League winner with Real Madrid. Kylian had been the undoubted star of the competition's most exhilarating match, France's 4–3 win over Lionel Messi's Argentina in the round of 16. Early on in the game, he outpaced half of the Albiceleste on a one-man counter-attack, only to be fouled just inside the box by Marcos Rojo as he homed in on Franco Armani's goal; Griezmann scored the resulting penalty. Argentina could not cope with Mbappé; that afternoon in Kazan, no other team under the sun could have. A similar explosion of pace left for dead the two Nicoláses, Otamendi and Tagliafico, who had no other option than to send him flying – but this time, inches outside of the box. His two second-half goals, the first one scored with the left foot, the second with his right, meeting Olivier Giroud's perfectly weighted through-pass without pausing to control the ball, left Argentina with a two-goal gap they could not quite close. As Kylian himself put it, 'I was given the chance to put my mark on history' – and he took it; but this was not quite enough. It was Varane's club team-mate Luka Modrić of losing finalists Croatia who was presented with the trophy. It was the first time since 2007 (Kaká of European champions Milan was the winner that year) that it had not been given to one of Cristiano Ronaldo or Lionel Messi, who had spent a whole decade playing their own personal game of Ballon d'Or snap.

Only once did Kylian come closer to receive it himself, in 2023, when he finished third behind Messi and Norway's goalscoring phenomenon Erling Haaland, who'd found the net 52 times in 53 games for Manchester City. He could blame Fifa's decision to move the Qatar World Cup to November and December for that. Though the trophy is awarded in view of performances over a calendar year, the timing of the vote precluded the judges from taking that tournament into account in the 2022 poll, as the final was played on 18 December in Doha. Irony of ironies, the trophy went to another Frenchman, Karim Benzema, who was back in Deschamps's good books after a five-year exclusion from the national team, but had been prevented from taking part in that World Cup because of a thigh injury and announced his international retirement the day after Argentina avenged themselves of their 2018 defeat to Les Bleus. Given the circumstances, it was hard to begrudge Benzema his Ballon d'Or. His record of 15 goals in 12 games had taken Real Madrid to their fourteenth European Cup or Champions League – his personal fifth. He had also played a key part in their La Liga triumph, thirteen points ahead of Barcelona, and added the Supercopa de España, the UEFA Super Cup and the Fifa Club World Cup to his list of honours that year – a year which, as far as the Ballon d'Or is concerned, had finished before what was supposed to be its crowning moment, too early for Kylian's hopes to be fulfilled.

'Is the Ballon d'Or the goal of a career? It depends,' he had told *L'Équipe* TV a year earlier. 'As to me, yes, of course, I want to win one, or several. There is a process to follow for that, but I think I am on course. I think that if you want to win it, you first must win the Champions League.' In another ironic twist, the club he joined in order to fill that gap in his *palmarès*, perennial favourites Real Madrid, fell to Arsenal in the quarter-finals of the 2024–25 edition after struggling to fight off Atlético de Madrid in the previous round, Kylian failing to score in any of those four games; while the club he had left, PSG, finally won it, and its chief goalscorer, his friend Ousmane Dembélé, became the fifth French player to receive the Ballon d'Or, after Kopa, Platini, Zidane and Benzema.

Mbappé still made the top ten (he finished seventh, just behind another PSG player he is close to, Achraf Hakimi), as he has done every single year since 2017, a record unmatched by any of his contemporaries. Consistency is not enough, however. 'You first must win trophies,' he said after scoring two penalties in Real Madrid's 2–1 win over Marseille in the Champions League, one week before Dembélé received the trophy. 'All I have to do is help my team win trophies. I don't think I break a taboo if I say that, if I have a successful year,

I will win the Ballon d'Or as well. Is it in the back of my mind? Of course. It's in the back of every player's mind. But the only trophy I can have a [direct] impact on is the Golden Boot' – which rewards Europe's most potent goalscorer after the strength of the respective leagues is taken into account, and which he won in 2024–25 for the first time. Some consolation, I suppose; but no consolation goal, if you'll forgive the play on words.

Not all Ballon d'Or winners have been greats of the game. Allan Simonsen of Borussia Mönchengladbach can be considered lucky to have been the recipient of the trophy in 1977, a fallow year in which there were no stand-out candidates, though Kevin Keegan and Michel Platini, who came second and third in the poll, a whisker behind the Danish winger, may have thought otherwise. But a case can be made that – almost – all the greats of the game who qualified for the award, which only considered non-European players from 1995 onwards, when Liberian striker George Weah won it, have been Ballons d'Or. There are a handful of exceptions. Thierry Henry deserved it more in the eyes of many, myself included, than Juventus midfielder Pavel Nedved in 2003, and Steven Gerrard would have made for a very popular winner in 2005. That Mohammed Salah never even made the top three, unlike Virgil van Dijk who did once, in 2019, is unfathomable. Yet, read through the list, and here they all are, players who, almost to a man, were blessed with what we perceive as greatness, the Eusébios, Cruyffs and van Bastens. Does Kylian Mbappé belong in that kind of company, the company he so clearly wants to keep? Goals and titles are a must, yet not enough – think of Raúl, who scored and won plenty in his sixteen years at Real Madrid, a club legend no doubt, but who lacked that special something which his team-mate Fernando Redondo possessed. More is needed: an element of mystique, a degree of romance, a suggestion of jeopardy, qualities which are bestowed on a select few but which have yet to be associated with Kylian Mbappé, and which no 'project' or no measure of control can conjure. Exercising control, in fact, has the opposite effect. Control acts as an insurance against failure, when the possibility of failure heightens the eventual achievement. One day, perhaps as soon as this year, Mbappé may well win the Champions League title which he still lacks, but it will be with Real Madrid, for whom it is no dream, but a recurrent exercise of their God-given right, achieved through stockpiling the most expensive talent available. Had he won it with Paris Saint-Germain, who went from disappointment to disaster to catastrophe in Europe while he was there – well, I would be telling a very different story. Many PSG fans felt he was abandoning ship when the long-awaited move to Real took place, an unfair judgement in view of all that Mbappé had done for their club. One thing they got right, however, was that PSG was always meant to be the penultimate stop in the glory trip to Madrid, not the final destination.

What made Michel Platini France's greatest was not only the 1984 Euros victory in the Parc des Princes, but what had happened before that: the penalty wrongly given to Argentina in the 1978 World Cup, when it looked as if the hosts could fall to a young, thrilling French team; Harald Schumacher's unpunished assault on Patrick Battiston in Sevilla, 1982, when the French captain held the hand of his team-mate when he was stretchered off the field. What happened afterwards too: the 1986 World Cup, a sublime game of football against Zico's Brazil in the quarter-finals and West Germany, again, blocking the way to what would have been Les Bleus' first-ever final in that competition. Mbappé has known failure with Les Bleus, most notably at the 2020 and 2024 Euros; but these failures had nothing glorious or heroic about them. France, among the favourites in both tournaments, had been a painful watch, and Kylian well below his best on both occasions. Les Bleus deserved what came to them, and good riddance, said the rest of the world. Being flawed is fine. Being just plain bad is not. I'm not so sure the French would revere Zinédine Zidane as much as they do if he hadn't headbutted Marco Materazzi in the 2006 World Cup final. We prefer our heroes that way. Or is it that 'prefer', here, should be used in the past tense?

There is no translation of the French adjective *lisse* into English which conveys what it means when applied to a person's character or public persona. 'Smooth' won't do, and neither will 'slick' or 'sleek'. Smoothness, slickness and sleekness come into it, but miss the essential point: in that context, the word primarily refers to the lack of visible asperities which one can hang onto to relate to the person in question, to develop an emotional attachment which may be one-sided, but is no less fervent for that – the kind of attachment I felt for Eric Cantona and, when all was said and done, for Thierry Henry, and which I struggle to find when it comes to Kylian Mbappé. Respect, admiration and gratitude are not substitutes. This would not matter if I were the only one to feel that way, but I am not. The very nature of the 'project' has seen to that. The irresistible playfulness of the teenage Mbappé has gone. The 'shrimp' of Monaco has grown into a superb athlete who no longer looks like he's playing in the wrong age category. He is in many ways suited to an age in which the experience of football has been increasingly fragmented and de-materialised, in which slow can no longer be beautiful and cameras jitter and fidget to give an illusion of urgency. Rio Ferdinand exclaiming 'skills!' on TV. Pre-game, fast-edited showreels in which every ball must end up in the top corner. Match reports illustrated by spectacular photographs which bear no relation to what happened on the pitch. I have a particular one in mind here, an action shot of Kylian attempting a scissor-kick a metre off the ground which was used by *Der Spiegel* above their account of the Real Madrid–Marseille game I mentioned earlier, suggesting that it had been a scintillating affair in which the French acrobat had shone more brightly than anyone, when he had shinned the ball into Row Z of the Santiago Bernabéu. Kylian's game lends itself naturally to this type of gamification, in which players become increasingly undifferentiated from their digital avatars and 'connecting' with them means plugging a charging cable into your mobile phone. He hasn't programmed himself that way: he is a natural fit in an age of unnaturalness. He and his 'project' chime with our time, in which affect matters less than instant effect, that is all.

But could the 'Mbappé project' be successfully replicated by, say, Lamine Yamal or Désiré Doué, the two teenagers whom he is often compared with today? Both are in some respects ahead of where Kylian was at their age, Yamal in terms of early impact and Doué in his all-round game. The parallel with Doué is particularly striking. Like Kylian, Désiré comes from a mixed-race family; like Kylian's father Wilfrid, Doué's father Moho was born in French-speaking Africa, the Ivory Coast in his case, while his white mother comes from the Loire valley. Like Kylian, he joined a club known for its remarkable record in identifying and nurturing exceptional talent: Mbappé went to Monaco, Doué to Stade Rennais, where current French internationals like Real Madrid's Eduardo Camavinga, PSG's Ousmane Dembélé and Tottenham Hotspur's Mathys Tel all signed their first professional contracts; and like Mbappé, his next step was a move to PSG, if at a lower price (€50 million) than Mbappé's record transfer to the perennial French champions. Like Kylian,

Désiré exploded onto the scene on the Champions League stage, the former in AS Monaco's run to the semi-finals in 2017–18, the latter in even more spectacular fashion, scoring two goals and assisting another in PSG's 5–0 annihilation of Internazionale in the 2025 final, earning himself a Player of the Match award as well as a place in UEFA's European XI of the year and a ten out of ten rating in *L'Équipe*, a score which only eighteen other players had been given previously in the history of the paper. He followed that by being voted the outstanding player in Fifa's 2025 Club World Cup. Like Kylian in the 2017 Euros, Désiré was the key player in France winning the U17 European title in 2022, graduating to the French Olympic team – silver medallists in the 2024 Paris Games – then to the senior side in a matter of months: Didier Deschamps simply could not ignore such a phenomenal talent any more than he could have left Mbappé out after his performances for France's youth teams and the Monégasques. Like Kylian, Désiré had been guided all along by his father Moho and, if anything, his family's football pedigree is even more impressive than Mbappé's. While Kylian was inspired by the example of his elder brother Jirès – another Stade Rennais product, as it happens – Désiré followed in the footsteps of his sibling Guéla, his senior by two-and-a-half years, who chose to represent Ivory Coast at international level and currently plays right-back at RC Strasbourg. His cousin Yann Gboho, also capped by the Ivory Coast, also trained at Stade Rennais, joined Ligue 1's Toulouse FC last summer, while another cousin, Ambroise Gboho, recently signed for Luxembourg's top division club FC Swift Hesperange. Uncle Désiré Doué Normandiez, the 2011 African referee of the year, completes an impressive collection of footballing relatives. So is there, or could there be a 'Doué project' taking its cue from the way Mbappé, his family and his advisors defined and controlled his trajectory?

The plain answer is no; there isn't, and there couldn't be. Doué's ascent was unprogrammed, absurdly fast, and surprised some of the coaches who looked after him in his boyhood and his teenage years, whereas Kylian was 'one to follow' from the age of 8. They loved Doué's attitude ('he's a dream to work with,' Rennes's manager Bruno Génésio said of him when he joined the senior squad), warmed to his sunny personality, thought he had what it takes to make a career out of football, but did not expect him to become 'the next Kylian'. At the age of 20, Doué has yet to endorse a single sponsor, whereas Mbappé became a Nike athlete at 8. His family has stepped back from the management of his affairs, entrusting them to London-based agent Moussa Sissoko, whom he was introduced to by his PSG team-mate Ousmane Dembélé. No 'Doué' trademark has been registered with WIPO yet, though it must only be a question of time until someone insists he takes advantage of a family name which means 'gifted' in French. Searches for companies associated with him or his family yield no results. If there is a 'project' at work, it is all about football and, for the time being at least, football only.

Lamine Yamal's case is different and, at least superficially, closer to the Mbappé model: the young Spaniard, who only turned 18 in July 2025, has trademarked his name and endorsed over half a dozen brands over the past couple of years. Two companies, L.Y. Sports Management, S.L. and LY304 FC, have been set up by his lawyer Alejandro Liotta to look after his image rights. A marketing firm called The Underdogs, founded by one Bernardo San Torcuato, takes care of his social media accounts, communication and promotional campaigns. The – crucial – difference is that Yamal himself does not have anything like the measure of control over his own affairs which Mbappé was given by his parents from an early age. The Underdogs, for example, is a subsidiary of Gestifute, the company founded and fully owned by super-agent and Cristiano Ronaldo mentor Jorge Mendes, who poached the Barcelona prodigy from former player-turned representative Ivan de la Peña when he broke through the ranks at Barça's academy. It is Mendes who calls the shots, it is Mendes who picked the team which looks after his charge's interests. Yamal's close relatives remain present in his everyday life but play no part in the management of his career. His cousin Mohamed Abde serves as his chauffeur and companion, alongside childhood friend 'Souhaib', and that is as far as the family involvement goes. There was no 'Yamal Project', and there could not be. His father Mounir left home when he was a toddler. His mother Sheila worked in a McDonald's. The Rocafonda neighbourhood where the boy grew up was as tough as they come. There were no private tutors for the young Lamine, no trips to Dubai for the summer holidays, no electric cars for Christmas, only a Barça scarf which had been given to him by his mother and which accompanied him everywhere. There was no plan, only a prodigious raw talent whose stroke of luck was to attract the attention of the FC Barcelona youth coaches and to be given a new home, La Masia de Can Planes, the academy where he soon flourished like no other academy student since Lionel Messi. The rest – the contracts, the businesses, the advertisements – followed in due course; not so for Kylian, whose future was mapped before his voice had broken. This is not to belittle what Kylian has achieved and will achieve in years to come, the just reward of talent, ambition and far-sightedness; more to reflect that, while there could not have been an 'Mbappé project' in another, not-so-distant era, there may not be another one in ours. The planets smiled on him and aligned like a guard of honour, but he still had to walk the walk, take care of the most difficult part and deliver what was expected of him on the football field; off it too, sacrificing what most of us take for granted, starting with childhood and, later, privacy.

He is only halfway there; in fact, probably not that far yet. Plenty of boxes remain unticked: the Champions League, the European Championships, the Ballon d'Or he so craves. When the time comes to dress up in a suit rather than in shirt and shorts, and not just to visit the Elysée and attend award ceremonies, the player will reinvent himself as a manager, or a club owner, or a businessman. There will be a plan for that, as there's been a plan for everything else. He will be unique. No two players are alike. There is only one Kylian Mbappé, and this is how it will remain.

Kylian Mbappé Milestones

1998
20 December: Born in the 19th arrondissement of Paris.

2004
Joins US Bondy, age 5.

2006
First sponsorship contract, with Nike.

2011
Joins the Institut National du Football, Clairefontaine.
Has a trial at Chelsea in the spring and is invited to come back for a second one. His mother Fayza turns down the offer.

2012
16 December: Invited by Real Madrid, he and his family watch Cristiano Ronaldo score at the Santiago Bernabéu stadium. After a very short trial, the Mbappés turn down the offer of a place at Real's academy.

2013

Joins the academy of AS Monaco.

2014

First international call-up, with France U17 team.

2015

Debuts in Ligue 1 as a late substitute against SM Caen on 2 December.

2016

20 February: Scores his first Ligue 1 goal for AS Monaco, against Troyes.

6 March: Signs his first professional contract with Monaco.

24 March: Makes his debut for France U19 against Montenegro, and scores his first international goal at any level two days later, against Denmark.

21 May: Wins the Coupe Gambardella (Youth Cup) with Monaco, scoring twice in the final.

24 July: Crowned U19 European champion. Scores five goals in five games and is named in the UEFA 'Team of the Tournament'. Passes his baccalauréat in management studies, at the second attempt.

27 September: Makes his Champions League debut for Monaco in a group game against Bayer Leverkusen, as a late substitute.

2017

21 February: Scores his first Champions League goal in a 3–5 away defeat to Manchester City.

25 March: Capped by France at senior level for the first time, coming on as a late substitute in a World Cup qualifier against Luxemburg.

17 May: Crowned French champion with ASM, finishing Ligue 1's fifth-best goalscorer.

14 June: Becomes an official sponsor of children's charity Premiers de Cordée, which has received all of his France appearance bonuses since.

30 August: Files registration requests for his name and his goal celebration with the European trademark organisation EUIPO.

31 August: Joins Paris Saint-Germain on loan (with automatic buy-out clause). Scores his first senior international goal for France (against the Netherlands) the same day.

7 September: Plays his first game and scores his first goal for PSG in a 5–1 win over FC Metz.

12 September: Makes his European debut for PSG and scores, against Celtic.

23 October: Receives the Golden Boy award for the most promising young player in Europe. Makes his first appearance in the Ballon d'Or top ten, in seventh place.

2018

21 February: Invited by French president Emmanuel Macron to the Elysée Palace for the first time.

31 March: Wins the first of his twelve major trophies with PSG, being chosen as 'Man of the Match' in the League Cup final, a 3–0 win over his former club Monaco.

15 July: Wins the Fifa World Cup with France in Moscow, having scored 5 goals in the tournament, including 1 in the final won 4–2 by the French against Croatia.

7 October: Scores the first quadruple of his professional career, in the space of thirteen minutes, when PSG beat Lyon 5–0 in Ligue 1

at the Parc des Princes. Chosen as the 2018 World Cup's 'Young Player of the Tournament' by Fifa.

4 December: Awarded the Kopa Trophy, given by the Ballon d'Or jury to 'the best under-21 player in the world'.

31 December: Receives the Légion d'honneur from president Macron, alongside his World Cup-winning French team-mates.

2019

23 February: Becomes the youngest player in Ligue 1 history to reach 50 goals at 20 years, two months and one day. Tops the Ligue 1 goalscoring charts for the first time, with 33 goals in 29 games.

19 May: Voted France's 'Best Young Player' and 'Player of the Year' by his peers.

10 October: His foundation Inspired by KM is launched.

2020

In early March, COVID puts a premature end to the Ligue 1 season, with PSG crowned champions and Mbappé finishing top scorer once again.

23 August: Plays his first Champions League final, which PSG lose 0–1 to Bayern Munich.

5 December: Reaches the 100-goal mark for PSG (in all competitions) in a 3–1 victory over Montpellier.

2021

28 June: Misses France's last of five attempts in the penalty shoot-out against Switzerland in the COVID-delayed Euro 2020 round of 16.

10 October: Scores in France's 2–1 victory over Spain in the UEFA Nations League final, his second trophy with Les Bleus, and is awarded the tournament's Golden Boot by UEFA.

11 November: Publication of *Je m'appelle Kylian*, the self-published autobiographical graphic account of his career so far, which sells a quarter of a million copies in France.

2022

21 May: Signs a vastly improved new two-year contract (with the option of an extra year) with PSG and celebrates it with a hat-trick against FC Metz on the same day.

24 June: Announcement of a partnership between Mbappé's newly created US company Zebra Valley and the National Basketball Association (NBA).

18 December: Plays in his second World Cup final, lost on penalties to Argentina. Scores a hat-trick in this game, finishing the tournament with eight goals and the Fifa World Cup Golden Boot trophy.

2023

4 March: Becomes PSG's all-time greatest goalscorer, with 201 goals so far, after scoring in a 4–2 win over FC Nantes at the Parc des Princes.

20 March: Named captain of the France national team (on a permanent basis) by manager Didier Deschamps.

Early July: travels to his father Wilfrid's native country Cameroon and visits two schools which have been part-financed by his Inspired by KM foundation.

21 July: PSG manager excludes Mbappé from pre-season touring team after the announcement by the player that he would not stay at the club beyond June 2024: The player is reintegrated at the start of the season proper.

30 October: Finishes third in the Ballon d'Or vote, his highest ranking so far.

2024

10 May: Confirms that he will not activate his one-year contract extension clause and will depart PSG at the end of the season.

25 May: Plays his last game for PSG, a 2–1 win over Lyon in the French Cup final.

1 June: Shares first place in UEFA Champions League goalscoring charts with Harry Kane of Bayern Munich (eight goals each).

3 June: Real Madrid announces that Mbappé has signed a five-year contract with them.

16 July: Presented to 80,000 fans at the Santiago Bernabéu stadium.

31 July: The sale of Stade Malherbe Caen to Mbappé's investment company Coalition Capital is announced.

14 August: Makes his debut for Real, scoring both goals in his team's 2–0 win against Atalanta in the UEFA Super Cup.

1 September: Scores his first two La Liga goals in a 2–0 victory over Real Betis.

2025

January: Voted La Liga's 'Player of the Month' for the first time.

26 May: Awarded the Pichichi award, given by *Marca* magazine to the top scorer in La Liga and wins the UEFA Golden Boot for the first time.

28 May: Voted Real Madrid's 'Player of the Season' and is included in La Liga's 'Team of the Season'.

29 July: Following the departure of Luka Modrić, Mbappé is awarded the number 10 shirt by the club.

13 November: On the tenth anniversary of the terrorist attacks which caused the death of 130 people in Paris, including at the Stade de France, scores his 56th and 57th goals for France in a 4–0 defeat of Ukraine which seals their qualification for the 2026 World Cup.

At the age of 26, Kylian reaches the 400 goals mark for club and country, a milestone previously attained by only two other French internationals, Karim Benzema (503) and Thierry Henry (411).

26 November: Becomes the first Real Madrid player to score a quadruple in a European competition for nearly ten years, netting all of his team's goals in a 4–3 victory over Greek champions Olympiacos.

Sources

All the statistics and data mentioned in this book were valid and correct as of 1 December 2025. Quotes were taken from hundreds of secondary sources, far too numerous to be mentioned in full here. Those that provided the greatest wealth of original material deserve to be mentioned, however, starting with the series of six articles ('Promo 98') written by Rémi Dupré and Henri Seckel for *Le Monde* in October 2011 that provided unique insight into the life of Kylian Mbappé and his fellow scholars at the Institut National du Football at Clairefontaine. *Personne ne peut vous interdire de rêver*, a collection of interviews with Kylian Mbappé, his friends and family, which were originally published in *L'Equipe* and *France Football* in 2017 and 2018, was published in book format by *L'Equipe* and Editions Solar in May 2019. No newspaper, not even *L'Equipe*, followed Kylian's career as closely as *Le Parisien*, to which his mother Fayza Lamari gave two in-depth interviews of particular interest. The first, in which she answered questions put to her by readers of the daily, was conducted by Frédéric Gouaillard, Arnaud Detout, Dominique Sévérac and Laurent Perrin and published on 6 October 2021. The second was conducted by Stéphane Bianchi and published on 17 July 2024. As

Kylian Mbappé's lawyer Delphine Verheyden hardly ever gives interviews, the conversation she had with Alexandre Mars for the *Pause* podcast in June 2022, as well as her exchanges with Barnabé Binctin for *Le Parisien* on 16 October 2021, and with Arnaud Huchet and Jean-Marcel Boudard for *Ouest-France* on 20 September 2022 were precious in this regard. Last, the 2018 documentary *Kylian Mbappé, hors normes*, directed by Sébastien Tarrago, Guillaume Dufy and Fabien Touati for L'Equipe TV, was invaluable in its account of the player's early years.

Books

France Football, *Kylian Mbappé: Personne ne peut vous interdire de rêver* (Solar, 2021)

Documentaries

'Kylian Mbappé, hors normes'. L'Equipe TV, 2018

Online articles

Arena, Stacie, 'Kylian Mbappé furax: ce jour où sa mère lui a fait "perdre 6 millions d'euros"'. Published on Femme Actuelle (18 January 2024) www.femmeactuelle.fr/actu/news-actu/kylian-mbappe-furax-ce-jour-ou-sa-mere-lui-a-fait-perdre-six-millions-deuros-2121003

Auger, Constance, 'Neymar a répondu aux accusations de viol et révèle avoir été violent à la demande de son accusatrice'. Published on *Closer* magazine (14 June 2019) www.closermag.

fr/people/neymar-a-repondu-aux-accusations-de-viol-et-revele-avoir-ete-violent-a-la-demand-982044

Chaillou, Clément, 'PSG: pourquoi les retrouvailles entre Mbappé et l'entraîneur de Pau risquent d'être tendues'. Published on RMC Sport (20 January 2020) https://rmcsport.bfmtv.com/football/coupe-de-france/psg-pourquoi-les-retrouvailles-entre-mbappe-et-l-entraineur-de-pau-risquent-d-etre-tendues_AV-202001200370.html

Davies, Rob. 'British gambling regulator prosecutes Sorare football game'. Published on *The Guardian* (26 September 2024) www.theguardian.com/business/2024/sep/26/british-gambling-regulator-prosecutes-sorare-football-game

Demarle, Xavier, 'Révélations sur les comptes très inquiétants de Sorare, l'ex-star de la French Tech'. Published on L'Informé (12 June 2025) www.linforme.com/tech-telecom/article/revelations-sur-les-comptes-tres-inquietants-de-sorare-l-ex-star-de-la-french-tech_2943.html

Dupré, Remi and Secke, Henri, 'Les yeux dans les petits Bleus'. Published on *Le Monde* (13 October 2011) www.lemonde.fr/sport/article/2011/10/13/les-yeux-dans-les-petits-bleus_1587358_3242.html

Eurosport, 'Officiel: Kylian Mbappé signe au PSG'. Published on Eurosport (31 August 2017) https://www.eurosport.fr/football/ligue-1/2017-2018/officiel-kylian-mbappe-signe-au-psg_sto6311912/story.shtml

Georges, Alain, 'Le PSG prêt à verser 25 millions d'euros au Real Madrid pour un défenseur?' Published on Real Madrid Actu (29 May 2025) https://realmadridactu.com/2025/05/29/le-psg-pret-a-verser-25-millions-deuros-au-real-madrid-pour-un-defenseur/

Gouaillard, Frédéric; Detout, Arnaud; Sévérac, Dominique and Laurent Perrin, 'Sa famille, l'avenir de son fils, l'argent: les confessions de Fayza Lamari, mère de Kylian Mbappé'. Published on *Le Parisien* (6 October 2021) www.leparisien.fr/sports/football/psg/sa-famille-lavenir-de-son-fils-largent-les-confessions-de-fayza-lamari-mere-de-kylian-mbappe-06-10-2021-24OQERZEIVFQJJ7QYFES6WRFRE.php

Holyman, Ian, 'Jean-Kevin Augustin faces punishment for refusing France under-21 call-up'. Published on ESPN (12 September 2018) www.espn.com/soccer/story/_/id/37561556/jean-kevin-augustin-faces-punishment-refusing-france-21-call-up,%20for%20example.

Huchet, Arnaud and Jean-Michel Boudard, 'PORTRAIT. Mbappé, Mayer, Fourcade . . . L'avocate Delphine Verheyden façonne l'image des champions'. Published on *Ouest France* (20 September 2022) www.ouest-france.fr/sport/football/kylian-mbappe/rencontre-delphine-verheyden-l-avocate-de-kylian-mbappe-qui-faconne-l-image-des-champions-eac90a02-37ff-11ed-8ce0-a7ed58f597f6

Hytner, David, 'Benoît Assou-Ekotto: "I play for the money. Football's not my passion"'. Published on *The Guardian* (1 May 2010) www.theguardian.com/football/2010/may/01/benoit-assou-ekotto-tottenham-hotspur

L'Equipe, 'L'avocate pénaliste de Kylian Mbappé dénonce une campagne de dénigrement'. Published 16 October 2024 www.lequipe.fr/Football/Actualites/L-avocate-penaliste-de-kylian-mbappe-denonce-une-campagne-de-denigrement/1514048

Le Figaro, 'Ligue des nations: Un comportement de starlettes, le coup de gueule de Maignan dans les vestiaires après la défaite des Bleus'. Published 7 September 2024 www.lefigaro.fr/sports/football/ligue-des-nations/ligue-des-nations-un-comportement-de-starlettes-le-coup-de-gueule-de-maignan-dans-les-vestiaires-apres-la-defaite-des-bleus-20240907

Le Gall, Aymeric, 'Mes parents m'ont envoyé en France pour que j'ai une meilleure vie'. Published on So Foot (22 March 2016) www.sofoot.com/articles/mes-parents-mont-envoye-en-france-pour-que-jai-une-meilleure-vie-emirats-al-nasr-interview-jires-kembo-ekoko

Mallais, Hugo, 'Kylian Mbappé a passé sept ans au Conservatoire, sa professeure raconte: "Il voulait toujours jouer en premier!"' Published on *Télé 7 Jours* (22 December 2022) www.programme-television.org/news/musique/artistes/kylian-mbappe-a-passe-sept-ans-au-conservatoire-sa-professeure-raconte-il-voulait-toujours-jouer-en-premier-4699717#google_vignette

Mathers, Daniel, 'Paris' Uneasy Relationship with Mbappe: He could fire France to World Cup glory again, but in his home city some feel he embodies football's grubby side of greed and excess' Published on the *Daily Mail* (8 December 2022) www.

dailymail.co.uk/sport/football/article-11518059/Kylian-Mbappe-fire-France-World-Cup-glory-Paris-feel-embodies-greed-excess.html

France Info 'Quand Kylian Mbappé a failli signer au RC Lens'. Published on France Info (7 November 2017) https://france3-regions.franceinfo.fr/hauts-de-france/quand-kylian-mbappe-failli-signer-au-rc-lens-1361221.html

Sévérac, Dominique, 'Kylian Mbappé, une étoile est née'. Published on *Le Parisien* (21 July 2018) www.leparisien.fr/sports/football/kylian-mbappe-une-etoile-est-nee-21-07-2018-7828908.php?ts=1763465820347

Tassel, Victor; Gouaillard, Frédéric and Detout, Arnaud, 'Sur les traces de Kylian Mbappé à Bondy, la ville de son enfance'. Published on *Le Parisien* (17 October 2018) www.leparisien.fr/sports/football/sur-les-traces-de-kylian-mbappe-a-bondy-la-ville-de-son-enfance-17-10-2018-7920855.php

Index

Note: page numbers in *italics* indicate images

Abidal, Eric, 207
Abramovich, Roman, 143
Accor hotel chain, 107, 116–17
Afflelou, Alain, 95
Aftonbladet newspaper, 193, 197–8, 200
Agence France-Presse, 230, 232
Agent de Sportifs: Pleins feux sur une profession en développement (Verheyden), 91
Ahmad, Ahmad, 160
Al Jazeera Sport, 126
Al-Khelaifi, Nasser, *121*, 124, 126–8, 140, 143–5, 148–50, 167, 173, 177–80
Al Thani, Hamad bin Jassim, 128
Al Thani, Sheikh Tamim bin Hamad, 127–8, 167
Alcaraz, Carlos, 111
Algeria national team, 67, 118
Alonso, Xabi, 234
Amoros, Manuel, 80
Ancelotti, Carlo, 20, 125, 194
Ancón, Peru, 118
Anelka, Nicolas, 67, 133, 207

Anquetil, Jacques, 90
Antonetti, Frédéric, 35, 97
Arconada, Luis, 208
Aréola, Alphonse, 125
Argentina national team, 166, 237, 258–9
Arles Avignon FC, 82
Armani, Franco, 259
Arsenal FC, 83
AS Bondy, 7, 19, 23, 34, *39*, 42, 55
AS Monaco, 7, 18, 79–86, 113
  Mbappé's transfer to PSG, 123–5, 129–31, 161
Assini (Mbappé company), 99, 109
L'Assomption de Bondy school, 58–9
Assou-Ekotto, Benoît, 51
Augustin, Jean-Kévin, 22–3, 26

Bale, Gareth, 130
Ballon d'Or, 10, 23, 133, *253*, 255–63
Baltazar, Bruno, 244–5, 247
Barcelona FC, 53, 129
Barcola, Bradley, 220, 234
Barthez, Fabien, 158

INDEX

Bassette, Norman, 247
Batelli, Ludovic, 24–6
Bath, Neil, 19
Battiston, Patrick, 262
Beckenbauer, Franz, 206
Beckham, David, 125–6, 242
Belanov, Igor, 257
Bellerin, Hector, 242
Bellingham, Jude, 183, 220
Ben Yedder, Wissam, 149
Benalla, Alexandre, 163, 164n
Benna, Ziyed, 43
Benzema, Karim, 113, 130, 147, 259–60
Bertrand, Jean-Jacques, 90–91
Best, George, 5, 135, 257–8
BFM-TV, 199, 201
Bielsa, Marcelo, 23
Blacquard, François, 67
Blanc, Laurent, 65, 66, 68, 73, 83, 125, 158, 207–8, 230
Bocanegra, Carlos, 35
Boga, Daniel, 19
Boga, Jérémie, 19
Bognini, Céline, 59
Boli, Basile, 159
Bolt, Usain, 107
Bondy, France, 41–7, 61
  see also AS Bondy
Bordeaux FC, 77, 250
Bowie, David, 191
Boyd, William, 191
Brahimi, Bilal, 246
Briand, Jimmy, 35
Brochen, Jean-Michel, 258
Buffon, Gianluigi, 140

Caballero, Willy, 98
Cabaye, Yohann, 125, 208
Cabinet Flechner (patent lawyer), 100
Caen see Stade Malherbe Caen
Camara, Souleymane, 79, 80
Camavinga, Eduardo, 264

Cameroon, 67, 118
Campos, Lúis, 82–3, 89, 149
Canal+, 53–4, 127
Le Canard enchaîné, 163
Cantona, Eric, x–xi, 90–91, 158, 229, 263
Canu-Bernard, Marie-Alix, 95, 195n, 199–201
captaincy, 205–21
Capton, Pierre-Antoine, 242
'Carlito' (social media influencer), 165–6
Carragher, Jamie, 206
Casillas, Iker, 208
Cavani, Edinson, 83, 125, 130, 136, 140
Cazarre, Julien, 140, 146
Cazorla, Santi, 242
Chamalières, France, 157
Champel, Eric, 127–8
Champions League, 84, 98, 129, 131, 136, 140, 145, 147, 174, 183, 184, 225, 260
  2024–25: 233
Charlton, Bobby, 258
Chaumier, Denis, 256–7
Chelsea FC, 18–19, 143
Cherki, Rayan, 89
Chevalier, Lucas, 209
Chilavert, José-Luis, 206
child football training camps, 52–3
Chirac, Jacques, 158–9, 162
Clairefontaine National Football Centre, 34, 59, 65–73, 78–9, 156, 227
  l'affaire des quotas and, 65–7
Clay, Thomas, 181, 183
Clichy, Gaël, 252
Clique (TV programme), 202
Club World Cup, 183, 233
Coalition Capital, 114–16, 243, 251
Cognard, Jean-Rémi, 91
Collective Motion, 110
Collège Catherine de Vivonne, Rambouillet, 72
Coman, Kingsley, 125, 166

INDEX

Compton, Denis, 5
Coulibaly, Amedy, 199
Les Coulisses d'une victoire (documentary), 160
Coupe de France, 136, 177
Coupe Gambardella, 84
Courtois, Thibault, 147
COVID pandemic, 166
Croatia national team, 225, 227
Crowe, Martin, 135
Cruyff, Johan, 29, 135, 261
Cubillas, Téofilo, 29
Cultural Factory, 110

Daily Mail, 41–2
Daily Mirror, 205
Danso, Kevin, 216
De Gaulle, Charles, 155–6
De la Peña, Ivan, 267
Debouzze, Jamel, 133, 149
Delapierre, Quentin, 116
Dembélé, Moussa, 125
Dembélé, Ousmane, 132–3, 234, 260, 264, 266
Democratic Republic of Congo, 31–2
Der Spiegel, 264
Der Zakarian, Michel, 246–7
Deschamps, Didier, 86, 126, 162, 167, 175, 194, 200, 206, 209–16, 218–20, 225–6, 228, 232, 259, 265
Di María, Ángel, 83, 130, 141
Di Stéfano, Alfredo, 5, 66, 184
Diallo, Philippe, *121*
Diarra, Alou, 207
Digital Big Brother (DBB), 174
Digne, Lucas, 125
Diop, Issa, 26
Dior, 107, 117
Direction Technique Nationale, 65, 67
Djébalé, Cameroon, 44–5
Dobrage, Frédéric, 91
Domenech, Raymond, 207, 230

Donnarumma, Gigi, 145, 147
Doué, Désiré, 234, 264–6
Doué, Guéla, 265
Doué, Moua, 264–5
Doué Normandiez, Désiré, 265
Draxler, Julian, 130, 141
Drogba, Didier, 160, 206
Ducos, Françoise, 59
Dugarry, Christophe, 175–6
Duluc, Vincent, 118
Dumas, Franck, 78
Dunga (Carlos Verri), 104
Dupré, Rémi, 69, 71

EA Sports, 107
Edouard, Odsonne, 82
Edwards, Duncan, 5
Ejnès, Gérard, 128–9
Elysée Palace, 160, 162–4
Emery, Unai, 130, 141
Endeavor entertainment group, 111
Enrique, Luis, 142, 175–6
Envoyé Spécial (TV programme), 131, 150
L'Équipe newspaper, 54–5, 69, 85, 124, 149, 164, 174, 184, 186, 196, 207, 218, 226, 231, 265
Erdős, Éva, 48, 48
Eriksson, Sven-Göran, 206
Escalettes, Jean-Pierre, 228
Estanguet, Tony, 91
European Championships
 1984: 157, 262
 2016: 25–6, 162
 2020: 96, 99, 262
 2024: 169–70, 215–19
European Club Association (ECA), 127
Eusébio, 236, 258, 261
Expressen newspaper, 193, 197, 200–201

Fabinho (Fábio Henrique Tavares), 18, 125

285

INDEX

Fachetti, Giacinto, 258
Falcao, Radamel, 85, 125
Ferdinand, Rio, 263
Fifa, 127–8
    technical committee, 167, 209
    women and, 250
FLA (Mbappé company), 110
Fontaine, Just, 148
Fourcade, Marin, 91, 93
France
    French FA, 65–7, 180
    legislative elections (2024), 168–70
    Ligue 1, 84, 129, 136
    Ligue 2, 247–51
    national sports, 155–60, 168
    parental football obsession, 51–3
    see also France national team
France Football magazine, 17, 20, 255–6
La France Insoumise, 170, 227
France national team (Les Bleus), 42, 86, 162–3, 166–7, 184, 228–31
    captaincy, 206–21, 225–30
    France U23s (Les Bleuets), 66, 84
    Knysna scandal (2010), 207, 228–9, 231
    Mbappé's 'strike', 230–33
    sponsors, 230–32
Fraser, Jim, 19
French Football Federation (FFF), 228–33
Fuzier, Claude, 46

Gaddafi, Muammar, 159
Gadocha, Robert, 29
Gainsbourg, Serge, 59
Galtier, Christophe, 175
Gandini, Umberto, 127
Garande, Patrice, 78, 248
Gboho, Ambroise, 265
Gboho, Yann, 265
Génésio, Bruno, 266
Gerrard, Steven, 256, 261

Gérson (Gérson Santos da Silva), 29
Gestifute, 266–7
Ghazi, Bilel, 89
Gignac, André-Pierre, 207
Giha Brigneti, Maria Fe, 118
Ginola, David, 186
Giresse, Alain, 32
Giroud, Olivier, 184, 215, 217, 235, 237, 259
Giscard d'Estaing, Valéry, 156–7, 160
Giuntini, Jean-Claude, 82
Glaize, Laurent, 75, 78–9
Glazer, Jonathan, 191
Goldman, Patricia, 95, 198
Gomis, Tidiam, 248
Gonçalves Santos, Nadine, 106
Good Goût, 117, 231
Grace, W. G., 4–5
Greaves, Jimmy, 5
Griezmann, Antoine, 67, 114, 162, 175, *203*, 209, 211–15, 219–20, 235–7, 258–9
Groupe Scolaire Assomption, Bondy, 45
Guardiola, Pep, 3, 18
Guendouzi, Mattéo, 231
Guérin, Yann, 186
Gueye, Idrissa, 186

Haaland, Erling, 259
Habyarimana, Juvénal, 33
Hadlee, Richard, 135
Hakimi, Ashraf, 97, 145, 149, 260
Halys, Quentin, 47
Hammoud, Ziad, 243, 245–6, 249
handball, 47–8
Henry, Antoine, 55
Henry, Thierry, x–xi, 7, 18, 24, 55, 67, 80, 128, 186, 210, 228, 237, 252, 261, 263
Heskey, Emile, 206
Hollande, François, 159
Hountondji, Andréas, 247

286

INDEX

Hublot, 107, 116
Hurst, Geoff, 205, 209
Hurtis, Muriel, 47

Ibrahimović, Zlatan, 21, 83, 125–6, 136, 186
Ikoné, Jonathan, 47, 125
Ilanga, Mwepu, 30–32
Infantino, Gianni, 160, 183
L'Informé (investigative website), 115
Iniesta, Andrés, 193
Inspired by KM (IBKM) foundation, 116–19
Institut National du Football *see* Clairefontaine National Football Centre
Interconnected Ventures, 109–10, 112, 115, 118, 243
Intertoto Cup, 244
Irlès, Bruno, 80–82
Isco (Francisco Suárez), 130

Jacquet, Aimé, 159, 211
James, C.L.R., 5
Jardim, Leonardo, 17–18, 82, 84–5
Je m'appelle Kylian (book), 54, 118
Jean-Philippe, Clarissa, 199
'Jeremy' (bodyguard), 195
Johansson, Scarlett, 191
Jordan, Michael, 142
Journal de 20 heures (TV programme), 162
Journal du Dimanche newspaper, 210
Juventus FC, 6

Kaká (Ricardo Izecson dos Santos Leite), 259
Kang, Michelle, 250
Kanté, N'Golo, 225
Karanka, Aitor, 15–16
Karembeu, Adriana, 159
Karembeu, Christian, 159

Kassovitz, Mathieu, 41
Keegan, Kevin, 257, 261
Kembo Ekoko, Jirès, 19, 32–8, 45, 48, 70–71, 80, 265
Kembo, Jean Uba, 27, 31–2, 35
Kimmoun, Jean-Louis, 47
Kimpembé, Presnel, 175
Knysna scandal (2010), 207, 228–9, 231
Konaté, Ibrahima, 169, 225
Kopa, Raymond, 210, 236
Koundé, Jules, 169
Kovrig, Marie-Anne, 182–3
Krantz, Katrin, 200
Kvaratskhelia, Khvicha, 234
'Kylian Mbappé Lottin', 110

Labrune, Vincent, 180
Lacombe, Guy, 35
Lafargue, Jean-Claude, 69
Laffont, Perrine, 91
Lamari, Fayza, 19, 33, 38, 42, 45, 47–8, 86, 87, 193
  AS Monaco and, 83
  business affairs, 108–12
  IBKM and, 118–19
  Kylian's career and, 69, 72, 78–80, 89–90, 93–4, 99, 107–8, 131, 142, 148, 150
  Kylian's education and, 57–60
  Le Parisien interview, 96–9
  split with Wilfrid, 94
  Stade Malherbe Caen and, 249–50
Lamouchi, Sabri, 244
Lampard, Frank, 256
Larios, Jean-François, 235
Lasry, David, 78, 242
Lato, Grzegorz, 29
Lavezzi, Ezequiel, 21, 125
Lavillenie, Renaud, 91
Law, Denis, 258
Le Graët, Noël, 228–30, 232
Le Pen, Marine, 42, 166, 169, 227

287

INDEX

Lefebvre, Nicole, 60
Lemar, Thomas, 18, 125
Lens FC, 77
Létang, Olivier, 83
Ligue de Football Professionnel (LFP), 127
Lille FC, 129
Liotta, Alejandro, 266
Lizarazu, Bixente, 91
Lloris, Hugo, 163, 206–9, 214, 221, 230, 232, 235
Lobanovskyi, Valeriy, 257
Loewe, 107
Lycée Jean-Jaurès, Rueil-Malmaison, 59

Macron, Brigitte, 160, 163
Macron, Emmanuel, *121*, 151, *153*, 159–70, 210
Maignan, Mike, 125, 133, 194, 209
Maison, Hector, 155
Maldini, Paolo, 241
Malouda, Florent, 207
Manchester City FC, 3, 17, 143
Mandanda, Steve, 207, 209
Mandžukić, Mario, 162
Mansour, Sheikh, 143
Maouassa, Faitout, 25n
Maradona, Diego, 4, 43, 135, 205, 237
Marche, Roger, 206
Marie Antoinette, Queen of France, 3, 255
Marquinhos (Marcos Aoás Corrêa), 175
Marseille FC, 124
Martigues FC, 247
Martinez, Emiliano, 166
Masters, Richard, 180
Mata, Juan, 192–3, 242
Materazzi, Marco, 205, 263
Matthäus, Lothar, 228
Matuidi, Blaise, 126
Mbappé, Ethan, 9, 34, 45, 80, 117, 131, 150, 193

Mbappé, Kylian, *101*, *121*, *171*
   agents and team, 89–97, 241
   Al-Khelaifi and, 173–4
   AS Bondy and, 23–4, 56
   AS Monaco and, 18, *75*, 79–86, 123–4, 129
   bad behaviour, 97
   Ballon d'Or, *253*, 258–63
   Bondy (town) and, 45–6, *49*
   business affairs, 108–17, 242–3
   cars, 113–14
   Champions League and, 17–18, 90, 174–5, 233
   charity work, 116–19
   Chelsea FC, and 18–19
   childhood, 10, 37, 42–5, 54–6
   Clairefontaine and, *13*, *63*, 65, 68–73, 78–9, 242
   criticism of, 219–20, 233–5
   early football career, 10–11, 17–26, 56, 58
   education, 56–62
   Euros (2016), 25–6, 169–70, 215–19, 262
   first-team debut, 7
   France national team (Les Bleus), 86, 175–6, 184, 194, 206–18, 225–33
   France U17s, 82
   France U19s, 25, 82
   France U23s (Les Bleuets), 84
   French captaincy, 206–21, 225–8
   friends, 132–3
   goal scoring, 134–6, 144, 235–7
   Golden Boot, 135, 209, 261
   IBKM charitable foundation, 116–19
   image, 100, 107–8, 142–3
   intelligence, 56, 60
   Je m'appelle Kylian (book), 54, 118
   Jirès and, 37
   Macron and, 160–70, 210
   milestones, 269–75
   moves to Paris, 130–31

murals, 42, 54
music and, 59
nicknames, 70
obsession with football, 54–6
penalties, 235–6
personality, 68–9, 97–8, 227–8, 263
'Player of the Season' trophy, 139
'Player of the Year' trophy, 136
police violence and, 168
politics and, 168–70
private life, 192–3, 202
projet Mbappé, 52–4, 61, 263–4, 267–8
PSG and, 21–3, 97, 123–4, 129–31, 134–6, 139–51, 161, 174–87
Real Madrid and, 19–20, 123, 136, 144–5, 177–8, 183–4, 220, 225, 233–4
security, 195–7
signs first professional contract, 84, 90
Silver Ball award, 167
sponsors, 106–8, 113–17, 178, 231, 266
Stade Malherbe Caen and, 77–9, *239*, 241–52
Stockholm affair, *189*, 193–202, 225
superstardom, 7–10, 131–2
taxes, 113
trademark, 100
visits to Elysée Palace, 160–64, 167, 210
wealth, 113–15
World Cup (2018), 162–3, *203*, 209–10, 225, 258–9
World Cup (2022), *153*, 166–7, 173, *223*, 259
World Cup 2026 qualifiers, 234–5
Mbappé, Pierre, 19–20, 38, 48, 57, 80–81
Mbappé, Wilfrid (Elie), 19, 23–4, 33–4, 38, 42, 44–5, 47, 59, 98
  AS Monaco and, 85
  business affairs, 108–12
  Kylian's career and, 7, 20, 55–6, 69, 71–2, 77–80, 89, 93, 150

Kylian's education and, 59
split with Fayza, 94
Mbappé-Bessemé, Philippe, 44–5
Mboma, Alain, 38, 57
Mboma, Patrick, 81
'McFly' (social media influencer), 165–6
Meazza, Giuseppe, 5
Mediapart (investigative website), 65–6, 174
Mélenchon, Jean-Luc, 166, 170, 227
Mendes, Jorge, 100, 256, 267
Mendes, Nuno, 145
Mendy, Benjamin, 18, 125
Mercato (film), 133
Merzouk, Nahel, 168
Messi, Lionel, 5, 8–9, 23, 86, 105, 107, 112, 145–7, 166, 175, 178, 236–7, 259, 267
Mexès, Philippe, 207
Michel, Henri, 229
Michu (Miguel Pérez Cuesta), 242
Middlesbrough FC, 15
Milo of Croton, 3, 6
Mitterrand, François, 157–8
Mobutu Sese Seko, 30, 32
Modrić, Luka, 259
Mombaerts, Erick, 66
Momège, Allan, 72
'Monchi' (Ramón Rodríguez Verdejo), 16–17, 21
Le Monde newspaper, 69, 73
Montpellier FC, 129
Moore, Bobby, 205–6
Motta, Marcos, 104–6
Motta, Thiago, 125
Moura, Lucas, 21, 83, 125
Moutinho, João, 18, 125
Muani, Kolo, 47, 215, 217, 220
Mugoša-Antić, Svetlana, 48
Mukiele, Nordi, 196
M'vila, Yann, 244

INDEX

Nasri, Samir, 207
Nations League, 194, 225, 227, 232
Navas, Jésus, 16
Nedved, Pavel, 261
Netherlands national team, 237
Neville, Gary, 241
Neville, Phil, 206
Newpie (Mbappé company), 109–10
Neymar Jr, 8, 86, 97, 103–7, 112, 126, 129–30, 134, 140–42, 144–7, 161, 174–5, 186–7
Neymar Sr, 103–7
Neyou, Yvan, 68
Ngijol, Thomas, 149
Nike, 19, 42, 54, 70, 106–7, 117, 178, 229
Nouveau Front Populaire, 170

Oakley glasses, 107, 117
Oaktree Capital Management, 242–3, 247, 250
Ohzora (Mbappé company), 110
Olmo, Dani, 217
Olympe de Gouges primary school, Bondy, 57–8
Olympic Games
    Atlanta (1994), 158
    Paris (2024), 265
    Tokyo (1964), 155
Olympique de Marseille FC, 159–60
Orelsan (Aurélien Cotentin), 251–2
d'Ornano, Maxime, 251–2
Ornstein, David, 177
Orta, Victor, 16, 21–3, 26
Otamendi, Nicolas, 259
Ouest France newspaper, 90
Oukidja, Alexandre, 97
Owen, Michael, 206, 257

Panini, 107
Parc des Princes, Paris, 156
Paris, France, 108–9, 130–31
    riots (2005), 43–4

Paris Match magazine, 165
Paris Saint-Germain (PSG), 10, 21–3, 53, 77, 83, 123–7, 134–6, 173–87, 233–4, 262
    Champions League and, 136, 142, 145, 147, 233
    DBB and, 174
    Mbappé extends contract, 148–51, 176
    Mbappé leaves PSG, 177–83, 185–6, 234
    Mbappé's dissatisfaction with, 139–49
    Mbappé's legal claim, 179–85, 198
    Mbappé's transfer to, 123–31, 161
    'Player of the Season' trophy, 139
    Qatar Sports Investment and, 124–8, 143
    Sarkozy and, 127, 159
    smear campaign, 200
Le Parisien newspaper, 96–8, 133, 149, 150, 186, 199
Pastore, Javier, 83, 130
Pauleta, Pedro, 10, 186
Pause podcast, 107
Pelé, 6, 104, 225
Pereira, Danilo, 175–6
Perez, Florentino, 19, 168
Péria, Guillaume, 69–70
Petit, Emmanuel, 216
Piqué, Gérard, 24, 114
Pirès, Robert, 91
Platini, Michel, 32, 127–8, 135, 157, 206, 210–11, 228, 235, 237, 261–2
Players' Tribune, 45, 54
Pochettino, Mauricio, 144, 146–7
Pogba, Paul, 128, 163
Pompidou, Georges, 156
Prêcheur, Gérard, 68, 71, 249
projet Mbappé, 52–4, 61
Puel, Claude, 24
Puskás, Ferenc, 184

Qatar, 127–9, 143, 148, 150, 159, 167, 173
Qatar Sports Investments, 89, 124–9

Rabiot, Adrien, 174
Rai (Raimundo Souza Vieira de Oliveira), 186
Rainea, Nicolae, 31
Ramos, Gonçalo, 220
Ramos, Sergio, 16, 175
Rangnick, Ralf, 23
Rashford, Marcus, 140
Rassemblement National, 168–70
Raúl (Raúl González Blanco), 261
Real Madrid FC, 9, 19–20, 78, 113, 123, 130, 135, 147–8, 183–4, 194, 233–4, 260, 262
    La Fábrica, 20
    Mbappé's transfer to, 144, 177–9
Redondo, Fernando, 261
Rennes FC, 77
Rensenbrink, Rob, 236
Reyes, José-Antonio, 16
Riccardi, Antonio, 23–4
Rice, Declan, 66
Rimowa, 107
Riner, Teddy, 91
RMC radio network, 226–7
Rodri (Rodrigo Hernández Cascante), 133, 256
Rodrygo (Rodrygo Silva de Goes), 183, 220
Rojo, Marcos, 259
Ronaldinho (Ronaldo de Assis Moreira), 7, 34, 256
Ronaldo, Cristiano, xii, 7–9, 19, 61, 86, 99–100, 107, 112, 130, 184, 192, 220, 236, 256–7, 259
Ronaldo *Fenômeno*, 220, 241
Rothen, Jérôme, 225–6
Roux, Guy, 158
Rüdiger, Antonio, 234

rue Henry Monnier, Paris, 108–9, 114, 116
Rybolovlev, Dmitry, 18, 79, 125

SailGP team, 116–17
Saint-Aubert, Yannick, 57, 61, 86
Salah, Mohammed, 261
Saliba, William, 47
San Torcuato, Bernardo, 266
Santos FC, 105
Sarkozy, Nicolas, 42, 127, 150, 159, 167
Saziley (Mbappé company), 99, 109
Schumacher, Harald, 262
SCI Falam (Mbappé company), 110
Seckel, Henri, 69, 71
Seube, Nicolas, 244, 248
Sevilla FC, 21
Shirakova, Maria, 197, 200
Silva, Bernardo, 18, 125
Silva, Thiago, 21, 125
Silver, Adam, *101*
Simeone, Diego, 212
Simons, Xavi, 125
Simonsen, Allan 260
Sindelar, Matthias, 5
Sissoko, Moussa, 266
Smerecki, Francis, 66
Sochaux FC, 77
social media, 7–9, 232
Solskjaer, Ole-Gunnar, 140
Sorare (video game), 107, 114–15
Le Sportif et son Agent (Bertrand and Verheyden), 91
Stade Malherbe Caen, 7, 10, 20, 71, 77–9, 116, *239*
    Mbappé's acquisition of, 241–52
Stockholm, Sweden, *189*, 194–201
Suárez, Luis, 43
Sud Ouest newspaper, 218
Świątek, Iga, 111
Szarmach, Andrzej, 29

INDEX

Tagliafico, Nicolas, 259
Tapie, Bernard, 159
Tathou (Mbappé company), 110
Tchaga, Brice, 150
Tchouameni, Aurélien, 166, 225
Tchouméo, Audrey, 47
Tel, Mathys, 264
ter Stegen, Marc-André, 51
Theagenes of Thasos, 4
Thépot, Alex, 208
Thomas, Romain, 246
Thomassin, Sylvine, 61
Thuram, Lilian, 68
Thuram, Marcus, 68, 169, 215
Tiafoe, Frances, 111
Tigana, Jean, 32
Tostão, 29
Tottenham Hotspur FC, 84, 208
Traoré, Bouna, 43
Trézéguet, David, 80
Tuchel, Thomas, 140–41, 144

UEFA Youth League, 82
Uzzan, Barbara, 95–6

Valverde, Federico, 183
van Basten, Marco, 261
van der Wiel, Gregory, 125
van Dijk, Virgil, 261
Varane, Raphaël, 209, 258
Varley, John, 205
Vaucelle, Christophe, 248
Verheyden, Delphine, *87*, 90–97, 99, 107–8, 180, 182–3, 230–31
Verratti, Marco, 125, 141–2, 175
Vertonghen, Jan, 216
Vesterloppe, Marc, 77
Vicault, Jimmy, 47
Villa, Vincent, 85
Vinicius Jr (Vinícius José Paixão de Oliveira Júnior), 133, 183, 220, 256
Vivian, Dani, 217

Weah, George, 160, 186, 261
Wenger, Arsène, 18, 21, 83
White, Ben, 51
William Morris Entertainment, 111
Williams, Serena, 114
Wilson, Ray, 205
World Cup
  1958: 148, 156, 225
  1962: 156
  1966: 205–6, 209
  1974: 29–32
  1978: 262
  1986: 262
  1994: 158
  1998: 159, 166
  2006: 263
  2010: 207
  2018: 21, 162–3, *203*, 209–10, 225, 258–9
  2022: 41, 127–8, 134, 143, 148, 159, 166–7, 173, 209, *223*, 259
  2026: 111, 184, 234–5
Wristcheck, 116

Xavi (Xavier Hernández Creus), 193

'Yaëlle' (personal assistant), 195–6
Yamal, Lamine, 217, 219, 264, 266–7
Yashin, Lev, 133
YouTube, 165–6

Zaïre, 32–3
Zaïre national team, *27*, 30–32
Zebra Valley LLC, 96, 110–11, 117
Zecler, Michel, 168
Zico (Arthur Antunes Coimbra), 262
Zidane, Zinédine, 19–20, 43, 67, 68, 128, 130, 133, 162, 166, 192, 205, 210–11, 228, 263
Zig, Thierry, 47
Zubizarreta, Andoni, 208